Educational Research: The Importance
and Effects of Institutional Spaces

Educational Research

VOLUME 7

Aims & Scope

Freedom of inquiry in educational research can no longer be taken for granted. Narrow definitions of what constitutes 'scientific' research, funding criteria that enforce particular research methods, and policy decision processes that ignore any research that is not narrowly utilitarian, in many countries, create a context that discourages scholarship of a more speculative, exploratory, or critical sort.

In this series, internationally leading scholars in *philosophy and history of education* engage in discourse that is sophisticated and nuanced for understanding contemporary debates. Thus social research, and therefore educational research, is again focused on the distinctive nature of what it studies: a social activity where questions of meaning and value must be addressed, and where interpretation and judgment play a crucial role.

This educational research takes into account the historical and cultural context and brings clarity to what actually constitutes science in this area. The timely issues that are addressed in this series bear witness to the belief that educational theory cannot help but go beyond a limited conception of empirical educational research to provide a real understanding of education as a human practice. They surpass the rather simple cause-and effect rhetoric and thus transgress the picture of performativity that currently keeps much of the talk about education captive. The authors are united in the belief that 'there is a place within the social sciences in general', and within the discipline of education in particular, for 'foundational' approaches that enable the systematic study of educational practice from a discipline-orientated approach.

For further volumes:
http://www.springer.com/series/8398

Paul Smeyers • Marc Depaepe • Edwin Keiner
Editors

Educational Research:
The Importance and Effects
of Institutional Spaces

 Springer

Editors

Paul Smeyers
Faculty of Psychology
  and Educational Sciences
Ghent University and Katholieke
  Universiteit Leuven
Belgium

Marc Depaepe
Campus Kortrijk
Subfaculteit Psychologie en
  Pedagogische Wetenschappen
Katholieke Universiteit Leuven
Belgium

Edwin Keiner
Erziehungswissenschaftliche Fakultät
Universität Erlangen-Nürnberg
Germany

ISBN 978-94-007-6246-6   ISBN 978-94-007-6247-3 (eBook)
DOI 10.1007/978-94-007-6247-3
Springer Dordrecht Heidelberg New York London

Library of Congress Control Number: 2013932706

Printed on acid-free paper

Springer is part of Springer Science+Business Media (www.springer.com)

Earlier Volumes in this Series

Contents

Chapter 1
Exploring a Multitude of Spaces in Education and Educational Research

Paul Smeyers and Marc Depaepe

The various faces of educational research have been at the centre of many sophisti-cated debates. This collection discusses the importance and effects of institutional spaces and frames for the shaping of educational research and knowledge, their production, dissemination and reception in international contexts. A historical and a philosophical focus are combined to understand different institutional spaces of educational research, but attention is also paid to their potential and limitations. Different meanings of 'space' are distinguished such as what this means at the level of the practice of education, for example, in a classroom, at the level of the institutions, and last but not least, when the focus is on the academic discipline of education. Thus, the perspectives on the multifaceted diversity of institutional spaces are addressed as well as the theoretical and methodological constructions of institutional spaces educational research is embedded in. The contributions to this volume dis-cuss, among other things, the steps to investigate the social and epistemological communication patterns of historical and philosophical educational research, their disciplinary peculiarities and commonalities and their disciplinary boundaries. Thus, they offer a revitalisation of methodological reflections and approaches and strengthen the disciplinary self-observation and self-governance. Significant perspectives of investigation on institutional spaces of educational research are also

P. Smeyers (✉)
Faculty of Psychology and Educational Sciences, Ghent University
and Katholieke Universiteit Leuven, Belgium
e-mail: paul.smeyers@ped.kuleuven.be

M. Depaepe
Campus Kortrijk, Subfaculteit Psychologie en Pedagogische Wetenschappen,
Katholieke Universiteit Leuven, Belgium
e-mail: marc.depaepe@kuleuven-kortrijk.be

P. Smeyers et al. (eds.), *Educational Research: The Importance and Effects of Institutional Spaces*, Educational Research 7, DOI 10.1007/978-94-007-6247-3_1,
© Springer Science+Business Media Dordrecht 2013

dealt with; in addition to newly emerging 'hybrid' structures, networks and joint ventures, which take on functions of mediation, and control 'knowledge management' in the process of global adjustment, are focused on. Thus, the question is raised whether and under what conditions they are able to transnationally integrate national knowledge diversity according to common goals and perspectives. Already in medieval times and to a large extent apart from the local (spatial) constraints, a community came into existence which looked for a way to gather universal knowledge.

As can be witnessed from the existence of the many learned societies, the oldest of them founded in the fourteenth century, space, that is, an intellectual space, has been central to scholarly work in all academic disciplines. In some sense, 'globalisation' has changed this—as physical presence (geographical space) to take part in a debate, for example, is no longer necessary—yet in another sense, it foregrounds perhaps even more than in the past the embeddedness in 'local settings' and/or discussions. Spaces, as argued by Burbules in this collection, are relatively objective, defined by the contours of natural or architectural structures and locations—though they might already contain cultural markers and meanings. But *places* are spaces that have become personally or socially significant, because of their history, uses and cultural significance. Spaces are sometimes designed with the intention of making them places (a public square or a tourist attraction in a natural park), and sometimes they become so. But it is often the case that serendipitous events and circumstances make a space into a place that no one intended; other times, an existing place evolves over time to take on certain architectural or locational (spatial) features because it is where people actually gather and do things of cultural significance—here, the place defines and reshapes the space. The notion of 'place', therefore, raises issues about the relation between natural or human structures and dynamic processes of historical, cultural and social change, Burbules continues. Something can be a place and then lose that quality over time as people forget or as practices change; a space may acquire some new significance or meaning; or we might see 'place conflicts' when a particular space has different meaning and value as a place for different groups, thus far Burbules. The mental space, the way things are experienced ('privatised'), is correlative to what is offered in the public space. Some places become spaces; others become unfamiliar. Educationalisation may bring the 'private' and the 'public' in competition. In some contexts such as child-rearing (see Schreuder & Dekker, Chap. 5, this volume), the educational space has increased in the sense that it is now more object of public scrutiny by professionals (correlatively the parents' space to shape the upbringing of their children is narrowed). In other instances such as in the case of the curriculum, one observes a growing tendency to control the content of the curriculum (together with the educational processes). This dynamic seems to be crucially important: it delimits not only what one is allowed to think (e.g. in cases of censorship) but more importantly also what one *can* think (sometimes referred to by 'cultural-historical geographies of knowledge'), in other words what one is initiated in. 'Space' is potentially a very rich notion: it has references to society, to interpretation and action; it allows for specificity such as in 'mathematical space' and invites to take up (challenging) opportunities and what is not yet conceived; finally, it admits to situate (individual) research projects.

In this collection, attention is paid to different disciplinary cultures, cognitive textures and languages, often locked into traditions of both national research cultures and educational systems. These disciplinary approaches form communicative spaces more or less separated from each other and use different concepts and criteria of methodological standards and scientific quality. Reference is made to different concepts, modes and structures of coupling or decoupling research and practice, and how this influences educational policy advice, raising the question whether and under what conditions educational policy and administrations are able to govern educational research into politically designated directions—including which criteria are used to justify, to evaluate and to analyse these directions. At present one finds a dominant tendency across the educational research cultures which introduce new developments: these include blurring the boundaries between research and technique, steering by results, radical shifts in communicative spaces, the appearing of distorting output indicators and new criteria for promotion. These affect the traditional research cultures and create new similarities and differences, new coalitions and resistances. In times of transition and uncertain and unclear situations, a contribution is made to investigate traditional and newly emerging institutional patterns of educational research, that is, disciplinary profiles of knowledge production, justification, reception and distribution, demands and expectations of educational professions and contemporary and historical policies in educational research in an international and comparative perspective.[1]

This is not the first time that the *Research Community 'Philosophy and history of the discipline of education'*,[2] established by the Research Foundation Flanders FWO, Belgium (Fonds voor Wetenschappelijk Onderzoek—Vlaanderen), addresses an area that is central for educational research. In both the first (1999–2003) and second (2000–2008) periods, which focused on *'Evaluation and evolution of the criteria for educational research'*, various positions were scrutinised (see Smeyers & Depaepe, 2003, 2006). In the present (third) 5-year period of this *Research Community* (2009–2013), the overall interest is *'Faces and spaces of educational research'*, which is divided into four subthemes (respectively addressed during the conference in 2009, 2010, 2011 and 2012): the ethics and aesthetics of statistics; the attraction of psychology; the institutional space, designs and material culture; and finally, the representation of educational research. The chapters published in this volume were first presented at the 2011 *Research Community* conference. Scholars from philosophy and history of education (some of whom are particularly interested in history and philosophy of science) combine their efforts to study 'institutional space' as part of both the academic discipline of education and the broader educational context. The chapters in this collection address a variety of topics such as how space in the geographical sense has helped to shape researchers' mental structures, how institutional spaces for young children emerged, how the parochial was dominant in the shaping of the American system of higher education and how the concept of space can help us to understand classroom practice. Texts (always in need of interpretation) are spaces too and such can also be claimed concerning the multilayered discursive space of research itself. An interesting area is mathematics education, and so are virtual spaces such as Web 2.0 to which other chapters turn. That all of this has implications for the attitude of the researcher working in an environment of 'innovation' which may be one day possibly the virtual university is the focus of some other contributions.

In Chap. 2, *Lynda Stone* takes up the topic of institutional spaces in two regards, one the conception of democracy and the other in two times and exemplars of potentially democratic practices. The latter are first as a 'failing institution' particularly targeting youth in the USA today and second as a 'successful institution' in an innovative experiment at a psychiatric hospital in the late 1950s. Following the first setting, the central focus of the chapter is the theorising and its implementation of democratic character and institutional democratic development from political psychologist Harold Lasswell.[3] The last is in the form of research and its reporting. To begin with, the first section describes three contemporary instances of institutional failure: school discipline, the school to prison pipeline and the war on terrorism. At the least, these are a reminder that American democracy cannot be taken for granted and must be renegotiated again and again. The next sections introduce Lasswell, synthesise his text *Democratic Character*, describe and exemplify implementation of the innovation and offer an assessment by researchers Lasswell and Robert Rubenstein. The conclusion summarises the chapter, returns to youth and schools and closes with a comment on educational research.

In Chap. 3, *David Labaree* addresses 'The power of the parochial in shaping the American system of Higher Education'. By the mid-nineteenth century, the United States had constructed the largest system of higher education in the world. Cobbled together without an overall plan, this system was characterised by wide geographical dispersion, radically localised governance and the absence of guaranteed support from either church or state. Only a small number of these institutions were creatures of the individual states and dependent on state appropriations. The modal institution was the independent college in a small town with a corporate charter and stand-alone finances. Most had the blessing of a religious denomination, which granted legitimacy and a source of students but provided little or no financial help. Instead, they had to survive on the tuition paid by students and the gifts of individuals from the town and from the larger church community. They operated in a very competitive market for higher education, where supply vastly exceeded demand and where their main selling points were that they were geographically accessible, religiously compatible, academically undemanding and relatively inexpensive. The purpose of this chapter is to show how this parochial and academically weak system rose from obscurity in the nineteenth century to world leadership in the twentieth century. By 1880, the system had developed a series of strengths that would serve it well in the emerging world of higher education: enormous capacity, spread across the landscape of a continental country; institutions that had the ability to survive in a highly competitive setting with little support from church or state; sensitivity to consumer demand, which allowed colleges to adapt quickly to changes in the marketplace; a broad base of popular support; and a reputation for providing a practical education. All the system needed was students and academic credibility, and the new model of the research university provided both. The rest is history.

In their chapter (Chap. 4), *Marc Depaepe, Lieven D'hulst and Frank Simon* deal with a remarkable historical example: 'Crossing the Atlantic to Gain Knowledge in the Field of Psycho-pedagogy: The 1922 Mission of Ovide Decroly and Raymond Buyse to the USA and the Travel Diary of the Latter'. They use a recent publication (Depaepe & D'hulst, 2011) reflecting the ubiquitous American influence on the construct of psycho-pedagogical sciences in Belgium, to clarify the extent to which space, in the geographical sense of the word, has helped shape researchers' mental structures, often for a lifetime. The publication contains the travel notes (in the original French and translated into English) of the future professor Raymond Buyse, made during his study trip to the United States—the country of choice for immigrants, at least that is the way in which it is impressed in our collective memory—together with Ovide Decroly in the spring of 1922. These notes are a gold mine for cultural-historical research into mental migration as well as into the related perception of the cultural context from which one wishes to import scientific opinions, ideas, theories, methods and techniques. On the other hand, they also reveal the reverse side of the scientific activity that these men went to study there, from the perspective of the history of science, among other things, as a consequence of their uncensored naiveté and stereotyping. The article is arranged into two parts: the first deals with the study trip and its mission, in relation with the general landscape of an emerging 'science of education' as well as with the individual careers of the travellers scientists. With some imagination, one can put this section under the heading 'macro space'. The second deals with some more specific aspects of the travel as reflected by the notes of Buyse. With the same imagination, one can call this the 'micro space' of the travel diary.

Pauline Schreuder and Jeroen Dekker continue with 'The Emergence of Institutional Educational Spaces for Young Children: In Pursuit of More Controllability of Education and Development as Part of the Long-Term Growth of Educational Space in History' (Chap. 5). They address both long-term developments and current manifestations of the continuous reshaping and growth of educational spaces, particularly in the Netherlands. From the nineteenth century onwards, those spaces developed together with the growth of educational ambitions as the notion of 'the child's best interest' became ever more prominent in policy, laws and in child-rearing theories. But there was no fixed understanding of what constitutes 'the best interest of the child'. Theories can be said to define mental space, that is, allowing for the dominance of certain understandings of the best interest of the child, resulting in the shaping of educational practices within the space that is allocated by laws. During this process, the boundaries between the private and the public, between the autonomy of the family and the jurisdiction of the state, fluctuate. Over time, the state has gained dominance over a larger educational space, while the autonomy of the family has decreased when it comes to deciding how to raise and educate children and how to decide on their best interest. The case of the Electronic Child Dossier is discussed as an example. New educational spaces in the Netherlands, developing within this long-term and gradual process of increasing influence of the public on the private educational space, became dominated by the notion of controllability. That notion can be found in the emphasis on procedures and systematic educational methods and on asking parents to monitor their children's development. It is concluded that thus the parents' mental space to understand and shape the upbringing of their children is narrowed and has become an object for public scrutiny by professionals. As a result, public educational ambitions shape the everyday life of young children and their parents.

The interest for child-rearing is continued by *Pieter Dhondt*'s 'A Different Training, a Different Practice:Infant Care in Belgium in the Interwar Years in the City and in the Countryside' (Chap. 6). Following the hygienic movement, the fight against infant mortality also became an important policy objective in Belgium around the First World War. Increasingly, the National Board of Child Welfare made an appeal to visiting nurses in order to give the mothers educational advice in their own environment and to control the children medically. The focus in this article is on the development of infant care as a specific educational space and how this received a somewhat different interpretation in the city and in the countryside, following on the training of visiting nurses in different nursing schools, themselves to be regarded as institutional spaces of educational research. The pillarisation of the education of visiting nurses along ideological lines resulted in a different approach of infant care. Whereas the catholic nursing school St. Elizabeth in Bruges regarded nursing primarily as a vocation and put an emphasis on the social role of the nurse in the countryside, the liberal *École belge d'Infirmières diplômées* decided in favour of an in-depth medical training, which resulted in a more professionalised medical approach of her work in the city.

Pieter Verstraete's chapter focuses on 'Disability, Rehabilitation and the Great War: Making Space for Silence in the History of Education' (Chap. 7). Although 'silence' can be considered a widespread educational instrument, until now historians of education have not devoted much research to the historical use made of it for educational purposes. In this chapter, he puts forward the fruitfulness of a historical exploration of the manifold and complex connections between silence and education. In particular he demonstrates how within a particular neglected subfield of the history of education, namely, the rehabilitation of Belgian disabled soldiers from the First World War, the silence or quietness one can encounter in particular spaces was thought to leave a stimulating impression on the mind of the mutilated soldiers. For those responsible of realising the rehabilitative measures towards (Belgian) disabled soldiers, silence was considered a pre-eminent educational tool that was intimately connected to the often heard pedagogical ambition of 'The right man on the right place'. However, by including the voices of the disabled soldiers themselves, it is also shown how silence at the same time was turned by the mutilated men themselves into a meaningful instrument, one that enabled them to resist the educational regimes of rehabilitation. The narrative enables us to steer away from the traditional interpretation of silence as being the opposite of language—and thus of the political. Silence, as will become clear, can and should be considered as something serving—whether intentionally or unintentionally—particular educational goals and bears in itself the outlook of particular world-views. Demonstrating this instrumentalisation, therefore, should be considered an important task to be carried out by historians of education in the twenty-first century.

Turning towards another kind of space, *Richard Smith* foregrounds 'Interpretation: The Space of Text' (Chap. 8). It is easy to forget that text too is an institutional space of educational research and one with distinctive forms in academic journal articles and books, forms that are often stranger and less innocent than they appear at first reading. If we suppose that text is a neutral and transparent medium for representing 'research findings', then we are unlikely to pay the attention we should to the forms that texts take, and in particular, we may not subject their more rhetorical and figurative manifestations to the criticism they deserve. As an example, he offers here a reading of a recent UK White Paper [*sic*] on Higher Education. Texts of course need to be interpreted: reflection on what constitutes sound interpretation moves us further away from the domination of empiricist paradigms of research in education and in social science more widely, and foregrounds the virtues of the good interpreter rather than shibboleths such as accuracy and 'rigour' that have their roots in scientific and empiricist paradigms. The strictures upon the written as opposed to the spoken word that can be found in a naive reading of Plato (especially of a notorious passage in *Phaedrus*) have played a part in obscuring the significance of text and interpretation, as has the tendency to think of interpretation as a methodology of criticism rather than as a methodology of the production of knowledge and ideas. Interpretation, whether of texts or of people, can never achieve certainty, but the good interpreter can offer us grounds for confidence in her readings, and this is all the warrant that we are entitled to seek and that we need.

Stijn Mus continues this interest in his 'Exploring Educational Research as a Multilayered Discursive Space' (Chap. 9). In this chapter, a spatial metaphor to describe the pursuit of educational research is explored. During the last decades, all the possible candidates to safeguard the legitimacy of meaning in qualitative educational research—from scientific detachment to subjective agency—have come under pressure. What was shared by many of these orientations was a firm belief in empiricism and realist aesthetics to grasp the true nature of its object. A possible way out of this impasse might be to focus on the discourse itself and pay closer attention to the way realist aesthetics functions. Therefore, the chosen angle here is to focus back from the reality behind the text to the operative dimension of the text itself. Different levels of meaning, operative as different registers are identified, before exploring the ways in which their tropes influence one another. This will allow to appreciate how scientific conventions itself function as rhetorical codes to construct meaning. Starting from the fact that the text itself is performative for the emerging meaning, it is argued that educational research could be conceived as a cultural discussion, which engages in the construction of possible meanings and provides them an intersubjective—that is, a shared, public—character by gaining them legitimacy and recognition on the cultural forum. As such, qualitative research is caught in a permanent cycle of feedback loops between cultural description and cultural performance. From this follows the epistemic priority of the imagination over empiricism to bridge the seemingly natural and the not yet conceivable.

The chapter by *Karen François, Kathleen Coessens and Jean Paul Van Bendegem* turns to 'The Spaces of Mathematics: Dynamic Encounters Between Local and Universal' (Chap. 10). No doubt mathematics is the last place (or face?) to look for 'situatedness', that is, to show that mathematics too is linked to places, to people, to instruments and to practices. Yet over the past years, evidence has been accumulating that mathematics too needs a context in order to be understood. This contextuality ranges from the high-level, abstract mathematical discourse that requires a strong social closure in terms of experts to the educational context where mathematical thinking and doing is transmitted including the hidden philosophical and universal claims and to the ethno-mathematical context where mathematics is supposed to integrate into society rather than the other way around. In short, universality requires some very special contextual conditions to demonstrate its full force (at least so it is claimed).

Ian Munday's chapter 'The Classroom Space: A Problem or a Mystery?' (Chap. 11) pays attention to another educational practice context. Though researchers from different backgrounds may perceive the classroom space in different ways, they arguably share one thing in common, namely, that they see it as a site for solving problems—teachers and children will be emancipated and students will become more effective learners. In this chapter, he considers what it might mean to think of the classroom as a space of mystery rather than a site for problem-solving. Here, he draws on the work of existentialist philosopher Gabriel Marcel: "A problem is something met with which bars my passage. It is therefore before me in its entirety. A mystery, on the other hand, is something in which I find myself caught up, and whose essence is therefore not before me in its entirety. It is as though in this province the distinction between *in me* and *before me* loses its meaning" (Marcel, 1949, p. 109). What might the loss of a distinction between 'in me and before me' mean for teaching and classroom research? This is discussed in relation to his own experience of both school teaching and working on a practitioner research course that employed the pedagogical model of blended learning (where most of the teaching took place online). He argues that the virtual spaces (forums and chat rooms) are suited to a pedagogy that favours problem-solving at the expense of mystery. During the paper, he considers the notion that cyber pedagogies fit in (too) 'neatly' with both current conceptions of practitioner research and school teaching more generally. All three are bound up in a libidinal drive to solve problems and delimit the classroom space.

The latter discussion is continued by *Nick Burbules* in his 'Spaces and Places in the Virtual University' (Chap. 12). He examines the transition of the traditional university into a partly *virtual university*, as we witness the growth of online courses and degree programmes as well as the increased uses of technology for the redesign of teaching and learning even within the traditional campus. He relies on the concepts of *space* and *place* to describe this transformation and relates these to changing understandings of knowledge, authority, and community within higher education. Finally, he relates this transformation to three key ideas in online education: the design of learning spaces; the social, collaborative nature of these spaces; and the potential and challenges of ubiquitous learning.

In 'Material Contexts and Creation of Meaning in Virtual Places: Web 2.0 as a Space of Educational Research' (Chap. 13), *Lynn Fendler and Karin Priem* offer further insights concerning the virtual space. They focus on the salient features of Web 2.0 as a space of educational research creation, distribution and interaction.

Web 2.0 is a relatively new reading/writing platform that cannot be fully understood without examining the history of reading and writing as cultural and literary phenomena. Drawing from the work of Roger Chartier and Bruno Latour, the paper highlights authorship and gatekeeping as salient cultural practices. Following a historical and epistemological approach, the paper has two main parts: (1) A Short History from Scroll to Screen: Materialities of Reading and Writing and (2) From Redaction to Compositionism: Epistemological Shifts in Web 2.0 Spaces. In the first part, they trace historical developments in reading and writing from scroll to codex to web-based formats, noting similarities and differences among various textual architectures and shifts in purposes of reading and writing. In the second part, they suggest that Web 2.0 spaces exemplify a shift from redaction to compositionism (Latour), which includes new displays of peer review comments and a redistribution of editorial gatekeeping. The paper concludes by suggesting that Web 2.0 spaces represent a historical shift in reading and writing practices for educational research, a recent shift that follows a long historical trajectory of previous shifts in the materialities of reading and writing. The architecture of the texts tends to be vertical (scroll-like) and multidimensional (hyperlinked). Authorship in Web 2.0 spaces tends to be dispersed, iterative and social, rather than individual, institutionally validated and static. The distinction between readers and writers has become blurred. The dynamic heterogeneity of compositionism is replacing hierarchical forms of redaction critique and authoritative reviewing mechanisms. Finally, Web 2.0 spaces have facilitated new research practices of data generation, community involvement, governance and surveillance.

In the final chapter, *Naomi Hodgson* discusses 'From Entrepreneurialism to Innovation: Research, Critique, and the Innovation Union' (Chap. 14). In the process of integration, Europe has been reframed as a different space. The Lisbon Strategy, which aimed to make the EU the most competitive and dynamic knowledge economy in the world, has recently been superseded by strategies for the creation of an Innovation Union. The recasting of the European Union as an Innovation Union recasts the role of the university and of the researcher. The shift not only affects institutions usually associated with knowledge production however; innovation is now a priority across all policy areas and for all actors to be able to adapt to and survive in current conditions. The creation of an Innovation Union brings about shifts of emphasis from a general entrepreneurialism to a more focused innovation and from learning to research. Current regimes of performance have been argued to effect an immunisation and thus a stifling, or domestication, of critique. The Innovation Union is constituted as a space by devices for measuring innovation and by actors acting in the name of such performance measures. The innovative researcher required of this space is a mobile, adaptable individual seeking permanently to rethink how she does what she does in the name of efficiency, sustainability and responsibility, for which she requires permanent feedback. The possibility of resisting this mode of governance requires a reorientation of the researcher's attitude to the present. This is explored with reference to the reconceptualisation of the university by Jan Masschelein and Maarten Simons and the attitude of exposition found in the work of Michel Foucault and Bruno Latour.

Notes

1. Some of the ideas used in the preceding paragraphs are based on the introduction that Edwin Keiner gave at the occasion of the 2011 conference.
2. For further information about previous work of the *Research Community*, see Smeyers, 2008.
3. For references to the works of the mentioned authors in this chapter, please see the list of references in the chapters that are dealt with.

References

Smeyers, P. (2008). Afterword. In P. Smeyers & M. Depaepe (Eds.), *Educational research: The educationalization of social problems* (pp. 227–237). Dordrecht, the Netherlands: Springer.

Smeyers, P., & Depaepe, M. (2003). Introduction. In P. Smeyers & M. Depaepe (Eds.), *Beyond empiricism: On criteria for educational research* (pp. 9–23). Leuven, Belgium: Leuven University Press.

Smeyers, P., & Depaepe, M. (2006). Introduction: On the rhetoric of 'what works'. Contextualizing educational research and the picture of performativity. In P. Smeyers & M. Depaepe (Eds.), *Educational research: Why 'what works' doesn't work* (pp. 1–16). Dordrecht, the Netherlands: Springer.

Chapter 2
American Democracy and Harold D. Lasswell: Institutional Spaces of 'Failure' and 'Success', Present and Past

Lynda Stone

> *We understand by democracy the practice of justice by majority rule…. [Government] of any kind is of the people; government by the people is majority rule; government for the people is the practice of justice.*
>
> *When we respect the capacity of every individual to contribute to the common life, we practice justice and achieve democracy.*[1]

2.1 Introduction

Given in 2011 what came to be called the Arab Spring, with southeastern nation after nation demanding human rights and government change, democracy as an institution is at the forefront of minds worldwide. Central questions concern what *it* would look like in countries long without practice and what would be comparisons to nations with established democratic traditions. A year later, there are 'success' stories in some places but retention of the previous nondemocratic status quo in others. One aspect seems certain: This is that democracy necessarily looks different in diverse locales.

The purpose of this chapter is to explore the institution of democracy in a US context beginning in the present in several domains that have educational import and returning to a theoretical, a philosophical, and an empirical past. The latter and principal focus is the writing and practical innovation in democracy by American scholar and political and social scientist Harold D. Lasswell who lived from 1902 to 1978.

As is commonly recognized, there are several meanings of 'institution'. As used in what follows, the general term names something established and customary in a social order. Institutional spaces, moreover, are of various kinds that range from

L. Stone (✉)
School of Education, University of North Carolina at Chapel Hill,
Chapel Hill, NC, USA
e-mail: lstone@email.unc.edu

P. Smeyers et al. (eds.), *Educational Research: The Importance and Effects of Institutional Spaces*, Educational Research 7, DOI 10.1007/978-94-007-6247-3_2,
© Springer Science+Business Media Dordrecht 2013

structures to conceptions. Herein a conception founds a structural innovation in democracy. Democracy, as the well-used phrase from the epigraph encapsulates, is government of, by, and for the people either directly or through representatives. The chapter has these sections: The first, entitled failing institution, sets out three examples of a seeming contemporary denial of democracy. The second section, introducing Lasswell, brings forth his career and character to a largely unfamiliar educational audience. The third, democratic character, explicates a text of the same name of his general theory of democracy. The fourth, innovation, tells of a democratic experiment conducted by Lasswell and a partner, Robert Rubenstein, at a psychiatric hospital in the late 1950s, of which the latter was a senior staff member. The fifth section, assessment, offers the researchers own evaluation of the innovation. The final section as conclusion summarizes the chapter and turns back to the point of section one to connect 'lessons' from Lasswell to American democratic practices today. These are important for society at large but especially for youth and schools. A brief comment on educational research closes the chapter.

Even though many forms of democracy exist or potentially exist for modern nation states, as an institution it entails commonalities; the introduction concludes with reminder of some of these. The institutional base of democracy is political but, in an evolving form, it is today understood that certain social and economic conditions are necessary for sustainability. Democracies seem not to do as well when people are insecure, hungry, homeless, out of work, and poor. Democracies are big and small, the size of nations, the size of neighborhood watch associations. Whatever the size, there is recognition of who members are, as individuals and/or groups. These members have rights and choices that in best senses include freedom of thought and action, of lifestyle, and of civic participation. Importantly, while participants need agreement among themselves for democratic activity, there must also be room for disagreement. Ironically, democracies flourish when dissent is centrally valued.

2.2 Institutional Failure

This section begins with a bold contention: The institution of American democracy today is failing if not broken; its practices in many respects no longer embody just and equitable governance that are the ideals of its formulation. Instead, within hierarchical social structures, a rampant fear of uncertainty has led to a culture of behavior regulation, legal sanction and infraction, and severe consequences. This has resulted in what broadly may be termed a punishment and imprisonment society. Three present-day examples follow: The first is school discipline, the second is the 'school to prison pipeline', and the third is the 'war on terrorism'. All three, it is emphasized, almost entirely target the young.

School discipline today is often harsh and inflexible. It reflects a general impression, actually dating across a generation or more, that 'they' no longer are controllable and at any moment might revolt against their elders. Beginning especially with the

Columbine school shooting and heightened by September 11, respectively, in 1999 and 2001, this fear has resulted in a demand for 'safety' and 'security' at any cost. In schools, this is seen in very common discipline practices of entry metal detectors, surveillance cameras, police guards, drug-sniffing dogs, and even strip-searching of youth. In *Homeroom security: School discipline in an age of fear*, criminal justice scholar, Aaron Kupchik, describes the situation thus: "Schools define appropriate responses to misbehavior so narrowly that teachers, disciplinarians, and administrators tend to pursue only a single goal: following the school's code of conduct and prescribing the appropriate punishment" (Kupchik, 2010, p. 6).

A school's code of conduct quite typically is based in zero tolerance. This means that once a rule is in place, any infraction is treated in a same way, usually by suspension or expulsion from school. A child who unthinkingly brings a pen-knife in a lunchbox for cutting fruit is treated similarly as an adolescent victim of peer threats who for protection also carries a knife. Each instance is a 'crime', and criminalization of the young has become commonplace (Stone, 2011). A good example is the enactment of anti-bullying laws, passed in almost all states in the last dozen or so years.[2] Now schools, and their adults, can claim that they are no longer accountable for serious harm from bullying on and by young people that occurs in their domain. Rather, bullying is a matter for police and courts to handle.

An additional note. Along with invasive school discipline and youth criminalization has come an intensification of academic standardization and accountability, especially through testing. Even though there are voices calling for calmer responses, the nation is obsessed with its international rankings and what is widely perceived as the failure of public schooling. Larger issues of poverty, income inequality, and racist organization of schools are perhaps too 'fearful' to combat. At the edge of a national consciousness, however, looms the realization that punishment does not work.

Fear of disorder in school has an analogue in fear of crime in society. The second example is the 'school to prison pipeline' composed primarily of minority male youth—African Americans, increasingly Latinos, and those with disabilities (with female numbers growing overall). The school end of the pipeline begins in suspensions that culminate in dropping out. Across several decades, rates of exclusion are on the rise. Furthermore, youth lacking school credentials have difficulties finding work and turns to drugs follow. At the prison end of the pipeline, a first manifestation is massive incarceration largely for drug-related offenses. A second effect mentioned subsequently—and relating to the other two examples—is creation of a 'penal state'. Numbers tell the story. The USA has the largest prison system of industrialized nations worldwide. A recent count of 2.3 million imprisoned persons means that 1 in 42 Americans at any time is confined. Social scientist Victor Rios (2007) breaks down the minority statistics. As of 2003, 12 % of all black males in their twenties were in prison or jail, almost 4 % of Latinos, and 1.5 % of whites. In recent years, states appear to be building more prisons; relating race and poverty, the lives of millions are tragic.[3]

The general result, creation of a penal state, is well described in a 2007 volume, *Governing through crime: How the war on crime transformed American democracy and created a culture of fear*, written by legal scholar, Jonathan Simon. Even as statistics of adult violent crime show a decrease in recent years (as does youth violence), the generalized 'fear' of crime and need for safety remain. Simon offers this contemporary metaphor of a social classed society reacting to perceived threat. Across the USA,

> the gated community style of subdivision and the oversized sport utility vehicles (SUVs) both reflect a priority on security and on reinforcing the distance that middle class families seek from crime risks they associate with the urban poor.... [This emphasis on fortification makes such communities] even more reliant on a command-and-control police and penal state. (Simon, 2007, p. 7; see also Western, 2006 and Marable, 2007)

The third example is the 'war on terrorism'. Since 9/11, emphasis on personal safety from crime has been extended in the American imaginary into a desperate need for national security. This means to be free from attack at home and to engage in war abroad. The focus, fueled by religious fundamentalism, is Muslims 'suspected of being terrorists'. Punishment for al-Qaeda, for example, has resulted in imprisonment practices unheard of since the twentieth-century world wars. In a relatively recent essay in *The New York Review of Books*, English, journalism and politics professor Mark Danner applies Italian philosopher Giorgio Agamben's term 'the state of exception' to America. If at first glance the first two examples of this section do not seem to relate directly to denial of democracy, this example is surely one of failure. Agamben relates that the state of exception is "a position at the limit of politics and law... an ambiguous, uncertain borderline fringe" (Danner, 2011, p. 2, citing Agamben, 2005, p. 1). Danner's specific topic is the practice of official torture that previously was "'illegal' and 'anathema'... [and] today... is a policy choice" (Danner, p. 3).

Policy, issued right after the 9/11 attack by the then President George W. Bush, called on the Central Intelligence Agency to 'disappear' perhaps in total as many as 100,000 persons into secret prisons around the world. No habeas corpus, no due process—as Danner puts this, "without legal status or even government confirmation that they are alive and in custody.... [such prisoners become the objects] of 'indefinite detention'" (Danner, 2011, p. 5, citing Agamben, 2005, pp. 3–4). Different from earlier excesses by the CIA, this time the agency insisted on explicit approval for everything it did. Along with this, attorneys for the US Department of Justice actually explored and documented whether 12 torture techniques including the infamous waterboarding actually violated internal criminal and international agreements. In 2006, the US Congress granted approval in the Military Commissions Act.

Move closer to today. Public all along, gradually, these utterly severe practices of imprisonment and torture became more and more widely revealed. Media reports, Congressional hearings, investigative exposes, and former Vice President Richard Cheney's proud memoir, *In My Time*, are confirmation. Under President Barak Obama, American policy is supposedly changed, but Guantánamo Bay remains open and 'disappearance' has been extended even for prisoners who are known to be innocent. As Danner concludes,

> Americans, believing themselves to stand proudly for the rule of law and human rights, have become for the rest of the world a symbol of... a society in which lawbreaking, approved by its highest officials, goes unpunished. (p. 12; see also Cole, 2011)

If these three examples are indicative of an American democratic institution that is failing, it must be said that all is not lost. This past year also saw the Occupy protests over deeply troubling economic disparities and, as well, the American presidential primaries. The right to 'have a say' is still alive in the USA—even though ironically, political Super PACS (organizations raising millions and millions of dollars for candidates) have a lot of control over who can win the election. At the least, recent and present events are a reminder that democracy in America cannot be taken for granted and must be renegotiated again and again. One way to 'rethink' democracy is perhaps to turn to the past in theory and practice. The focus of the remainder of this chapter is the writings in the first decades of the twentieth century by political psychologist Harold D. Lasswell and their implementation in an experimental democratic innovation.

2.3   Introducing Lasswell

Harold D. Lasswell devoted his career to the pursuit of understanding and facilitating of democracy in America. Not only did he desire its widespread institutionalization, but he might even be called an institution in his own right because of his unique theorizing and research. As this section reveals, classifying him within a standard history of American social science is not easy. He published 60 volumes and more than 300 articles—as well as several hundred reviews and commentaries (Almond, 1987, p. 265).[4] In a recent account, Lasswell's student William Ascher describes his contribution in a contemporary context: "[His] distinctive intellectual history elucidates how he succeeded in bringing psychodynamic functional theory into political psychology in accordance with the principles of pragmatism" (Ascher & Hirschfelder-Asher, 2005, p. 13).[5] More succinctly, he is chief among modern fathers of American policy sciences. One biographer, Bruce Lannes Smith, names him "a kind of Leonardo de Vinci of the behavioral sciences" publishing across anthropology, international relations, political philosophy, empirical political science, economic policy, labor relations, psychiatry, quantitative semantics, and "even law… of outer space" (Smith, 1969, p. 41). Lastly, in addition to these numerous fields and disciplines, Lasswell is known for the many new and enhanced research concepts, methods, and skills which he utilized.

Early biographic facts are these: As mentioned above, Lasswell lived from 1902 to 1978. He came from a midwest small town, was a high school prodigy, and at 16 entered the young, exciting University of Chicago in 1918. There, he was greatly influenced by the multidisciplinary Chicago School of 'sociology' of which Dewey had been a part. He did undergraduate, graduate, and early teaching there and was probably most influenced by eminent political scientist, Charles Edward Merriam. Over some years, Merriam issued a series of challenges to his young protégé that helped establish some of the major threads in Lasswell's research. Among them was the role of propaganda in political behavior that led to Lasswell's dissertation. As Gabriel Almond spotlights, also significant for Lasswell was Merriam's interest in "the psychological and personality aspects of leadership and the uses of the abnormal in the explanation of the normal" (Almond, 1987, p. 252). The latter culminate in Lasswell's very important book, *Psychopathology and Politics*, from 1930, with some reappearance in *Democratic Character* in the early 1950s, turned to below. Publishing early, and completing his dissertation, he was appointed Assistant Professor at the University of Chicago in 1926. Across these few years, Lasswell traveled to Europe several times to study, and, as biographers emphasize, this included the reading of Marx and especially psychoanalysis. He underwent therapy and joined in discussion and other endeavors with important European devotees. In an interest that remained throughout his lifetime, among noted neo-Freudians mentioned in his writings are Harry Stack Sullivan and Karen Horney.

Almond, cited previously, identifies three phases of Lasswell's career. The first lasted until 1938 and, as just indicated, comprised of his major writings in political theory. Heady, professionally and personally fulfilling at first, a decade after his appointment at Chicago, things changed. Under the presidency of humanist Robert Maynard Hutchins, Lasswell and colleagues were subject to strong criticism and lack of support. Thus, he left the university for Washington, DC, and had the opportunity to join Sullivan and anthropologist Edward Sapir to form a research institute.

The second phase began with the failure of this enterprise and lasted through World War II. As Joseph Goldsen (1979) recounts in a memorial statement, it was during this time that Lasswell continued but greatly expanded a role as consultant and government adviser; all his life, he did this also with colleagues and students. In his early career, among experiences, he had worked with Indian affairs and farm resettlement and in 1939–1940 consulted with the Rockefeller-funded General Education Board. Between 1940 and 1945, Lasswell's activities centered in the US Department of Justice and the Office of War Information and extended across other federal executive departments and agencies. As a listing of his appointments and accomplishments attests, he was a very busy man. Notably in this second phase, Lasswell began a 30-year association with the Rand Corporation.

The third phase was initiated with Lasswell's appointment in 1946 as professor in Yale University's School of Law. In this period, his career achieved further distinction. By the time of his research with Rubenstein, he held a distinguished chair and was awarded another at his retirement in 1970. He initiated new scholarly foci in theory of law, practices of jurisprudence research and decision-making, and legal education. He continued collaborations with scholars and researchers that had also characterized previous work (see Smith, 1969, p. 47). Among them was his Yale colleague, Myres S. McDougal, with whom he primarily undertook this new work. In the early 1950s, his first books on political theory were reprinted, and he published the monograph, *Democratic Character.* In addition, a partnership with Abraham Kaplan produced *Power and society: A framework for political inquiry* (1950) that brings forward Lasswell's political theory into a broad philosophical background. The era is also one in which Lasswell received many honors. These included presidencies of the American Political Science Association and the American Society of International Law and several honorary degrees. He became a fellow in the American Academy of Arts and Sciences and the National Academy of Sciences. Harold Lasswell died in 1978 following a massive stroke and a year's illness.

Before concluding this section, and as transition to the next on 'character', it seems appropriate to relate something of Lasswell's person. Across his life, he appears to be somewhat eccentric, charming to most. He never married but had many friends. Here is an illustration of affectionate memories from a colleague:

> Lasswell is perennially youthful. His prevailing mood is ebullience…. [He] is sometimes exhausting but always inexhaustible…. He has a ravenous, a ferocious, an insatiable appetite for every conceivable aspect of living. He is surely the most indefatigable talker, drinker, eater, traveler, conferee… bibliophile, and notetaker in the world. (Rosten, 1969, pp. 7–8; see Rogow, 1969)

He was known for entertaining and ever-articulate monologues in long dinner evenings with friends.

In summary, Lasswell might well be seen as quintessentially 'American' for his generation: middle-class roots, extraordinary rise to prominence, utilizing multidisciplinary, multifaceted research interests and methodologies in the context of the promise of empirical science. He lives across the century of America becoming a 'superpower'. In this era, the nation succeeds culturally and intellectually to break free from Europe; participation in world wars actually leads to social and economic progress; the Great Depression, even, is the basis for widespread reform and creation of a 'model' welfare state that has only recently been virtually dismantled. It just might be said that at various points in the century as they cared for themselves, prosperous Americans also cared for others (see also Rogow, 1969 and McDougal, 1979 on Lasswell).

As his biography above and his work demonstrate, however, Lasswell's contributions are not a simple representation of the era. He does undertake research characteristic of his times but the breadth and depth of his interests, topics, and methods of inquiry stand in the face of what is also a century of increasing and often narrow specialization. Serving as transition to the next section, as many of his day, Lasswell's work—and his own character—manifests an underlying faith in the promise of democracy. But, while the institution realizes increases in opportunity in many domains of American life and for more and more persons, into the next century, this faith, at the least, comes or ought to come under scrutiny.

2.4 Democratic Character

The epigraph of this chapter begins a small volume that Lasswell publishes in 1941. Entitled *Democracy through public opinion* (Lasswell, 1941), it was one of the many opportunities for him to disseminate aspects of a comprehensive theory of democratic political theory first developed, as indicated above, in the early 1930s. Although America was not at war (yet), he was well aware of the larger world scene: Who could not be? And he 'knew' that there was no immunity from the war. He writes, "On the surface the crises of our time are crises of destructiveness. Deeper yet, they are crises of self-respect. We have brought destructiveness upon ourselves and one another because we have not learned how to conserve the dignity of man" (p. 2). In this volume, Lasswell's focus is on the role of public opinion in democracy, related to themes of communication and decision-making prominent in his work.

Ten years later, Lasswell puts forth another synthesis, *Democratic Character* (Lasswell, 1951). In it, he sets out 'criteria' for individuals and collectives to be democratic. The work is systemic and systematic, written as a sort of manual, taking the reader through a set of definitional and descriptive categories for the institution toward a conceptual aim. It is in a logical, textual sense, 'empirical'. His democratic political psychology relates to a dominant interest in 'personality theory' of his day. Although he does mention Marxist views, discussion and elaboration centers on his reading of psychoanalysis. Even with his renown, however, Lasswell's reliance of explanatory "Freudian conceptions" (Ascher & Hirschfelder-Asher, 2005, p. 68) may have been a matter for strong criticism in twentieth-century mid-decades. Today, it seems safe to say that psychoanalytic theorizing is not part of mainstream theoretical and empirical psychiatry and psychology or political science in the American context. In the rest of this section, a way to conceive of Lasswell's theory of democratic character is through a layered analysis.[6]

First layer: character and constitution. As in American liberal, and western thought, Lasswell begins discussion with a return to philosophical traditions, classical and modern. From Aristotle and Plato, a premise is connection of 'character' and 'constitution'. The former, coming down to contemporary times, refers to individual capacities and contributions.[7] The latter is an interesting usage. Lasswell explains that in the classical era, "Aristotle… had in mind 'a scheme of life, directed to attain a particular quality of life… a culture'" (Lasswell, 1951, citing Barker on Aristotle, 1946, pp. 332, 465). The modern approach, in contrast, moves away from universal propositions to scientific procedures in order to understand specific individuals and groups in particular settings and circumstances. As Lasswell says, it is "through self-understanding… or the self-understood action of others" (Lasswell, 1951, p. 469). To this empirical base, he marries the aim of 'democratic community'. Here is an initiating definition that elaborates on his signature phrase about human dignity mentioned above: "A democratic community is one in which human dignity is… characterized by wide rather than narrow participation in the shaping and sharing of values" (ibid., p. 474). Values, for Lasswell, which he names as "preferred events", are what man strives for through institutions and their resources (ibid.). They are of two types: "deference" values personally attributed by self and others and "welfare" values impersonally attributed.[8] Illustrative but not definitive, seven values are power, respect, rectitude, well-being, wealth, skill, and enlightenment. The deference category is constituted in the first four values and welfare the other three. Their application is that any community can be described according to "who gets what (values) when and how" (ibid., 475).

Second layer: character and personality. As just mentioned, personality is a central construct of twentieth-century American social psychology. Lasswell offers this view: "[A personality is the] comprehensive term for enduring traits of an individual…

[which] are manifested in interpersonal relationships" (ibid., p. 480). It incorporates attitudes, skills, and knowledges as well as basic drives and their automatic and unconscious restrictions, compulsions, and mechanisms. In traditional psychoanalytic categories, the personality is divided into the ego, the superego, and the id. Developed from Sullivan and George Herbert Mead, Lasswell names the ego "the self-system" (ibid., p. 481). Experiencing this system includes not only self and not-self—identifications—but also demands and expectations of this system. Thus, "character… is the self-system… [along with] the degree of support, opposition or non-support received from the unconscious parts of the personality" (ibid., p. 482). Significantly, while personality is the self-system, character is the predispositional element as well as demands, expectations, and projections and, turned to below, an "energy" or "intensity system" (ibid., pp. 481–483; Ascher & Hirschfelder-Asher, 2005, pp. 68–70).

Third layer: subsystem and democratic character. In the next layer, Laswell applies the general picture of constitution, personality, and character to a potential realization of democracy. Important for the innovation to follow, he writes thus:

> It is… to be understood that the present sketch is designed to serve as an aid to empirical inquiry and that the 'theoretical model' of the democratic character will undoubtedly undergo extensive modification as scientific work in this area gains scope and depth. (Lasswell, 1951, p. 495)

In application, within the subsystem, three elements are central for democratic character. These are the open ego, multiple and shared values, and confidence in human potentialities.

With reference to identifications, the first element, open ego, is an attitude toward other persons that is, in the scientist Lasswell's terms, warm, inclusive and expanding, capable of friendship, and to "sense the feelings and viewpoints of others in the life of an entire group" (p. 496). The second element, with reference to demands, multiple and shared values, is a disposition not to hoard or monopolize; importantly to the democratic character, in these, "the exercise of power… [holds little] value" (p. 498). The third element, in expectations as confidence in human potentialities, is this: the development of trust in human benevolence.

Fourth layer: energy system and democratic character. Lasswell continues description of democratic character by expanding more specifically into the unconscious. He poses this: "The ideal conception of the democratic character includes the specification that the self-system shall have at its disposal the energies of the unconscious part of the personality" (ibid., p. 503). For him, these energies form a supporting 'subsystem' that is manifest in both positive and negative ways but is largely "tied down to the task… [of prevention of]… destructive drives" (ibid., p. 509). Negative manifestations range from psychosomatic disturbances to prejudices to those he believes are most significant, anxieties. Taken from Sullivan, and typical of other self-system, psychoanalytic origins in infancy, across their lives, humans experience an 'uncanny emotion' often described as awe, dread, or loathing (ibid.). This is Lasswell's definition of anxiety.

Fifth layer: discussion. For any individual, patterns of enduring activity are formed throughout a life that exhibits the 'maximization principle', that is, "the tendency to maximize the indulgences of the system as a whole" (ibid., p. 512). With regard to democratic character, Lasswell writes that

> we have in mind the development of the self and energy systems which withstand adversity on behalf of democratic patterns of value and practice…. The task is nothing less than the drastic and continuing reconstruction of our own civilization…. This calls for a reconsideration of adult-to-adult and adult-to-pre-adult relationships… [to provide] continuing support for democratic performance…. [and] to bring into being a democratic equilibrium in societal relations. (Lasswell, 1951, p. 513)

Discussion in *Democratic Character* concludes with a turn to empirical study and need for development of a 'continuing trend survey' of democratic character for democratic community. Lasswell cautions that such surveys are always situational and trends not universal. In a foreshadowing of the innovation with Rubenstein undertaken just a few years later, he offers this negative hypothesis: "[Failure] to develop democratic character is a function of interpersonal relations in which low estimates of the self are permitted to develop" (ibid., p. 521). For Lasswell, the occupation of psychiatry in adults is to 'reeducate' for a positive self.

2.5 Innovation

This section now turns to a particular experiment in the institution of democracy in an unusual social site, a psychiatric hospital. The innovation is, in effect, his effort to put a conception into operation—to try it out. Rubenstein and Lasswell begin their reporting in *The sharing of power in a psychiatric hospital* (1966) with a particular psychological and institutional situation. The role of the family is the initiating factor in the life of a growing, maturing individual who must find fulfillment therein and in his communities. Growth always entails conflicts that need to be worked out. Some persons, they assert, have historically had few resources for individual control: "'Negroes,' women, students and patients are still disadvantaged" (Rubenstein & Lasswell, 1966, p. 2). With regard to psychiatric patients, a broad societal view had traditionally been held: They have to be taken care of because "they are ill, incapacitated, or defective" (ibid., p. 3). Over time, moreover, specialized institutions were created to "reprocess behavior and the needs of… [the ill]" (ibid., p. 4). These include schools, monasteries, work communities, prisons, and hospitals. Significantly in the latter around mid-twentieth century, the psychiatric 'therapeutic community' changed and developed in order that patients prepare themselves for successful participation in the larger society—this preparation was to occur within the hospital.

The particular setting of the innovation was the Yale Psychiatric Institute established as part of a larger institution in human relations in 1930. In its early history, the institute specialized in diagnosis and evaluation believing (in the tradition above) that severely mentally ill patients would remain ill. In the mid-1940s, seemingly earlier and different from most other similar places, the institute's emphasis turned to psychoanalysis and psychotherapy. Interdisciplinary research in the social sciences was also emphasized with the hospital conceived as a small society (ibid., p. 37). It is important to note that prior to the mid-1950s, what patients regarded as "pro forma" participatory government had existed. According to the Rubenstein and Lasswell report, it was characterized by "patients' apathy… [and] contempt… [because the] staff alone exercised power and made all of the important decisions in the hospital" (ibid., pp. 37–38).

Given this background and the matching interests of Rubenstein and Lasswell, the chief innovation is the initiation of the YPI patient-staff meeting.[9] Here follows a brief description of the study. Attended by as many as 60 people, the meetings were initiated in late 1956, and the period of research covered regularly scheduled bimonthly events between July 1, 1957 and June 30, 1958. Of the latter, two tape recordings were selected for verbatim presentation and analysis in the body of the report, and two others were added to the appendix without elaboration. The analysis consists of two dimensions, the actual wording and commentary. The latter itself has two parts, one quantitative which includes value analysis and decision process and one qualitative which characterizes participants' tactics in the meetings. The first coding was conducted by a research staffer and validated by the researchers/authors, and the second was by them.

The flavor of the meetings and of the research process is best demonstrated in two brief text exemplars around the value of power; they also specifically tie Lasswell's institutional conception of democracy to the jointly undertaken research process.

Power. The values list in *Democratic Character* names power first. Its foremost place seems appropriate given the focus on innovation at YPI. To begin with, here follows Lasswell's definitional listing of 'shared power' (see Lasswell, 1951, p. 476):

1. Power is shared when the political myth favors the pattern of general participation in the making of decisions.
2. Power is shared when in fact there is general participation in decision-making.
3. Shared power means that it is assumed that office-holders can be criticized without fear of serious retaliation.
4. Shared power means that the shaping of decisions depends upon values to which access can be had on the basis of merit.
5. Shared power includes the freedom to challenge the lawfulness of applying general rules to concrete cases.
6. Power is shared when there is effective presumption against the politicizing of human relations.
7. Power is shared when there is a presumption against the use of power in great concentration, particularly in the form of regimentation, centralization, and militarization.

In the rest of this section and the next, all material is taken from *The sharing of power in a psychiatric hospital* (1966, hereafter *Sharing*). In the first transcript, the chairman of the meeting who is the YPI Director, and the only one wearing a lab coat, begins the meeting (the third of the year). Behind on a blackboard is a cartoon of him drawn by a patient. Here is an excerpt (both paraphrased and verbatim) in which multiple values including—and ultimately—power is involved. What begins to be revealed in the analysis is the interweaving and complexity of values events. The three participants are the Director, Dr. Fleck, and two patients, Betty and Adam, and the example concerns the opening of the meeting (Rubenstein & Lasswell,

1966, pp. 110–112). All italics are verbatim transcriptions as they appear in the report; numbers refer to sequences of interactions for each patient; the numbers are comprised of both the statements and the researcher commentary.

Chairman (Dr. Fleck) 1.: *Did you want to speak, Betty?*
....

Betty (patient): 2: *Well, I just announced that you were here, Fleck* (laughing), *Dr. Fleck. The people that I was pointing out, I've heard people call 'nurse' (calls it out), instead of.... And I've heard people say, "O.K. Oakland" instead of Miss Oakland (a staff nurse present in the meeting), and I don't know, but she doesn't—do you mind it, Miss Oakland? (short pause). Then I don't think Dr. Fleck should like it, if I called him "Fleck." (There is general laughter in the group)*
....

2. [Betty] imposes a *respect* deprivation upon the Chairman by omitting his title. Her laughter suggests that she is enjoying the exchange with him.... [She makes the same deprivational reference to 'nurses' in general and to a particular nurse.... Led by Betty, [the group] laughs at... [the Director], and thus as a group *deprive* him with regard to *respect*..... [Although the teasing suggests affection, this exchange continues with an entry by Adam.]
....

Adam (patient) 3: *If I may, you ought to call Dr. Fleck, "Steve." (pause)*
3. Adam then carries this teasing further, flaunting and provoking the power of the Chairman-Director, testing how far he can go, he deprives him in *respect*, and at a deeper level, of *power*. Adam and Betty are learning how far they can go in depriving the Director, exploring the limits of toleration of the environment before counter deprivations begin.... Adam takes the spotlight from Betty, *depriving* her and *indulging* himself in *respect* as the challenger of authority.

The first transcribed meeting took place in July 1957; the second occurs the following September. The issue herein is the welcoming of a stranger to the group: Dr. Dunn is a foreigner whose English is limited, thought by patients at first to be a 'staff-type visitor' but who turns out to be a patient. As discussed subsequently, ultimately, the instantiation of shared power, of democratic practices and responsibilities, has a therapeutic purpose. In this example, the category of power is not prevalent but it is the underlying key focus (ibid., pp. 153–154, 157–158). At this point in the meeting transcript, Dr. Dunn has attended and left. She has equivocated over her lack of English and, as well, her personal confusion. But she asks a vital question about not understanding the purpose of the meeting that resonates with (the other) patients. After discussing the issue of welcome, several patients turn to the central question.

Fred 103: *Well, I think maybe one of the reasons why ah people ah more or less were sarcastic, was because she was new here. But I don't think that was the only reason.... I felt the general feeling of annoyance at this meeting... because we come here and we talk about the same thing over and over again... just like a record playing over and it gets rather boring after a while.*
103. A rebellious deprivation of the ideology... [of shared power and of increasing responsibility by patients for the community].
....

[Exchanges 104–130, all mediated through the Chairman, in which seven patients and one resident speak, most briefly. Fred enters the conversation again.]

Fred 130: *Well, I think it's rather strange... when Dr. Dunn asked the question of what this meeting is for, nobody could really give a decent answer, including the doctors... who made this meeting.... And, as for ah... ah... the trouble that Dunn had, I think that perhaps if one of the doctors was... to introduce the new patient to all the other patients and to the other doctors, then the problem... would be eliminated.*

130. An impatient and blunt confrontation which is calculated both to *enlighten* and discomfort. He makes explicit the reaction expressed earlier in laughter by the group in response to Dr. Dunn's questions about the meaning of these meetings.

Chairman 131: *Edward.*

Edward 132: *While Fred is talking today I think this is a good theme we should get on, talking about definiteness versus vaguery... how many people here actually said something new to their physician once they've gotten a story out and started... It all goes around one theme.*

132. Edward purports to support Fred's effort to face issues squarely, but then... [turns] to the topic of repetitively saying nothing in psychotherapy.

Results. Analysis of the tapes includes frequencies of participation: Overall, patients speak approximately 80 % of the time, and staff members speak 20 %. Summary of the first category of values analysis, as just illustrated, reveals that for all persons, deprivational statements are more prevalent than indulgent statements. Recall according to the maximization principle that the latter or favorable attributions, both to self and to others that ought to increase along with a development of a 'we' community (see ibid., pp. 180–181). Both given the therapeutic purpose and the 'mental state' of patients, staff members are subjected to more deprivational statements than are patients. Summary of the second category of the decision process is similarly analyzed. The process is divided into seven phases: intelligence, appraisal, promotion, invocation, application, prescription, and termination. Each subcategory is operationalized. For example, intelligence statements have nearly a dozen forms. These include what does and will happen, planning, fact assertions, predictions and formulations of consequences, and mentions of policy solutions. Again, precise frequencies are counted with patients far outspeaking staff. About these combined results, Rubenstein and Lasswell comment,

> It might be asserted that power is divided as talk is divided, that if patients and staff talk the same amount it is probable that they exercise equal power.... However, this 'equal talk' criterion may be rejected since in these meetings the top power elite encouraged the rest of the community to talk. (ibid., p. 183)

They continue that talk might in fact be an expression of powerlessness in patients, their reaction. Further, the amount of deprivational statements by staff is interesting but also a bit misleading. As the year progresses, patient and staff talk participation becomes more equal as the latter are more confident about their roles (ibid., p. 184).

2.6 Assessment

Continuing from the previous section, in *Sharing* Rubenstein and Lasswell provide their own assessment of the innovation, hospital practices, and power relations that occur after patient-staff meetings are instituted. Overall, they describe a changed 'post-innovation hospital' (beginning p. 205). For the patient, the general ideology of the institution shifts away from the notions of family blame and terminal illness. Over time, the reputation of YPI changes with the emphasis on psychotherapy.

The aim is the return of the patient to a full life as person and citizen outside of the hospital, a shared goal to which all aspects of the institution must be committed. Overall, these changes occur: increase in admission numbers and in who enters treatment; they are often younger patients, single and educated but not financially 'independent'. Note that along with the new psychological emphasis comes the increase in drug therapies, characteristic of the field of psychiatry in the mid-decades and since. The researchers are unclear about the effects of this last change.

The 'daily life' of patients is also altered as their own engagement in its planning and structure develops. One patient-led enterprise is the welcoming of new patients—a decided improvement over the case of Dr. Dunn above. Moreover, previous days spent in "interminable sitting" (ibid., p. 207) are now filled with activities such as work, recreation, classes, and meetings. As patients are more engaged democratically in their own lives, they move from inside to outside the hospital; work is even paid. It is emphasized that these changes do not detract from the core of hospital responsibility, individual therapy. What is somewhat different are patient-resident doctor relationships since difficulties and complaints are more public. One question asked in the assessment concerns why patients did not take an even more powerful role—and this is returned to. Here significantly are issues of motivation, of alienation, of unwillingness to 'step up' that are common in the larger democratic society.

Lives, expectations, and activities of all staff change too. In the study's results, the researchers stress personal changes for resident therapists and nurses. This deserves comment because just as patients,

> [staff] members are limited by personal immaturity, long exposure to and incorporation of authoritarian values, and the resulting conflicts when confronted with freedom, responsibility, and opportunities to create and sustain constructive action with others. (ibid., p. 217)

One important effect of issues for staff members who are to be role models for patients is 'constraint' on the latter's visions of what a future holds. Indeed, a patient's overall picture of the hospital grows out of a relationship with the psychotherapist. Rubenstein and Lasswell offer that

> the hospital is perceived as hostile and unfriendly and its staff arbitrary and unfeeling... when the therapist is experienced as aloof and unconcerned... [rather than] warm and nurturing when the therapist seems considerate and helpful. (ibid., p. 209)

When the patient-therapist relationship is supportive and other factors 'are indulging' as well, one ironic result may be that the patient feels safest and happiest in the institution rather than in the outside world. Psychic improvement, of course, involves what ought to be an eventual desire to leave and take personal control.

From the question above, the following element of the assessment is vital to understand for the 'success' of the innovation: Although power is shared on some matters by patients and staff, the general authority structure remains in place at the top, seated in the director and his delegates. At his discretion, group decisions may be overruled; sometimes unilateral and seemingly arbitrary and unexplained policies are put in place. As Rubenstein and Lasswell explain, this has particular effect on patients "[who strive] to participate in the full realization of the therapeutic community... [and are] confused and exasperated by the knowledge that power is incompletely shared on grounds that remain ambiguous" (ibid., p. 217).

Before turning to a final assessment on democratic sharing of power, something needs be said about the research process. Rubenstein and Lasswell are careful to distinguish what they have undertaken from a classical scientific experiment, seeing innovation as standing between experiment and official intervention (ibid., p. 268). They name their work "prototype" and distinguish three phases: pre-introduction, introduction, and post-introduction. It is characterized overall by a process of working things out over time.[10] Beyond an initiation phase, an innovation is 'introduced' when its operation is underway, relatively stable, and supported favorably in terms of possible success by key participants. Likewise, there needs to be time for those opposed to leave. In the case of YPI, residents and other staff recruits were hired because they believed in and accepted a 'democratic' therapeutic ideology for individuals and groups. Important too is the agreement to engage in continuous refinement of assumptions, procedures, and objectives. Contributing to the social science of their day, the researchers do envision the use of prototypes leading to experiments (ibid., p. 273), but they also see much value in a broad use of this form of research in and of itself.

A concluding judgment of the YPI innovation in democracy, interestingly, concerns an 'incipient revolution', and the question asked is this: "Why wasn't the revolution more revolutionary?" (ibid., p. 257). In answer, and as results indicate, the researchers posit that power is shared and individuals and the community are changed. But, to continue from the central point above, an irony if not a contradiction remains as the top authority structure of the institution stays in place, even as the director and his senior staff 'consent' to the democratic ideology and even as those less powerful consent as well. Although there is a forum for discussion and even strong criticism of staff by patients, once decisions are made, they are rarely modified or undone. About this retention of power, the researchers have three thoughts: One is that given that YPI is a hospital, the top staff does have some responsibilities that cannot realistically be shared. The second, however, is that open discussion is not undertaken regarding this issue—and its implications for the hospital experience and for 'the real world' are not explored. There are power differentials elsewhere of course. The third concerns conflict between an authoritarian structure and the aims of psychotherapy itself, of individuals taking control of their lives as mentally well. These possible 'conflicts of conscience' for top staff are "assuaged by the limited steps toward power sharing that... [are] undertaken" (p. 260). At bottom here is the researchers' judgment: In YPI, those 'typically' powerless continue to see themselves so. For them, what is affected is more so the appearance of democracy than its actuality (ibid., p. 257).

One last connection is made by Rubenstein and Lasswell for what they name as 'the policy sciences of democracy' emerging in their day. The innovation, its successes and limitations, displays analogy to the larger political order. First, in order for it to be a 'harmonizing of the ideology and behavior of democracy' (ibid., p. 284), each individual, as each patient and staff, "[must seize] opportunities to participate with others in... [power shaping and sharing,] in building and sustaining a social context in which he believes" (ibid., p. 285). If a traditional power structure is to change, this means participation and change at both the top and the bottom. The innovation in democracy at YPI made some strides in this direction but fell short of 'revolution'.

2.7   Conclusion

This chapter has presented a study of institutional spaces that begins and now concludes in a present moment but principally focuses on past work of Harold Lasswell from the first decades of the twentieth century. As a political psychologist, among the range of his professional affiliations, he developed a conception of democracy that he then implemented. In the chapter, democracy exemplifies 'institution' as does the psychiatric hospital, its practices, and research therein. Of course schools, prisons, and federal government practices are also institutional. This section offers a summary of the chapter followed by a return American democracy today and its effects on society, especially for youth and schools. There is brief comment on educational research at the close.

The study has three elements that in conclusion need to be brought together. The first element is the biography and 'character' of Lasswell; he appears as a remarkable scholar and researcher of his day—an 'institution' himself. One important factor is both the breadth and depth of his interests that belie a century's increasing emphasis on narrow specialization in research. Another factor is his faith in democracy and commitment to its shaping. Throughout an illustrious career, a particular vision of politics was his preoccupation and occupation. Significantly, while he may have been quintessentially 'American' and liberal, he does not seem naïve.

A second element in the chapter is Lasswell's conceptual theorizing about democracy. In *Democratic Character* and elsewhere, he poses a complex picture of values and processes. The vision originates in classical western thought on character and constitution and extends to personality theory in the social sciences of his day. He means for each individual to contribute to community through the realization of a goal of universalized but particularized human dignity. Theoretically, what is especially interesting is the application of psychoanalytic insights into 'self-system'. A third element is the innovation in democracy by Lasswell and Rubenstein. In the mid-1950s, it is conducted at the Yale Psychiatric Institute, a mental hospital in which for medical reasons, values of democracy are traditionally absent. The study takes place over a year in which a forum of patient-staff meetings is instituted. For Rubenstein and Lasswell, the central value of democracy is 'power' and they document its practice through meeting transcripts, presentation of detailed data, and its analysis. Their method is 'content analysis' in which speaking events are coded by the values and processes set out in the previous theoretical work. Definitions and two brief examples provide a flavor of the research enterprise. They conclude their research process with an assessment of the innovation by the researchers.

Several results are interesting that indicate some 'success'. Through participation in the patient-staff meetings, in the long run, the hospital was changed. Further, in terms of democratic character and practice, the daily lives of patients were altered that could potentially contribute to their return to life outside the hospital. Staff lives changed also as they had to adapt to different relationships. Given public and more open communication at the meetings, the researchers were 'disappointed' that the patients did not assume stronger roles and more power. Their answer is that the overall authority structure of the hospital remained in place. Patients recognized this limitation and continued to envision themselves as "relatively powerless… [and living under] an appearance of democracy" (ibid., p. 257).

The appearance of democracy may indeed be the current state of American society and in many of its social institutions. The nation, the government, has lost respect both at home and abroad. It seems clear that safety and security are not guaranteed by discipline and punishment. Further, what is particularly pernicious today is that denial of democracy by many people is taken for granted. As the first section of the chapter indicates, failure illustrated in school discipline, the school to prison pipeline, and the war on terrorism especially target children and youth. Given these practices, several educational questions are evident to which there appear no easy answers. How could a nation committed to democracy in the ideal condone these practices and how might they be changed now? Given this present state, how can youth learn to be democratic adults? What might society and schools do to contribute to changes toward more democracy?

As negative as this state is, some positive steps toward change are underway. At the level of society, the first is that there is attention to each of these and other instances in the media and in research that is critical: Citations above are illustrative. At the school level, a good example is the growing recognition that zero-tolerance discipline is absurd. Unfortunately, other practices of surveillance and imprisonment appear more entrenched—and the school accountability movement remains strong as well.

From this chapter, Lasswell's overall contribution to the present moment is a reminder that a conception of democracy is available and that its implementation should and can be enacted—again and again. This is even if its success at any moment is not universal and for all.

To close, one intent of the chapter for this volume has been to demonstrate research in democratic theory and practice from mid-twentieth century—and the beginning of policy sciences—to an educational research audience today. Given the qualitative research process, the verbatim transcript analysis, the researchers' interpretive commentary, and their own 'self-assessment', the model seems very contemporary. In addition to lessons for the institution of democracy, for American society and its youth, from Lasswell's work, there are lessons for the research 'institution' as well.

Notes

1. See Harold D. Lasswell, *Democracy Through Public Opinion*, published in 1941.
2. See Bully Police USA, http://www.bullypolice.org, retrieved October 30, 2011.
3. This information is from Ask.com, US Prison Population, http://www.ask.com/web?q=US+prison+population&search=&qsrc=0&o=2815&l=dir,   retrieved October 10, 2011. Another source is the US Bureau of Justice Statistics in 2009

that counts 7.2 million Americans in jail, prison, or on probation. This is 1 in 32 persons. Also reported for 2010 is a decline in US violent crime across all age groups. Youth alcohol and marijuana use far outstrips use of all other drugs combined. See Bureau of Justice Statistics, http://www.bjs.gov, retrieved October 30, 2011. Finally, a 2008 story from Global Research offers the illustration of thirteen states with 'third strike' laws for felons leading to the building of a large number of new federal prisons. See Pelaez, 2008, http://www.global-research.ca/index.php?context=va&aid=8289, retrieved April 3, 2012.

4. Other sources cite less volumes; this number might well include significant reprints in the 1950s of original publications on politics from the 1930s.

5. William Ascher introduced me to Lasswell at Soka University of America in March 2011. I am most grateful for this gesture and the significant text. See Ascher and Hirschfelder-Asher (2005).

6. This is my account of Lasswell's categories as layers.

7. In today's terms, Lasswell might well be identified as a theoretical liberal. He might even approve of the content of the USA character education movement but, given his theorizing and experiment in democracy, he might well be critical of its didactic pedagogy. See Christina Hoff Sommers (2002), for the movement's citation of Aristotle.

8. The material on values is somewhat interpretive as I have attempted to understand Lasswell's use of the concept of value.

9. The terms 'innovation' and later 'prototype' are important for Rubenstein and Lasswell to distinguish their research from classical experiments with controls, variables, and generalizations. See also Rubenstein (1969), on their collaboration.

10. Philosophical development of power, alongside democratic institutions, forces, and participants, is found in Lasswell and Kaplan (1950).

References

Agamben, G. (2005). *State of exception* (K. Attell, Trans.). Chicago: The University of Chicago Press.

Almond, G. (1987). Harold Dwight Lasswell, February 13, 1902—December 18, 1978. In *Biographical memoirs, National Academy of Sciences of the United States of America* (Vol. 57, pp. 248–274). Washington, DC: National Academy Press.

Ascher, W., & Hirschfelder-Asher, B. (2005). *Revitalizing political psychology: The legacy of Harold D. Lasswell.* New York/London: Psychology Press.

Bully Police USA. Retrieved October 30, 2011, from http://www.bullypolice.org

Bureau of Justice Statistics. Retrieved October 30, 2011, from http://www.bjs.gov

Cole, D. (September 29, 2011). After September 11: What we still don't know. *The New York Review of Books*, pp. 1–11. Retrieved October 30, 2011, from http://www.nybooks.com/articles/archives/2011/sep/29/after-september-11-what-we-still

Danner, M. (October 13, 2011). After September 11: Our state of exception. *The New York Review of Books*, pp. 1–17. Retrieved October 30, 2011, http://www.nybooks.com/articles/archives/2011/oct/13.after-septemb

Goldsen, J. (Contributor) (1979). *Harold Dwight Lasswell, 1902–1978, In commemoration and continuing commitment* (pp. 78–81). New Haven, CT: Yale Law School, Policy Sciences Center, The Ogden Foundation.

Kupchik, A. (2010). *Homeroom security: School discipline in an age of fear*. New York/London: New York University Press.

Lasswell, H. (1941). *Democracy through public opinion*. Menasha, WI: George Banta.

Lasswell, H. (1951). Democratic character. In *The political writings of Harold D. Lasswell* (pp. 465–525). Glencoe, IL: The Free Press.

Lasswell, H., & Kaplan, A. (1950). *Power and society: A framework for political inquiry*. New Haven, CT/London: Yale University Press.

Marable, M. (2007). Introduction: Racializing justice, disenfranchising lives: Toward an antiracist criminal justice. In M. Manning, I. Steinberg, & K. Middlemass (Eds.), *Racializing justice, disenfranchising lives: The racism, criminal justice, and law reader* (pp. 1–14). New York: Palgrave Macmillan.

McDougal, M. (1979). *Harold Dwight Lasswell, 1902–1978, In commemoration and continuing commitment*. New Haven, CT: Yale Law School, Policy Sciences Center, The Ogden Foundation. (Editor not named in publication)

Pelaez, V. (2008, March 10). The prison industry in the United States: Big business or a new form of slavery. *Global Research*. Retrieved April 3, 2012, from http://www.globalresearch.ca/index.php?context=va&aid=8289

Rios, V. (2007). The hypercriminalization of Black and Latino male youth in an era of mass incarceration. In M. Manning, I. Steinberg, & K. Middlemass (Eds.), *Racializing justice, disenfranchising lives: The racism, criminal justice, and law reader* (pp. 17–23). New York: Palgrave Macmillan.

Rogow, A. (Ed.). (1969). *Politics, personality, and social science in the twentieth century: Essays in honor of Harold D. Lasswell*. Chicago/London: The University of Chicago Press.

Rosten, L. (1969). Harold Lasswell: A memoir. In A. Rogow (Ed.), *Politics, personality, and social science in the twentieth century: Essays in honor of Harold D. Lasswell* (pp. 1–13). Chicago/London: The University of Chicago Press.

Rubenstein, R. (1969). The study of political processes in psychiatric illness and treatment. In A. Rogow (Ed.), *Politics, personality, and social science in the twentieth century: Essays in honor of Harold D. Lasswell* (pp. 147–154). Chicago/London: The University of Chicago Press.

Rubenstein, R., & Lasswell, H. (1966). *The sharing of power in a psychiatric hospital*. New York/London: Yale University Press.

Simon, J. (2007). *Governing through crime: How the war on crime transformed American democracy and created a culture of fear*. Oxford/New York: Oxford University Press.

Smith, B. L. (1969). The mystifying intellectual history of Harold D. Lasswell. In A. Rogow (Ed.), *Politics, personality, and social science in the twentieth century: Essays in honor of Harold D. Lasswell* (pp. 41–105). Chicago/London: The University of Chicago Press.

Sommers, C. H. (2002). How moral education is finding its way back into America's schools. In W. Damon (Ed.), *Bringing in a new era in character education* (pp. 23–41). Stanford, CA: Hoover Institution.

Stone, L. (2011). Fear of uncertainty, control, and the criminalizing of youth. In J. DeVitis & T. Yu (Eds.), *Character and moral education: A reader* (pp. 283–294). New York: Peter Lang.

US Prison Population. Retrieved October 10, 2011, from http://www.ask.com/web?q=US+prison+population&search=&qsrc=0&o=2815&l=dir

Western, B. (2006). *Punishment and inequality in America*. New York: Russell Sage.

Chapter 3
The Power of the Parochial in Shaping the American System of Higher Education

David F. Labaree

The roots of American higher education are extraordinarily local. Unlike the European university, with its aspirations toward universality and its history of cosmopolitanism, the American college of the nineteenth century was a hometown entity.[1] Most often, it was founded to advance the parochial cause of promoting a particular religious denomination rather than to promote higher learning. In a setting where no church was dominant and all had to compete for visibility, stature, and congregants, founding colleges was a valuable way to plant the flag and promote the faith. This was particularly true when the population was rapidly expanding into new territories to the west, which meant that no denomination could afford to cede the new terrain to competitors. Starting a college in Ohio was a way to ensure denominational growth, prepare clergy, and spread the word.

Alternatively, colleges were founded with an eye toward civic boosterism, intended to shore up a community's claim to be a major cultural and commercial center rather than a sleepy farm town. With a college, a town could claim that it deserved to gain lucrative recognition as a stop on the railroad line, the site for a state prison, the county seat, or even the state capital. These consequences would elevate the value of land in the town, which would work to the benefit of major landholders. In this sense, the nineteenth-century college, like much of American history, was in part the product of a land development scheme. In general, these two motives combined, as colleges emerged as a way to advance both the interests of particular sects and also the interests of the towns where they were lodged. Better to have multiple rationales and sources of support than just one (Brown, 1995).

As a result, church officials and civic leaders around the country scrambled to get a state charter for a college (but with little or no state financial support), establish

D.F. Labaree (✉)
Stanford University School of Education, Stanford, CA, USA
e-mail: dlabaree@stanford.edu

P. Smeyers et al. (eds.), *Educational Research: The Importance and Effects of Institutional Spaces*, Educational Research 7, DOI 10.1007/978-94-007-6247-3_3, © Springer Science+Business Media Dordrecht 2013

a board of trustees made up of local notables, and install a president. The latter would rent a local building, hire a small and modestly accomplished faculty, and serve as the CEO of a marginal educational enterprise, which sought to draw tuition-paying students from the area in order to make the college a going concern. With colleges arising to meet local and sectarian needs, the result was the birth of a large number of small, parochial, and weakly funded institutions in a very short period of time in the nineteenth century, which meant that most of these colleges faced a difficult struggle to survive in the competition with peer institutions. Having to operate in a time and place when the market was strong, the state weak, and the church divided, these colleges found a way to get by without the kind of robust support from a national government and a national church that universities in most European countries enjoyed at the time.

In this chapter, I examine some of the consequences of the peculiarly dispersed circumstances in which American colleges had their origins. These colleges proliferated to such an extent that by the mid-nineteenth century, the USA had the largest number of institutions of higher education in the world. They were not only geographically localized but also quite parochial in intellectual and academic stature. Quantity not quality was the driving force, and supply vastly exceeded demand. As a result, enrollments at individual institutions were small, and colleges had to drum up business every way they could. When a broader societal rationale for pursuing higher education began to emerge late in the nineteenth century—arising from the German model of the research university and from middle-class demand for socialization and credentialing that would give students advantageous access to the emerging white-collar occupations—the large number of existing colleges provided a widely distributed and fully operational infrastructure to make a huge expansion in student enrollments easy to accomplish. Only at this point did research begin to emerge as a central part of American colleges and universities.

This historical background helps explain how American higher education in the twentieth century rose from being an intellectual backwater to a world leader. These institutions enjoyed a broad base of political and financial support, which was at the same time populist (educating large numbers of local students at the undergraduate level), elite (educating a small number of graduate students and producing high-level academic research), and practical (providing professional training and useful inventions to serve the needs of the community).

For educational research on higher education, this structure has posed distinctive limitations. Researchers are concentrated in institutions at the top of the structure, and as a result research on higher education has tended to focus on places like Harvard and Yale rather than the community colleges and regional state universities that employ the large majority of faculty and enroll the large majority of students. In addition, the extreme geographical dispersion and decentralized governance of the system has led researchers—especially in the history of education—to focus on the distinctive characteristics of individual colleges rather than on the characteristics of the overall system.

3.1 Rapid Expansion and Dispersion of US Colleges in the Nineteenth Century

In 1790, at the start of the first decade of the new American republic, the United States already had 19 institutions called colleges or universities (Collins, 1979, Table 5.2; Tewksbury, 1932, Table 1). The numbers grew gradually in the first three decades, rising to 50 by 1830, and then started accelerating. They doubled in the 1850s (reaching 250), doubled again in the following decade (563), and in 1880 totaled 811. The growth in colleges vastly exceeded the growth in population, with a total of 4.9 institutions per million population in 1790 rising to 16.1 institutions per million in 1880. As a result, the United States during the nineteenth century had by far the largest number of colleges and universities of any country in the world.

By contrast, the United Kingdom started the nineteenth century with 6 institutions and had 10 by 1880, while in France the number of universities rose from 12 to 22. In all of Europe, the number of universities rose from 111 to 160 during the same period (Rüegg, 2004). So in 1880 the United States had five times as many institutions of higher education as all of the countries in Europe combined. Why did this remarkable explosion of college expansion take place in such a short time and in such a cultural backwater?

One answer is that the large majority of these American institutions were colleges in name only and had but the weakest of claims to being purveyors of higher education. These colleges were very small. Because of the dispersed and marginal nature of these institutions, it is hard to determine their size and even their number until the federal government began to collect statistics in 1870. But the figures collected by Colin Burke (1982, computed from Tables 1.5 and 2.2) suggest that the average private liberal arts college (excluding the small number of state universities) had an enrollment of 42 students in 1830, rising to 47 in 1850. This varied widely by region. New England colleges—the earliest institutions, which in turn served the largest population—had an average enrollment of 128 students in 1850, while, in the rapidly expanding educational arena of the Midwest, colleges had an average of only 23 students. By 1880, the average institution of higher education had 131 students (Carter et al., 2006, Table Bc523). In 1870, the first year for which we have data on professors, the average American college faculty had 10 members, rising to 14 in 1880 (Carter et al., Table Bc571). The total number of degrees granted annually per college was only 17 in both 1870 and 1880 (U.S. Bureau of the Census, 1975, Series H 751).

Not only were these colleges very small, but also they were widely scattered across the countryside, the large majority located far from a major city. Burke's survey of liberal arts colleges showed that in 1850 only 7 % were in New England and 15 % in the Middle Atlantic regions, the two centers of population at the time, while 28 % were in the Southwest and 31 % in the Midwest, the most sparsely populated sections of the country. In addition to being geographically dispersed, the sponsorship for these colleges was also widely dispersed across a large number of religious denominations. He estimates that 87 % of the private colleges in 1850 were denominational in origin, with 21 % Presbyterian, 16 % Methodist, 14 % Baptist, 10 % Catholic, 8 % Congregational, 7 % Episcopal, and the rest scattered across seven additional denominations (Burke, 1982, Table 1.9).

Another sign of the lowly status of these nineteenth-century colleges is that they were difficult to distinguish from the variety of high schools and academies that were also in abundance across the American landscape. For students, it was often a choice of going to high school or to college rather than seeing one as the feeder institution for the other. As a result, the age range of students attending high schools and colleges overlapped substantially. And some high schools offered a program of studies that was superior to the offerings at many colleges. So, for example, in 1849 the Pennsylvania legislature gave the Central High School of Philadelphia the right to offer its graduates college degrees, including the bachelor of arts and master of arts (Labaree, 1988, p. 109).

If you delve into the histories of individual American colleges during the mid-nineteenth century, you find tales of woe: students rioting because of bad food, faculty salaries in arrears, no books in the library, and the poor beleaguered president trying to keep the whole shaky enterprise afloat. Take the case of Middlebury College, a Congregational institution founded in 1800, which has now become one of the premier liberal arts colleges in the country, considered one of the 'little ivies'. But in 1840, when its new president arrived on campus (a Presbyterian minister named Benjamin Labaree[2]), he found an institution that was struggling to survive, and in his 25-year tenure as president, this situation did not seem to change much for the better. In letters to the board of trustees, he detailed a list of woes that afflicted the small college president of his era. Hired for a salary of $1,200 a year, he found that the trustees could not afford to pay it and immediately set out to raise money for the college, including a $1,000 contribution of his own and gifts from the small faculty, the first of eight fund-raising campaigns that he engaged in. Money worries are the biggest theme in his letters (trouble hiring and paying faculty, mortgaging his house to make up for his own unpaid salary, and perpetually soliciting gifts), but he also complained about the inevitable problems that come from trying to offer a full college curriculum with a tiny faculty.

> I accepted the Presidency of Middlebury College, Gentlemen, with a full understanding that your Faculty was small and that in consequence a large amount of instruction would devolve upon the President – that I should be desired to promote the financial interests of the Institution, as convenience and the duties of instruction would permit, was naturally to be expected, but I could not have anticipated that the task of relieving the College from pecuniary embarrassment, and the labor and responsibility of procuring funds for endowment for books, for buildings etc., etc. would devolve on me. Could I have foreseen what you would demand of me, I should never have engaged in your service… (Labaree, 1975, p. 20)

At one place in the correspondence, he listed all of the courses he had to teach as president: "Intellectual and Moral Philosophy, Political Economy, International Law, Evidences of Christianity, History of Civilization, and Butler's Analogy" (ibid., p. 20).

The point is that these rapidly proliferating American colleges in the nineteenth century were much more concerned about surviving than they were about attaining academic eminence. Unlike the situation in the old world, where a small number of institutions could count on the support of a strong state and a unified church, they had to scramble to acquire financial resources and social legitimacy from a ragtag mix of small churches and small towns scattered across a lightly populated terrain. This does not sound like a formula for success in building a world-class system of higher education. But that, in the twentieth century, is exactly what happened. It turned out that these unimpressive origins contained key elements that enabled the system's later climb to distinction.

3.2 Sources of Strength in a Humble Collection of Colleges

By 1850, the United States had a large array of colleges that constituted a loosely defined system of higher education. Constructed without an overall plan, this system was characterized by wide geographical dispersion, radically localized governance, and the absence of guaranteed support from either church or state. Only a small number of these institutions were creatures of the individual states and dependent on state appropriations. The modal institution was the independent college in a small town with a corporate charter and stand-alone finances. Most had the blessing of a religious denomination, which granted legitimacy and a source of students but provided little or no financial help. Instead they had to survive on the tuition paid by students and the gifts of individuals from the town and from the larger church community. They operated in a very competitive market for higher education, where supply vastly exceeded demand and where their main selling points were that they were geographically accessible, religiously compatible, academically unde-manding, and relatively inexpensive. On the latter two points, gaining admission was not a problem, flunking out was not likely, and the cost was low enough to make it manageable for children from middle-class families with modest resources.

Already by 1850 there were other forms of higher education emerging on the American scene, including the state university, the land-grant college, and the normal school. In the next section, I discuss how these forms increased the complexity and added to the strength of the higher education system. But for now the key point is that these new forms entered a system where the basic model for the college was already established and where any newcomers would have to adapt to the same conditions that had shaped this model over the years.

At the heart of the college system was a strong and entrepreneurial president appointed by a lay board. Board members were the trustees of the corporation, who were responsible for maintaining its financial viability and who (as leading citizens of the town and members of the clergy) brought the college social legitimacy and helped it solicit donations. The president was the college's chief executive officer, who had to give the school academic and spiritual credibility while at the same time maneuvering the institution through the highly competitive environment within which the college had to operate. Survival was the first priority of every president, and, as we saw in the case of Middlebury College, the job involved a constant struggle to keep the institution financially afloat. This meant the president had to attract and retain credible faculty and to attract and retain tuition-paying students while at the same time raising donations and teaching a large number of classes. In the absence of steady streams of funding from church or state, these colleges had to depend heavily on the tuition dollars brought in by students. This was never enough to pay all the bills, so fund-raising from the various donor constituencies was critical, but tuition was the bedrock on which the college's financial survival depended.

This competitive environment produced a system of colleges that by the 1850s had managed to prevail in the struggle for survival. They were lean and highly adaptable organizations, led by entrepreneurial presidents who kept a tight focus on the college's position in the market while keeping an eye peeled for potential threats and opportunities on the horizon. Presidents, trustees, and faculty knew they had to keep the student-consumer happy with the educational product or he would attend college in the town down the road. Likewise, they had to keep the loyalty of local boosters, denominational sponsors, and alumni if they were going to maintain the required flow of donations.

3.3 Building New Capacity and Complexity into the System

On this landscape of numerous and widely scattered colleges in the mid-nineteenth century grew three new kinds of institutions of higher education, which came to comprise the major sources of growth in the number of colleges and enrollments: state universities, land-grant colleges, and normal schools.

3.3.1 State Universities

First to arise was the state university. Initially, the distinction between public and private institutions was unclear, since all of them received corporate charters from individual states and some of the 'private' ones (such as Harvard, from its earliest days in the colonial period) received state subsidies. But gradually a new kind of institution emerged, which was legally constituted as being under the control of state government and was not affiliated with a particularly religious denomination. The first was University of Georgia, founded in 1785. There were five such universities by 1800, 12 by 1830, and 21 by 1860. At the latter point, 20 states had established at least one state university, while 14 others had not (Tewksbury, 1932, Tables 12 and 13).

These institutions received more state funds and were subject to more state control than their private counterparts, but otherwise they were not very different. Deliberately located at a distance from major population centers, they continued the pattern of geographic dispersion. Landing one of these institutions was a major plum for town fathers, and there is much lore about the chicanery that often determined which town won the prize. These state universities initially were rather small, sometimes dwarfed by the preexisting private colleges. James Axtell discovered that in 1880 only 26 of the 881 institutions of higher education had an enrollment of more than 200 students. "Amherst [private] was as large as Wisconsin and Virginia [public], Williams [private] was larger than Cornell and Indiana [public], and Bowdoin [private] was near the size of Johns Hopkins [private] and Minnesota [public]. Yale [private] with 687 students was much larger than Michigan, Missouri, or the City College of New York [public]" (quoted in Thelin, 2004, p. 90).

State universities were similar to their private counterparts in another way as well. They were often the result of competitive pressures. States were reluctant to get behind in the race with other states in establishing a state university. Much like the kind of local boosterism that motivated small towns and religious denominations to support the founding of colleges, states saw the establishment of a public university as a way to support their claims to be considered an equal to their counterparts in the union, as centers of culture, commerce, and learning and as beacons of progressive public policy. Also, it helped that a state university provided a venue for doling out political patronage. For the most part, state universities developed outside New England and the Middle Atlantic states, where existing private colleges were already serving many of the same functions and effectively lobbied to head off state-subsidized competition.[3]

3.3.2 Land-Grant Colleges

Another form of higher education institution was arising only slightly later than the state university: the land-grant college. This uniquely American invention began as an outgrowth of efforts by the federal government to promote the sale of public lands in the new territories and states of the expanding nation. The Northwest Ordinance in 1787 set aside blocks of land in the new Northwest Territory (now the American Upper Midwest) for the support of public schools. This procedure became standard practice for new states and was extended to the support of higher education. Between 1796 and 1961, Congress made land grants for higher education to 17 new states. These grants ranged from 46,000 to 100,000 acres per state. The state was permitted to sell, lease, or donate these lands for the purpose of developing higher education. State governments frequently followed suit by donating public land to colleges instead of providing cash appropriations.

Initially the support was for higher education in general, but quickly the pattern developed that these land-grant institutions were to focus on a particular form of learning that was in support of 'the useful arts'. This patterned was codified in the enormously influential Morrill Land Grant Act of 1862, which specified that the proceeds of the land should be used to support such practical programs of study as agriculture, engineering, military science, and mining. Several land-grant laws followed the initial model of the Morrill Act, expanding this process of infusing resources into practical education. The number of institutions created by the various Morrill Acts alone (1862–1890, not including the numerous land grants before 1862) totaled 107 (Ogren, 2005, pp. 363–364). Much of this money went to support existing universities, but often the money went to new land-grant schools that signaled their practical focus by including A & M (Agricultural and Mechanical) in their titles (Thelin, 2004).

These land-grant schools were public institutions, but they had a different orientation from the existing private colleges and state universities, whose curriculum was a traditional mix of liberal arts subjects. The new institutions sought less to prepare people for the clergy and high professions than to provide students with practical training in the skills needed to promote growth in the agricultural and mechanical sectors of the economy. And outside the classroom the faculty at these institutions focused their energies on providing support to the state's farmers and industrial enterprises—patenting inventions, solving mechanical problems, and setting up systems of agricultural extension agents throughout the state.

3.3.3   Normal Schools

A third group of institutions that emerged in the middle of the nineteenth century were initially more like high schools than colleges: normal schools. These were established by state governments (also by local municipalities and school districts) to prepare teachers for the public schools, driven by the rapid expansion of universal public schooling between 1830 and 1860 and the subsequent demand for new teachers. The first state normal school emerged in Massachusetts in 1839, but by 1870 there were 39 and by 1880 there were 76 (Ogren, 2005, calculated from appendix, pp. 370–390). These institutions focused initially on preparing students to become elementary teachers, and their course of studies included both pedagogy and instruction in the core school subjects. They functioned as vocational high schools for teachers, and during most of the nineteenth century, they were not considered institutions of higher education. As a result, their numbers are not included in the counts of such institutions given earlier.

But the reason for including them here is that by the end of the century, they had started evolving into colleges. By the 1890s, some of them were beginning to become teachers colleges, with the right of granting bachelor's degrees. By the 1920s and 1930s, they were beginning to drop the word 'teachers' in the titles and substituting the word 'state'. By the 1960s and 1970s, they became regional state universities. So, for example, one such institution in Pennsylvania was founded in 1859 as Millersville State Normal School; in 1927 it became Millersville State Teachers College, in 1959 Millersville State College, and in 1983 Millersville University of Pennsylvania (Ogren, 2005, appendix). In 100 years or so, these institutions rose from being high schools for training teachers to regional state universities offering a full range of university degrees.

As a result of this remarkable evolution, normal schools became a central part of the American system of higher education. And their history shows how the patterns established in the mid-nineteenth century shaped the subsequent development of the system. Like their predecessors—private colleges, state universities, and land-grant colleges—they were located mostly in small towns and were scattered widely across the countryside, so they were geographically close to a large number of students. Also like the others, admission was easy and costs were low. And because their number was so large (Michigan and Minnesota had four each; California had eight), these institutions were markedly more dispersed and accessible than state universities or land-grant colleges. Like the latter two, they were state subsidized but depended heavily on tuition, donations, and other sources of income in order to keep afloat. Their dependence on student tuition, and the consequent need to attract and retain student consumers, explains why they were so quick to move up the hierarchy to the status of university. This is what the students demanded. They saw the normal school less as a place to get trained as a teacher than as a more accessible form of higher education. As such, it would serve their purposes in opening up a broad array of social opportunities if it was able to grant college degrees, then offer programs in areas other than teaching, and eventually offer a full array of university degrees.

3.4 The System's Strengths in 1880

By 1880, the American system of higher education was extraordinarily large and spatially dispersed, with decentralized governance and a remarkable degree of institutional complexity. This system without a plan had established a distinctive structure early in the century and then elaborated on it over the succeeding decades. As noted earlier, with over 800 colleges and universities, the USA had five times as many institutions as all of the countries in Europe. They consisted of a heterogeneous array of institution types, including private denominational and nondenominational colleges, state universities, and land-grant colleges. In addition there were 76 normal schools that were already on a trajectory to become colleges.

Of course, the large majority of these colleges were neither academically elevated nor large in scale. Recall that the average institution in 1880 had 14 faculty and 123 students and granted 17 degrees. Only 26 of the 811 colleges had more than 200 students. The system had enormous capacity, but only a tiny part of this capacity was being put to use. At 16.1 colleges per million of population, it is probably safe to say that no country in the world has ever had a higher ratio of institutions of higher education to population than the USA had in 1880 (Collins, 1979, Table 5.2). This was a system that was all promise and little product, but the promise was indeed extraordinarily. Let me summarize the strengths that this system embodied at the moment its overcapacity was greatest and the boom era of the university was dawning.

3.4.1 Capacity in Place

One strength of the system was that it contained nearly all the elements needed for a rapid expansion of student enrollments. It had the necessary physical infrastructure: land, classrooms, libraries, faculty offices, administration buildings, and the rest. And this physical presence was not concentrated in a few population centers but scattered across the thinly populated landmass of a continental country. It had faculty and administration already in place, with programs of study, course offerings, and charters granting colleges the ability to award degrees. It had an established governance structure and a process for maintaining multiple streams of revenue to support the enterprise. And it had established a base of support in the local community and in the broader religious community. The main thing the system lacked was students.

3.4.2 A Hardy Band of Survivors

Another source of strength was that this motley collection of largely undistinguished colleges and universities had succeeded in surviving a Darwinian process of natural selection in a fiercely competitive environment. Since they could not rely on steady streams of funding from church and state, they had learned to survive by hustling for dollars from prospective donors and marketing themselves to prospective student who could pay tuition. And since they were deeply rooted in isolated towns across the country, they were particularly adept at representing themselves as institutions that educated local leaders and served as cultural centers for their communities. Often the college's name contained the name of the town where it was located (Middlebury College, Millersville State Normal School), and this close identification with people and place was a major source of strength when there were so many alternatives in other towns. If they had succeeded in surviving in the mid-nineteenth century, when the number of colleges was growing so much faster than the population and funds were scarce, then they were well poised to take advantage of the coming surge of student interest, new sources of funding, and new rationales for attending college.

3.4.3 Consumer Sensitivity

These colleges were market-based institutions that had never enjoyed the luxury of guaranteed appropriations, so they had become adept at meeting the demands of the key constituencies in their individual markets. In particular, they had to be sensitive to what prospective students were seeking in a college experience, since these consumers were paying a major part of the bills. This meant that they did not have the ability to impose a traditional curriculum, which would be self-destructive if they sensed that students wanted something different. So when the land-grant colleges grew in popularity, other colleges quickly adopted elements of the new practical curriculum in order to keep from being squeezed out of the market. Even publicly supported institutions, such as state universities and land-grant colleges, had to be sensitive to consumers, because their appropriations were proportional to enrollment numbers. And colleges also had a strong incentive to build long-standing ties with their graduates, who would become a prime source for new students and the largest source for donations.

3.4.4   Adaptable Enterprises

The structure of the college—with its lay board, strong president, geographical isolation, and stand-alone finances—made it a remarkably adaptable institution. These colleges could make changes without seeking permission from the education minister or the bishop. The president was the CEO of the enterprise, and his clear mission was to maintain the viability and expand the prospects for the college. So presidents had to become adept at reading trends in the market, sensing shifts in demand, anticipating the concerns of alumni and other constituencies, and heading off threats to their mission and intrusions into their educational terrain. They had to make the most of the advantages offered to them by geography and religious affiliation and to adapt quickly to shifts in their position relative to competitors concerning such key institutional matters as program, price, and prestige. The alternative was to go out of business. Burke (1982, Table 1.2) estimated that, between 1800 and 1850, 40 liberal arts colleges closed, 17 % of the total.[4]

3.4.5   A Populist Role

Clark Kerr (2001, p. 14) identified three forms of higher education that fused together to form the American university: the British undergraduate college, the American land-grant college, and the German research university. The first two were firmly in place by 1880 and the third was on its way. The undergraduate college was the populist element, which started with the residential and rural college experience developed in Britain and added to it some distinctively American components that opened it up to a larger array of students. By locating these colleges in small towns all across the country and placing them in a competitive market that made these colleges more concerned about survival than academic standards, the American system took on a middle-class rather than upper-class character. Poor families did not send their children to college, but ordinary middle-class families could, if they chose. Admission was easy, the academic challenge of the curriculum was moderate, and the cost of tuition was manageable. These elements created a broad popular foundation for the college that saved it, for the most part, from Oxbridge-style elitism. The college was an extension of the community and denomination, a familiar local presence, a source of civic pride, and cultural avatar representing the town to the world. Citizens did not have to have a family member connected with the school to feel that the college was theirs. This kind of populist base of support came to be enormously important when higher education enrollments started to skyrocket.

3.4.6 A Practical Role

Another key characteristic of the American model of higher education was its practicality. As Richard Hofstadter (1963) showed, the United States has had a long tradition of anti-intellectualism. Overwhelmingly, Americans have given more attention to those who make things and make money than to those who play with ideas. Its central figures of admiration and aspiration have been inventor-engineers like Thomas Edison and self-made businessmen like Andrew Carnegie rather than academic intellectuals like William James, who were considered 'European' (not a compliment). The American system of higher education, as it developed in the mid-nineteenth century, incorporated this practical orientation into the structure and function of the standard-model college. The land-grant college was both an effect and a cause of this cultural preference for usefulness. The focus on the useful arts was written into the DNA of these institutions, as an expression of the American effort to turn a college for gentlemen or intellectuals into a school for practical pursuits, with an emphasis on making things and making a living more than on gaining social polish or exploring the cultural heights. And this model, which was quite popular with consumers, spread widely to the other parts of the system. The result was not just the inclusion of subjects like engineering and applied science into the curriculum but also the orientation of the college itself as a problem solver for the businessmen and policy-makers in the community. The message was, "This is your college, working for you. We produce the engineers who design your bridges, the teachers who teach your children, and the farmers who produce your food. We develop better construction methods, better school curricula, and better crops". So in addition to the system's broad populist base of support, there was also a practical rationale that made the system of higher education a valued contributor to the community, which earned support even from people whose children were never going to enroll in it.

3.5 The Pieces Come Together with the Emergence of the Research University

When the German research university burst onto the American educational scene in the 1880s, the last piece of Kerr's three-part vision of American higher education fell into place. In this emerging model, the university was a place that produced cutting-edge scientific research and that provided graduate-level training for the intellectual elite. This provided a way out of the doldrums that had settled on the once vibrant university structure in Europe, which had become irrelevant while the major scientific work was being done elsewhere. And American scholars started flocking to Germany to acquire the union card of the new research-oriented scholar, the doctorate in philosophy, and to learn about the elements of the German model for transport back to the States. Johns Hopkins University, founded in 1876, was the first American institution designed around this model, but other newcomers quickly followed (Chicago, Clark, Stanford), and the existing institutions scrambled to adapt. Consider why this model was so attractive for the American system and how the system managed to incorporate it into the existing structure.

3.5.1 A Research Role

The situation facing American higher education in 1880 brought opportunity but even greater risk. The system had an enormous amount of excess capacity: all of those buildings and professors and programs to maintain with a thin and uncertain stream of revenue. Lacking reliable funding from church and state, it was heavily dependent on students, yet there were not nearly enough students available to support the 900 or so colleges and proto-colleges that were in existence at the time. In addition, whereas the higher education system had broad support as an institution that was both popular and practical, it was lacking in the one thing that would distinguish it from other popular and practical institutions (such as museums and trade schools and apprenticeship programs)—academic credibility. There were too many colleges for more than a tiny number of them to be academically distinguished (Harvard, Yale, and a few others), they were too small to hold a credible concentration of academic talent, and they were too widely dispersed across the countryside to create viable cultural communities of high intellectual caliber.

The German model of the graduate-oriented research university offered help with a key part of this problem. In short, it offered a way to put the higher into American higher education. It gave a parochial, benighted, and dispersed array of colleges and universities a way to attain some degree of credibility as institutions of advanced academic learning. Its professors would come to have the new scientific degree, the Ph.D., which certified their position at the cutting edge of academic attainment, and they would be evaluated based on their own research productivity. Its graduate schools would draw the best educated and most talented students in the country and induct them into the scientific methods of research and the habits of mind that would lead to authoritative scholarly publication. For this heterogeneous and barely academic structure of higher education, the German model offered the chance to attain serious academic standing in the community and even the world.

3.5.2 Merging the Populist, the Practical, and the Elite in the American System

So the German research ideal offered academic hope for the American system, but it also posed a number of problems. The model envisioned a university that was extraordinarily elite academically and radically more expensive per student than anything that had existed before in the USA. To pursue this approach in the unalloyed fashion that German universities were doing was impossible in the American system. The German approach called for strong state support, since small and elite graduate programs could otherwise provide lack both the flow of funds and the political legitimacy needed to keep them going. This would not work in the American setting, where state investment in higher education still paid only a fraction of the total cost and where student tuition was essential for survival.

So instead of adopting the German model, the American system of higher education incorporated a version of it within the existing structure. The most ambitious, best financed, and oldest institutions—spurred by competitive pressure from research-oriented newcomers like Hopkins and Chicago—sought to establish key elements of the model: organizing graduate schools, hiring professors with Ph.D.s, developing advanced graduate programs, recruiting academically talented graduate students, and shifting faculty incentives toward the production of research. But they did this without abandoning the elements of the existing model that were critically important if they were going to be able to survive and thrive within the market-based political economy of American higher education. And they were aided in this effort by a development that had little to do with the graduate university but a lot to do with the sudden surge in student interest in enrolling in an undergraduate program.

It would take a book to explain why going to college started to become de rigueur for upper-middle-class American families in this period, but fortunately others have written such books, which I can draw upon here (e.g., Bledstein, 1978; Veysey, 1970). One factor was that the sharp decline of small business and the sudden rise of managerial work in the new corporate economy meant that families of a certain means were unable to pass on social advantage directly to their children by having them take over the family business; instead they increasingly had to provide their children with educational credentials that would give them priority access to the new white-collar work. Another factor was that high school enrollment was beginning to increase rapidly in the 1880s, and the middle-class families that had relied on a high school education as a form of distinction began to look to college as a way to mark themselves off from the incoming horde of high school students. And a third factor is that the overbuilt higher education system was desperately looking for ways to attract students. So in the 1880s American colleges and universities invented (or copied from peers) most of the familiar elements the twentieth-century American undergraduate college experience, which made attending college attractive to so many students: fraternities and sororities, football, comfortable dormitory rooms, and grassy campuses adorned with medieval quadrangles in a faux gothic style. It was a mix that said: This is a place where you can pick up social capital, cultural capital, and a useful credential, enjoy social life in a comfortable middle-class style, and do all this in a setting adorned with newly created social traditions and with academic nods to the great universities of the old country.

The large infusion of tuition-paying undergraduates reinforced the populist role that the American college had long played. Now attending college was both attractive and useful for large numbers of young middle-class men and women. This sharp increase in student enrollments brought an equally sharp increase in tuition revenues, and the closer loyalty to alma mater engendered by the new all-inclusive college lifestyle made graduates into an increasingly reliable and wealthy source of future donations for the institution. All this new money helped to subsidize the growing graduate programs and increasingly expensive research-oriented faculty. The undergraduates supported the elite academic enterprise that now allowed the college to call itself a research university. And the growth of research and graduate programs gave the institution the academic credibility it needed, to offset what otherwise would have been little more than a party school for socially qualified but academically challenged undergraduates. And on top of these elements—the populist and the elite—was the continuation of the college's practical functions, serving business and society through applied work and the production of the higher end of the workforce.

This mix of the populist, the elite, and the practical has continued to characterize the middle and upper ranges of the American system of higher education from the time of its creation at the end of the nineteenth century. Ever since then, the central struggle for university presidents, admissions officers, and fund raisers has been to determine exactly what mix of these elements was right at a given time for a particular institution in a given market niche. And this in turn allowed the institutions to preserve their autonomy from the state, drawing on a rich combination of income streams and sources of legitimacy. The resulting structure displays a peculiar mix of traits. It is highly accessible and radically stratified; it is widely localized and remarkably homogeneous; it includes under the label of higher education some of the most exclusive and academically elevated institutions in the world and many more of the most inclusive and academically mediocre such institutions. And the entire structure still bears the marks of its modest beginnings in the penurious and parochial nineteenth-century college.

Notes

1. An earlier version of this chapter was presented at the international conference on "Institutional Spaces of Educational Research", *Research Community on Philosophy and History of the Discipline of Education*, Friedrich-Alexander-University Erlangen-Nürnberg, Germany, November 17–19, 2011.
2. Labaree was my grandfather's grandfather.

3. In one extreme case, the New York did not establish a state university until 1948.
4. Tewksbury (1932, Table 2) argued that the failure rate on the frontier was much higher than this. He calculated that, in 16 states outside of New England between 1800 and 1860, the college mortality rate was an astonishing 81 %. Burke (1982, p. 13), however, says that this estimate is much too high, because Tewksbury counted a college as being founded if it received a state charter, but many of these chartered institutions never opened their doors, and many were high-school-level academies rather than colleges. All of this confusion about what was a college and what was a failure underscores the fluidity and volatility of the situation facing American colleges in this period.

References

Bledstein, B. J. (1978). The culture of professionalism. In *The culture of professionalism: The middle class and the development of higher education in America* (pp. 80–128). New York: W. W. Norton.

Brown, D. K. (1995). *Degrees of control: A sociology of educational expansion and occupational credentialism.* New York: Teachers College Press.

Burke, C. B. (1982). *American collegiate populations: A test of the traditional view.* New York: New York University Press.

Carter, S. B., et al. (2006). *Historical statistics of the United States, millennial education on line.* New York: Cambridge University Press.

Collins, R. (1979). *The credential society: An historical sociology of education and stratification.* New York: Academic.

Hofstadter, R. (1963). *Anti-intellectualism in American life.* New York: Knopf.

Kerr, C. (2001). *The uses of the university* (5th ed.). Cambridge, MA: Harvard University Press.

Labaree, D. F. (1975). Labaree picks up the pieces. In *Middlebury's 175 anniversary* (pp. 18–23). Middlebury, VT: Alumni Association.

Labaree, D. F. (1988). *The making of an American high school: The credentials market and the Central High School of Philadelphia, 1838–1920.* New Haven, CT: Yale University Press.

Ogren, C. (2005). *The American state normal school: "An instrument of great good".* New York: Palgrave Macmillan.

Rüegg, W. (2004). European universities and similar institutions in existence between 1812 and the end of 1944: A chronological list: Universities. In W. Rüegg (Ed.), *Universities in the nineteenth and early twentieth centuries (1800–1945)* (A history of the university in Europe, Vol. 3). London: Cambridge University Press.

Tewksbury, D. G. (1932). *The founding of American colleges and universities before the civil war.* New York: Teachers College Press.

Thelin, J. R. (2004). *A history of American higher education.* Baltimore, MD: Johns Hopkins University Press.

U.S. Bureau of the Census. (1975). *Historical statistics of the United States: Colonial times to 1970, Part 1.* Washington, DC: U.S. Government Printing Office.

Veysey, L. S. (1970). *The emergence of the American university.* Chicago: University of Chicago Press.

Chapter 4
Crossing the Atlantic to Gain Knowledge in the Field of Psycho-Pedagogy: The 1922 Mission of Ovide Decroly and Raymond Buyse to the USA and the Travel Diary of the Latter

Marc Depaepe, Lieven D'hulst, and Frank Simon

Recently a remarkable document was published by Leuven University Press (Depaepe & D'hulst, 2011), reflecting the ubiquitous American influence on the construct of psycho-pedagogical sciences in Belgium. In light of the topic of this collection—*the Institutional Spaces of Educational Research*—we would like to use this text to clarify the extent to which space, in the geographical sense of the word, has helped shape researchers' mental structures, often for a lifetime. But in many cases there are no written sources available on such '*histoire(s) croisée(s)*' (entangled histories)—an exception could be Lawn (2005). Thus, one often has to rely on what has been handed down verbally—in interviews, whether through oral history or 'hearsay' in the field. That is why the recently published book—especially in light of the intellectual biography of the protagonists—may also serve as an eye-opener, the ultimate reason why we want to discuss it within the context of a research community, which has focused from the outset on the history and the philosophy of educational research.

The publication contains the travel notes (originally in French and translated to the English) of the future professor Raymond Buyse, made during his study trip to the United States—the country of choice for immigrants, at least that is the way in which it is impressed in our collective memory—together with Ovide Decroly in the spring of 1922 (Buyse, 1922). These notes are a gold mine for cultural-historical research into mental migration as well as into the related perception of the cultural context from which one wishes to import scientific opinions, ideas, theories, methods and techniques. On the other hand, they also reveal the reverse

M. Depaepe (✉)
Campus Kortrijk, Subfaculteit Psychologie en Pedagogische Watenschappen, Katholieke Universiteit Leuven, Belgium
e-mail: Marc.Depaepe@kuleuven-kortrijk.be

L. D'hulst
Campus Kortrijk, Subfaculteit Letteren, Katholieke Universiteit Leuven, Belgium

F. Simon
Faculty of Psychology and Educational Sciences, Ghent University, Ghent, Belgium

P. Smeyers et al. (eds.), *Educational Research: The Importance and Effects of Institutional Spaces*, Educational Research 7, DOI 10.1007/978-94-007-6247-3_4,
© Springer Science+Business Media Dordrecht 2013

side of the scientific activity that these men went to study there, from the perspective of the history of science. Anyone interested in the culture of science and in science as culture, in general cultural phenomena, in the transatlantic crossing, in internationalisation, in the appeal of and the fascination for a new superpower, the United States, or simply in everyday aspects, stereotypes and associated prejudices, will definitely enjoy this publication. Buyse's reflections make for a good read, but they also encourage a reflection, as a consequence of their uncensored naiveté and stereotyping. We will discuss this below. This chapter is arranged into two parts: the first deals with the study trip and its mission, in relation with the general landscape of an emerging 'science of education' as well as with the individual careers of the traveller scientists. With some imagination we can put this section under the heading 'macro-space'. The second deals with some more specific aspects of the travel as reflected by the notes of Buyse. With the same imagination we can call this the 'micro-space' of the travel diary.

4.1 Aspects of 'Macro'-space: Crossing the Atlantic to Gain Knowledge in the Field of Psycho-Pedagogy

The 32-year-old author of these notes, undoubtedly a talented researcher—a doctor of pedology, the physiological and psychological study of children—was at the beginning of his career (Gille, 1965). He had just been appointed inspector for primary education institutions in Brussels. His travelling companion, the 51-year-old neurologist, psycho-pedagogist and educational innovator, Ovide Decroly, on the other hand, was already world-famous at the time. As a result, he too probably felt that it was time to visit the paradise of the test movement, at the height of his career, and so he travelled to the United States, where the measurement of psychological and pedagogical phenomena (and intelligence in particular) had taken on unprecedented proportions, in line with Binet's teachings. Prior to his voyage to the United States—this is an assumption—Decroly probably was also encouraged by an acquaintance, Dr. René Sand (also a neurologist, who focused on social health/social work), to take this trip (Eilers, 2011). The government of (unoccupied) Belgium dispatched Sand to the United States on two occasions, immediately after the end of the war, to study Taylorism, which Buyse and Decroly also focussed on during their travels.

The mission of both scientists was clearly a very serious one, so do not expect to read an enthusiastic "New York New York, I want to be part of it, If I can make it there I can make it everywhere" (from the Scorcese film with Liza Minelli, also a Frank Sinatra hit), or the more reserved "I came to New York and in only hours, New York did what it does to people: awakened the possibilities. Hope breaks out" by Philip Roth; this mission related to the study as well as the promotion of the highly successful American test movement, with the necessary scientific output as a consequence. Buyse and Decroly, in their joint publication of 1923 on the application of psychology to modern life, which is widely considered the most recognisable 'product' of this study trip, the authors, for example, wrote that the principle of 'the right man in the right place' finally ensured the victory of the Allies (Decroly & Buyse, 1923).

Next to this their study programme also included vocational guidance, educational innovation, schools for special education and the institutionalisation of American academic pedagogy. To this end they criss-crossed the country from east to west, from Teacher's College in New York to Stanford in Palo Alto, meeting such luminaries as Stanley Hall, Dewey, Terman, Thorndike and Goddard—who notoriously said that Decroly was "the greatest man I have ever known"—in fact all the leading figures in their disciplines. You might say that this was a psycho-pedagogical Lewis and Clark expedition, except that it involved trains and automobiles and that it was situated somewhat more to the south, geographically speaking.

Buyse started jotting down his impressions in New York on March 27, 1922, and his notes cover a 3-month period. They returned to Belgium on July 2, from New York. Buyse, interestingly enough, makes no mention of the passage by ship, which, at the time, would have taken at least 10 days for a return trip. The trip was paid for by the University Foundation, with funding from the defunct Commission for Relief in Belgium and which was in charge of organising food supplies to the needy population during the First World War.

The fact that the manuscript was found is not that important; it was found years ago, after all. The moment of publication, however, is more relevant. After the dominance of the study of structures and processes, history, and cultural history in particular, is currently experiencing a period of rediscovery, of the return of the individual, and such a source, a travel diary, is a perfect example of this trend. It is impossible to ignore this trend, in any event as every bookshop and even newspaper store now has a large biographical section, with a huge variation of personalities, including film stars, pop stars, athletes, criminals as well as murderers and the usual politicians and immortal scientists: "Everyone becomes part of history whether they like it or not and whether they know it or not" (to quote Philip Roth again). But if you look carefully, upon reflection, you will notice that there are many titles, but there is a lack of reflection.

We have chosen to explicitly refer to biographies because, together with Angelo Van Gorp, we have already published some articles on Buyse's travelling companion, and we are currently also working on a biography of the man himself. It is both interesting and intriguing that Decroly is only mentioned three times in the travel diary, over a period of 3 months.

Decroly is everywhere and nowhere; there is a hint of respect, of distance—certainly in ideological terms but also in professional terms—and of a pious silence, which, to a certain extent, contributes to the myth that was woven around Decroly (see Depaepe, Simon, & Van Gorp, 2003). We will try to update the existing hagiographical literature from a biographical, social- and scientific-historical perspective. In any event, the relation with the 'master' Decroly, who was also a freemason—there are a number of naive, touching sections on American freemasonry; did he or did he not know about Decroly?—is quite relevant for any future biographer of Buyse, who was a Catholic. It is especially relevant because they did not remain as close, or at any rate, Decroly's entourage always preferred to shrug it off. Buyse, for example, is completely absent in the 500-plus-page *Hommage au Dr. Decroly* (Decroly, 1933), which was published 1 year after Decroly died and which is considered to be a privileged source for reconstructing

Decroly's network. He is registered among the subscribers—and even there his name is misspelt—which perhaps appears to be more than a case of '*Fehlleistung*'. In a letter of condolence dated February 21, 1933, to Mrs Decroly, Buyse complained about the way he is pushed aside by the 'Decrolyiens', including 'neophytes and climbers'.

But let us focus again on the travel diary. These notes clearly pave the way for gauging a personality, writing a biography, albeit a biography as we see it, a construction of multiple 'selves' (Margadant, 2000), which relies on access to specific aspects, to subjective experiences to understand general developments. A biography, in which we pluralise the social world and accept that individual lives and careers may be complicated and that individuals belong to different worlds. A biography in which we explore the future of the past by breaking through the temporal consistency, from birth to death, to instigate a process aimed at unmasking a person to the present day.

As already has been demonstrated elsewhere and in more depth (Depaepe, 1993), the breakthrough of the 'experimental' scientific model is very much indebted to the intellectual legacy of positivism. During the nineteenth century, the natural sciences had not only disenfranchised themselves from the tutelage of philosophy, but the natural-scientific paradigm also contributed to a large extent to determining the field of 'scientific' pedagogy. As a consequence of the successive successes since the seventeenth century, gradually the conviction that the sciences, or at least the natural sciences, were a cornucopia, which only brought blessings and salvation, took hold. The idea of a superior form of knowledge slowly started to take shape. Scientists hoped that the scientific method would lead to an 'objective' approach of nature as well as culture and that the technical control of both nature and culture would promote human happiness. Observation and experimentation, methods which hitherto had been confined to the realm of natural sciences, increasingly proved useful for the study of mankind and of society.

One example that illustrates this is the emergence of 'experimental' medicine, which is associated with the name of Claude Bernard and to whom Buyse (1935) would explicitly refer in the frame of his 'pédagogie expérimentale'. In this key work he incorporated the preface of Bernard's *Introduction à l'étude de la médecine expérimentale* verbatim in his introduction, albeit that he did adapt the medical terms in function of pedagogical science. Buyse became fascinated with medical science during his training. After his studies at the Catholic teacher college of Bonne Esperance in Hainaut, where he obtained the diploma of teacher in 1909, he frequented various of Brussels' leading pedologists and pedotechnicians, including non-Catholic physicians such as Ovide Decroly, Jean Demoor (who himself started out his career as teacher and was appointed in 1912 rector of the *Université libre de Bruxelles*) and Josépha Ioteyko (a Brussels pedologist of Polish origin, who also served as the promoter of Buyse's PhD in 1919). They would have a lasting influence on his further career.

Ioteyko thought that the dawn of the new century was characterised "*par une nouvelle conquête des méthodes expérimentales*" (by a new conquest of experimental methods). In this frame, she also emphasised the role of experimental psychology.

It is widely known that the 'first' experimental psychology laboratory was founded in 1879 in Leipzig by Wilhelm Wundt—an initiative which would be copied in Belgium before the end of the nineteenth century, in Ghent and in Leuven (respectively, in 1891 and in 1894). Jean-Jules Van Biervliet and Armand Thiéry, who had both trained with Wundt, established these institutions. Wundt exercised amazing appeal, especially in the United States, where the professionalisation and academisation of psychology had already started a few decades earlier. During the 1880s and 1890s, a host of trendsetters in Northern American psychology graduated from his facility, including James McKeen Cattell, who would go on to become the first American university professor, specialising in psychology, in 1881, at the University of Pennsylvania. Around 1890 he also introduced the notion of mental tests there, which is why he was included on Buyse's and Decroly's list of people to visit, in addition to the aforementioned Granville Stanley Hall, who would make a lasting impression on both men, as well as Charles Hubbard Judd and several other psychologists.

As far as pedagogues are concerned, a meeting with John Dewey was a given. They met him and reported on this meeting, in a 'touching' manner, completely in line with the time frame, in Buyse's individual notes on their voyage, as well as in their joint publication on Park School—the Walhalla of educational reform created during the Progressive Era. Dewey's 'pedagogical creed', which centred on so-called learning by doing, all in all, had a rather missionary ring to it. It was founded on the philosophy of pragmatism (with the underlying idea of the flexible usability of active and inventive citizens in the American way of life) but also and above all on the notion that American society, which was de facto conceived as a 'meritocracy', was superior: the land of daring and of unlimited possibilities, the Eldorado, where the fairytale of the newspaper boy who one day becomes a press magnate could be fulfilled at any time, at least if you had a sufficient amount of common sense and were a born entrepreneur. That is why Dewey postulated that education had to focus on solving real problems. In his book, *How We Think?* (1910), which Decroly would subsequently translate into French with the help of his associates, Dewey reduced the entire thought process to problem-solving behaviour—a process for which he would devise a pedagogical approach, the project method, after his retirement, at the renowned Teacher's College of Columbia University, New York, in 1921, together with William H. Kilpatrick.

It will come as no surprise then that Decroly and Buyse learned of this new method during their study trip and met with its promoters. According to Dewey and Kilpatrick, schools had to be democratic communities, where children were prepared for real life through scientific thinking and practice—'the pragmatic test of truth'. This philosophy significantly approximated the pedagogical ideas of Ovide Decroly, whose 'new education' school in Uccle, Belgium, which was founded in 1907, used the slogan '*l'école pour la vie par la vie*' (school for life through life). It is also worth noting that Decroly would subsequently be referred to as 'Dewey's European counterpart'. According to Decroly, school had to provide a practical introduction to life, based on the child's knowledge of his own personality on the one hand and a knowledge of the natural and social environment in which the child functioned, on the other hand.

In the USA, however, the pedagogical reform movement of progressivism was never incorporated as the heart of 'hard' empirical educational research, in spite of its many successes. This task was reserved for educational psychology, as established by Thorndike. In her historical study of American pedagogy, Ellen Condlife Lagemann (2000) concluded, as a consequence, that 'Dewey lost—Thorndike won'. Thorndike, who was the 'rising star' at Teacher's College but also a 'typical American', as Buyse noted, had developed a general educational theory, based on trial-and-error experiments with animals, which could also, in his opinion, be applied to humans. This so-called 'connectionist' learning theory was founded on the principle that learning is a process, whereby a (neurological) bond is forged between a given 'stimulus' and a given 'response'. That is why it is also known as the 'S-R bond' theory, which also pre-empted behaviourism. It is telling of American culture at the time that these principles, which seem so simple at first glance, were so readily adopted in applied psychology, in which Thorndike also expressed interest, in view of conquering this market. In 1913–1914, for example, he published a three-volume *Educational Psychology*, in which the psychology of learning was transposed to education. From 1903 he had also started measuring intelligence and in the 1920s he developed a series of tests for this. With his educational psychology, he wished to provide these professionals with 'facts' rather than with 'speculations'. He tried to find 'behavioural' explanations, based on quantifiable facts. In his opinion, pedagogy had always remained a speculative science—in voicing this idea, Thorndike lashed out at child study (à la Stanley Hall). One of the best-known assumptions of Thorndike is that everything that exists in a certain quantity and thus is measurable. These ideas were subsequently adopted and refined by his associate, William A. McCall, with whom Decroly and Buyse had more contact during their voyage. Subsequently, McCall, who published his renowned *How to Measure in Education* in 1922, would go on to become a major source of inspiration for Buyse's *expérimentation en pédagogie*.

Meanwhile, Decroly also ventured into the field of tests. Alfred Binet, and his associate, Théodore Simon, developed the so-called intelligence scale in Paris around 1905. Using various assignments, including questions, tests, problem and situational analysis, Binet tried to gain a direct insight in every child's intellectual status and the differences between them (also with a view to gathering students who were 'lagging' in education). Decroly was one of the first to put this scale into practice, together with his associate, Julia Degand. He sent his critical findings to Binet as early as 1906. In 1908 this led to an improved version of the Binet-Simon scale, which Decroly and Degand once again set to be applied in Brussels. Their results were striking: the mental age of their test population was approximately 1.5 year higher than that of Binet's reference group. The difference could be attributed to the social-cultural difference in terms of background: Binet worked with children from a workers' background, while Decroly's pupils came from a more privileged environment—which pointed to the influence of environmental factors. But the Americans would ultimately not be interested in this (cf. Zenderland, 1998).

Henry Goddard, whom we have already mentioned above and with whom Decroly also corresponded after his mission of 1922, apparently had learnt about

Binet's test in Belgium. This was the doing of Ovide Decroly himself, whom Goddard visited in 1908. The latter imported the Binet-Simon test to the United States (Vineland), where he published a translation in 1908 (which would be amended in 1911). Yet Lewis M. Terman's adaptation of 1916 constituted the foundation for the so-called Stanford-Binet test, named after the Californian university where Terman worked, and which would go on to become, by far, the most popular intelligence test in the United States. Buyse and Decroly also concluded this on the spot, which probably motivated them to include the West Coast in their itinerary.

Regardless, under the influence of Goddard, Terman and others, researchers in the United States had started to believe that an individual's IQ remained quasi-unchanged and thus was an important element in the prediction of the future development of the individual in question. By simply applying scientific management, as propagated by engineers as Frederick W. Taylor in business, psychology had succeeded in evolving from a pure science into an applied art, in the army, as well as in business, in education and in vocational guidance—a 'lesson' that Buyse clearly wishes to pass on to Belgians. '*Tayloriser l'instruction pour valoriser l'éducation*' (Taylorising instruction to valorise education) was the slogan that Buyse continued to apply in the frame of his *pédagogie expérimentale*.

We all know that tests and measurements—of an individual's mental abilities as well as of their academic progress, including the large-scale 'surveys' about educational attainment, which J. M. Rice launched around 1890 (Engelhart & Thomas, 1966)—became a real industry in the period between the two World Wars in the United States. The test movement increasingly started to coincide with the meritocratic ideal of the 'corporate liberal state' in which it operated. As such it fed the belief that merit was the consequence of a genetic predisposition (i.e. of differences in intelligence), combined with hard work. In a sense, American Calvinism was rediscovered in this way: intelligent people 'earned' their success because of their superior character. And more importantly, in the light of cultural history, this ideology would go on to be an essential element of social control. To a considerable extent it legitimised the existing social and societal inequality, including the underlying racism—for which Decroly and Buyse would also suggest the existence of 'suggestive correlations' in their publication of 1923.

The fact that Decroly's and Buyse's interest in 'mental tests' eventually coincided with a penchant for 'progressive schools' elicited some measure of surprise in the United States. Test psychologist, Rudolf Pintner, especially, with whom the Belgian pair often met during their travels, was so astonished about this that he even wrote about it in the tribute book for Decroly. According to Pintner (1933), this alliance of both spheres of interest could only be interpreted as a typically Belgian phenomenon. Such a combination was barely conceivable in the United States, by which Pintner probably referred to the underlying, often contradictory 'social' implications. As we have explained elsewhere in more detail (e.g. Depaepe, Simon, & Van Gorp, 2011), the Belgian reform movement had a nice and even bourgeois reputation. Educational reform was conceived as the school's 'adaptation' to modern life, even by Decroly and Buyse (1923), without questioning the meritocratic, liberal-capitalist social model. A society based on the principle of '*l'égalité dans la médiocrité* (equality in mediocrity) did not appeal to them. The efficiency of the existing school could be increased considerably, by differentiating and taking a more individual approach, which was only possible by measuring, selecting and grouping, nothing more, nothing less.

The 'missing link' for a better understanding of the Belgian situation, and in particular the situation in Brussels, probably lies in 'special' education for the 'abnormal'. As Decroly had already argued at several international conferences before the First World War, society had to be saved by science. The negative energy caused by social abnormality and more specifically by youth criminality—a field in which the Brussels school physician became increasingly interested from a professional perspective—had to be turned into a positive energy; the negative 'ballast', which caused social maladjustment, had to be used for the further development of society. Prophylaxis and treatment by doctors played a crucial role in this. And to underscore this message, all registers of the scientific rhetoric were used. The fact that Decroly and Buyse were interested in the medical-pedagogical treatment of various categories of 'abnormal' individuals in the United States is therefore obvious.

In the scientific output, which was a direct consequence of their trip to the United States, they also paid attention to all of these themes: tests, educational reform and the treatment of 'abnormal' individuals but also the development of an academic psycho-pedagogy at university.

From a life history perspective, it is clear that the trip to the United States and all the related events did not harm Buyse's academic career. On the contrary, in 1923—the year in which the University of Leuven, in line with the example of the University of Brussels in 1919, wanted to establish an '*école de pédagogie et de psychologie appliquée à l'éducation*'—Buyse was appointed '*maître de conférences*' (lecturer). This would mark the start of a career, which would also be followed with great interest abroad: Buyse's experimental-pedagogical and didactic research, for which he established a veritable 'laboratory' around 1927, would result in widespread recognition and prestige, especially in France and Spain (see, e.g. Montalbetti, 2002). In 1933, he was invited to teach in Columbia, as visiting professor, and in 1958, 1 year before his retirement, he became doctor honoris causa at Geneva.

But we will not discuss this here. In the following section we will elaborate upon some matters, which stood out in the margin of the production and processing of the travel diary, that is, his scribbles, the laboratory, the inherently educational nature of travel, the geo-cultural space and the travel diary genre within the literature (and its dealing with natural and institutional spaces).

4.2 Aspects of 'Micro'-space: Travel Notes as the Basis for Writing Biographies About Educational Researchers

You come upon a precious document that has never been studied before. But the thrill soon starts to wear off when you start reading it. Where to start with these scribbles, this spidery handwriting? A host of quaint words have been coined for this.

We have all come upon such documents in various forms: a diary, such as Buyse's; a letter; a note; a medical certificate or course notes, which are unable to decipher; drafts for own articles and fragments of the publications of others; and so on. Decroly wrote everywhere (on the train, in the tram or bus), on everything, with a predilection for the reverse sides of documents, the back of invitations, advertising, bills, letters announcing someone died or, another example, the little notes that scientists leave behind, which are such interesting sources for examining creative operations, the formation, the building of knowledge. Reading handwritten sources is fun; it can be quite satisfactory, but it can be equally difficult, at times discouraging, nerve-wracking, very laborious and sometimes insurmountable. The job never ends and the end result is all too often incomplete. In retrospect, there are still errors, and the interpretation is not always satisfactory as you had hoped. This is also the case here, albeit to a lesser extent.

Scribbles can also be found in labs, which is where Buyse and Decroly wanted to spend most of their time in the United States. They were interested in seeing the daily 'laborare' with their own eyes. Buyse describes how they succeeded in visiting a lab in Pittsburgh. Decroly knew the ropes, and he was probably interested in redoing the others' work (as he did with Binet's intelligence test, among others); to use a quote by Bruno Latour (1987), he knew that every lab was an anti-lab and that this would not be sufficient for a scientific sceptic and he always aspired to have the best lab.

Both of our travellers-scientists were all too well aware that place plays an important part in science (and concomitantly, that place and space are not immobile) and that place and space are a key aspect of scientific knowledge and practice. Science is carried out in places, crosses boundaries, and that is where science continues (Livingstone, 2003). Clearly Buyse and Decroly were also interested in seeing the daily practice of a lab and more specifically the material aspect of such a lab, the equipment used, the 'machinery and tools', those indispensable aids for scientists in the practice of observation and measurement (Guignard, Raggi, & Thévenin, 2011). This should come as no surprise. It is a well-known fact that the analogy between the human body and the machine has a long history. In the era of the second industrial revolution—the period during which Buyse and Decroly conducted experiments—scientists learned to see the body as an electrical machine, a type of accumulator, with nerves as the wires (these days they are correlated with functions). Decroly, the neurologist, was an adept of the then practice of electrical medicine and was completely under the spell of 'machines', which were used in medicine and psychology to read the body in order to penetrate the mysteries of the mind. But this was equally applicable to Buyse, as is evidenced from his journal, and the slogan we mentioned above (*'Tayloriser l'instruction pour valoriser l'éducation'*) also ties in perfectly with this. But Buyse and Decroly also experienced the sensory changes of trains and cars and saw the destructive, disfiguring and regenerative force of war. Moreover, Decroly was an active photographer and loved film. He was one of the first to use film to record experiments and these machines create a new space and time, of immediacy, of the moment. Buyse's and Decroly's visits to the leading psychological labs in the USA were therefore quite evident. It is no coincidence that

Buyse jotted down the word 'pèlerinage' in relation to his visit to Stanley Hall, the founder of the first lab for psychology (Johns Hopkins University) in the United States and the teacher of several renowned psychologists, including Arnold Gesell, Lewis Terman, James McKeen Cattell and John Dewey.

Moreover, there is always an aspect of education in travel: all journeys have an educational function, even if it is merely restricted to revealing a new and different reality to travellers. However, some journeys are more educational than others or are experienced in a different way or differently by each individual. It also depends on whether you are travelling with a companion or alone. In short, there are several variations possible. Here Decroly and Buyse travelled across the United States for several months, on a scientific mission, as a scientific duo with a professional interest in education. This is also evidenced in the publications, the scientific output of the journey, on which the editors of Buyse's travel notes elaborate in great detail in their introduction (Depaepe & D'hulst, 2011). This kind of journey ties in with a centuries-old tradition, especially in terms of science, well before it was science. If you look at the educational aspect of the 'introduction to other educational systems', this tradition goes back to the second half of the eighteenth century (Viñao, 2007). But as we already said above, this journey had so much more to offer. And Buyse travelled along with Decroly; he got to travel with the master (Decroly was called 'le maître'). Decroly, who is universally described as a charismatic figure, travelling for 3 months, with someone, who as we have already mentioned, writes nothing about him, although the company of such a figure must have been very instructive (just think of the exchanges of experiences over dinner, on the ship). How frustrating this all is for the biographer.

An account like this will need to examine the institutions visited by Buyse and Decroly in more detail: they are cited, analysed, enhanced or discredited as such in Buyse's journal, but at the same time their presence can also be felt more implicitly and is no doubt partly subconscious. On the one hand, Buyse's peers work in these institutions and the manner in which they establish close or distant ties with their Belgian guests, with their colleagues or their students enables the development of models of intellectual sociability. These may have correlatively influenced Buyse's view of the Belgian university which would shortly be his. On the other hand, these institutions cannot be separated from the wider geo-cultural space, which traditionally plays an important role in the travel story genre. This genre— and this is entirely in line with Buyse's romantic style—favours the emotional and sensory effects caused by the immediate perception of nature and further underscored by the comparison with the traveller's familiar surroundings. Can one imagine a bigger contrast, for example, than that between Buyse's native Tournai and the wide, open spaces across the Atlantic? A contrast which only serves to underline their strangeness leaves the author to reflect nostalgically: "On the horizon, from both sides, [the hills] peel away! I have the blues! I want to be in Belgium, in some corner of my Tournai, where in the great calm of the Sunday repose, at this hour, I would hear high mass ringing from the nearby steeple or some distant jingle elsewhere" (Depaepe & D'hulst, 2011, p. 112).

That said, the confrontation with the Other constantly gives rise to a more vivid responsiveness in travel stories, which is the result of shaken sensory and cognitive experiences. One of the specificities of the genre lies in the fact that the traveller expresses his wonder at unexpected or unusual things which catch him unawares: "You cannot imagine how many cars one sees here… In every street one can count two rows of them at rest and on the middle of the silent asphalt, it's an incessant to and fro movement… There is virtually no one who still goes walking… except us" (ibid., p. 68).

We have come to expect such attitudes all the more in a travelogue because they are simply an application of the genre's rules, familiar to both authors and readers. But these rules are not applied as a whole.

On the one hand, the narrator does not fear to pair his outbursts of admiration with critical remarks, which reflect his common sense; let us not forget that we are in effect reading a draft, a work that was not intended for publication: "Returning, we leisurely admire the magic light of Times Square. It's unimaginable: with the amount spent every week on this orgy of advertising one could build a school at home" (ibid., p. 87).

On the other hand, this diary reflects the constant mix of natural and institutional spaces, a mix which has no equivalent in travel literature. This switching back and forth between the two spaces also results in crossovers. The institutional spaces often are micro-spaces: labs, classrooms, faculty offices and so on. But these micro-spaces have not been clearly separated from the private or intimate spaces which include the cars, the train compartments, the restaurants as well as the hotels, the lounges and dining rooms into which the two Belgian travellers were invited. So not only do we need to separate the different types of spaces that surround and intersect with the institutional micro-space, but at the same time we also need to compare the relations between the attitudes inspired by the natural spaces and those that characterised the gaze of the young scholar confronted with an intellectual and cultural universe with which he is unfamiliar.

Below we will list some characteristics of the narrator's attitudes to institutional spaces. America, at the time, was partially known, thanks to the stories and guides which Buyse no doubt consulted prior to this trip, although he did not reference his sources. For instance, Les Etat-Unis: avec une excursion au Mexique (The United States: with an excursion to Mexico), Karl Baedeker's travel guide, which was published in 1894 and was frequently republished in 1905, 1910, 1914 etc., and Jules Huret's *En Amérique : De New-York à la Nouvelle-Orléans* (In America: From New York to New Orleans, published in 1907) are travelogues which help structure the unknown and give it some meaning, even if Buyse's journal does not bear any traces of having borrowed specifically from these guides (see Baedeker, 1894; Huret, 1907). Other than that, we have no information about how Buyse researched American universities or the professors with whom he became acquainted. But it is likely that Buyse was guided by more than just books and American scholars, for whom he had 'an affectionate devotion'. In fact, his travel companion is likely to have inspired him far more. Decroly was imbued with the importance of sociability, which oversteps the spheres of private and public life. His wife's testimony, for instance, reads as follows (Guisset, s.d., p. 21):

> The house was open to anyone who visited him and the meetings often ended with music. Mr Washburn from Winetka never forgot the experience. He used to say: after the material nourishment comes the intellectual pleasure. This was the only house where people were not officially received, he said. I wanted people to meet him in his family environment (our translation from the original French).

Buyse's account is filled with similar crossovers between the private and professional world: "A delightful dinner, with the family, pot luck, no formalities !!! A beautiful close-knit household, topped-off with two beautiful children, very well behaved. The conversation is rather critical of course and our candid minds record a number of funny references, sparkling words, shrewed remarks, points of... orthography! Typical of university life. Everything is put with the admirable precision of the French eye... delicious observations, delicate ironies, flawlessy dissecting the Anglo-Saxon heart with imperturbable coolness" (Depaepe & D'hulst, 2011, p. 77).

These close relationships—obviously—also have their downside: "The best universities all have their little cliques. Here, Professor Judd, director of the School of Education, has not seen fit to introduce us to his colleagues Messrs' Gray and Breed. And we only saw Professor Freeman due to indiscretion" (ibid., p. 83).

The confidence, the admiration even, thanks to which natural and cultural (and singularly intellectual) reality, imagined as well as documented, can be made to correspond through the mirage of spontaneous recognition did not prevent Buyse from distancing himself from certain aspects of American culture. The scholar was not necessarily inspired by the big university cities but by those in which the natural and institutional spaces coexisted harmoniously: "A divine spring day: bright sun, blue sky, cool breeze and the lovely surprise of a quiet bourgeois town filled with churches, temples, auditoriums and laboratories. How it must do one good to live here in the peaceful pursuit of a great idea" (ibid., p. 90). The contrast with the arrival at Harvard was considerable: "Ten minutes on the subway leads us to Cambridge where we find Harvard University. Ordinary campus that feels painfully like a barracks yard" (ibid., p. 91).

Finally, Buyse's strongest impressions and emotions seem to have been heavily inspired by enclosed spaces: "As in a small Chinese temple, discreet and silent we enter the charming studio of Professor Spaulding, a nice educator who then introduces us to his colleagues, Professors Gesell and Chapman" (ibid., p. 90). The same powerful emotions and feelings were elicited by the entrance in the enclosed world of Stanley Hall: "As we go on a pilgrimage, with loving devotion, we go to a pretty red cottage which is only inhabited by the great Stanley Hall. A 15 year old girl shows us in and there we are in the drawing-room of the master. He comes, still very big despite his age, a handsome old European head, eyes still bright behind his glasses. Very cordially, he listens to our questions and responds with precision. Then after a slight, but painful, reference to the undesirable deterioration of this work at Clark, he asks us to go up to his studio. In a strange jumble of books, sitting near the stove in the old style, he talks about his colleagues, now dispersed. Then, as it is the very day of his birthday, he gave each of us a book with a dedication.

Why did he give me this strange *Zeitgeist* message? Maybe because being the youngest, he thought I must have more life! We leave this house in silence where a man lived his long hard life of austere work, for the betterment of the world and where he is about to die far from everyone, with the scrutinity of a sage. This twilight of God has something very moving" (ibid., pp. 90–91). Such institutional spaces thus become real places of memory and their role in Buyse's social and intellectual imaginative world remains to be studied.

Did Buyse learn anything from this journey, from this confrontation with a different reality? Did Buyse still think—where did he get it?—of putting *Manneken Pis* on the head of the Statue of Liberty, this 'Marianne', when first beholding New York's skyline, upon his return? How about his prejudices, his commonplaces about the new and different society that he visited, the USA and its population? Were they changed after the journey? Popular images are characterised by the typical dynamics of media, discourse, genres, styles, narrative forms, ideologies and identity constructs, by relations of power, by commercial and political objectives. The material, mental and social culture are in a constant interaction/exchange and mutually model themselves. The challenge for Buyse's future biographer lies in constituting a narrative from all the above.

References

Archives

• K.U. Leuven, Leuven.
Buyse, R. (1922). [*Voyage d'Étude aux U.S.A. 1922*]. Archives of the University. Archives Raymond Buyse, box 22.
• Centre d'études decrolyiennes, Bruxelles.
Guisset, M.-A. (s.d.). [*Biographie de Ovide Decroly*]. Centre d'Etudes Decrolyennes, Documents bio-bibliographiques.

Literature

Baedeker, K. (1894). *Les États-Unis, avec une excursion au Mexique: manuel du voyageur*. Leipzig, Germany: K. Baedeker.
Buyse, R. (1935). *L'expérimentation en pédagogie*. Brussels, Belgium: Lamertin.
Decroly, O., & Buyse, R. (1923). *Les applications américaines de la psychologie à l'organisation humaine et à l'éducation*. Brussels, Belgium: Lamertin.
Depaepe, M. (1993). *Zum Wohl des Kindes? Pädologie, pädagogische Psychologie und experimentelle Pädagogik in Europa und den USA, 1890–1940*. Leuven, Belgium: Leuven University Press; Weinheim, Germany: Deutscher Studien Verlag.
Depaepe, M., & D'hulst, L. (2011). *An educational pilgrimage to the United States: Travel diary of Raymond Buyse, 1922*. Leuven, Belgium: Leuven University Press.

Depaepe, M., Simon, F., & Van Gorp, A. (2003). The canonization of Ovide Decroly as a saint of the new education. *History of Education Quarterly, 43*, 224–249.

Depaepe, M., Simon F., & Van Gorp, A. (2011). L'expertise médicale et psycho-pédagogique d'Ovide Decroly en action. Utiliser le "fardeau" qu'engendre inadaptation sociale au profit de la société. In A. François, V. Massin, & D. Niget (Eds.), *Violences juvéniles sous expertise(s) XIXe-XXIe siècles* [Expertise and juvenile violence 19th–21st century] (pp. 39–54). Louvain-la-neuve, Belgium: UCL Presses Universitaires de Louvain.

Eilers, K. (2011). *René Sand (1877–1953) – Weltbürger der internationalen Sozialen Arbeit.* Opladen, Germany: Verlag Barbara Budrich.

Engelhart, M. D., & Thomas, M. (1966). Rice as the inventor of the comparative test. *Journal of Educational Measurement, 3*, 141–145.

Gille, A. (1965). Raymond Buyse, promoteur de la pédagogie expérimentale. In A. Bonboir et al. (Eds.), *L'oeuvre pédagogique de Raymond Buyse* (pp. 19–35). Louvain, Belgium: Vander.

Guignard, L., Raggi, P., & Thévenin, E. (Eds.). (2011). *Corps et machines à l'âge industriel.* Rennes, France: Presses universitaires de Rennes.

Hommage au Dr. Decroly. (1933). Sint-Niklaas. Belgium: Scheerders-Van Kerckhove.

Huret, J. (1907). *En Amérique: De New-York à la Nouvelle-Orléans.* Paris: E. Fasquelle.

Lagemann, E. C. (2000). *An elusive science. The troubling history of education research.* Chicago: The University of Chicago Press.

Latour, B. (1987). *Science in action: How to follow scientists and engineers through society.* Cambridge, MA: Harvard University Press.

Lawn, M. (Ed.). (2005). *An Atlantic crossing? The work of the international examination inquiry, its researchers, methods and influence.* Oxford, UK: Symposium Books.

Livingstone, D. (2003). *Putting science in its place. Geographies of scientific knowledge.* Chicago: University of Chicago Press.

Margadant, J.-B. (Ed.). (2000). *The new biography: Performing femininity in nineteenth-century France.* Los Angeles: University of California Press.

Montalbetti, K. (2002). *La pedagogia sperimentale di Raymond Buyse. Ricerca educativa tra orientamenti culturale attese sociale.* Milan: Vita e Pensiero.

Pintner, R. (1933). Mental tests and progressive schools. In *Hommage au Dr. Decroly* (pp. 409–414). Sint-Niklaas (W.), Belgium: Scheerders-Van Kerckhove.

Viñao, A. (2007). Viajes que educan. In A. C. Venancio Mignot & J. Gonçalves Gondra (Eds.), *Viagens pedagógicas* (pp. 15–38). São Paulo, Brazil: Cortez Editora.

Zenderland, L. (1998). *Measuring minds: Henry Herbert Goddard and the origins of American intelligence testing.* Cambridge, UK: Cambridge University Press.

Chapter 5
The Emergence of Institutional Educational Spaces for Young Children: In Pursuit of More Controllability of Education and Development as Part of the Long-Term Growth of Educational Space in History

Pauline R. Schreuder and Jeroen J.H. Dekker

5.1 Introduction

Part of the long-term growth of educational space in history was the emerging of spaces for the education of young children (0–4 years). In the last few decades, these spaces became increasingly characterised by institutionalisation, professionalisation and supervision of children and parents as a result of the quest for more controllability of education and child development. In this chapter, we first address this phenomenon of controllability of the education and the development of the young, and its relationship with changing and increasing ambitions on child rearing (Sect. 5.3). Then, we focus on the emergence, in the 1970s, of new educational spaces for young children and on how a new culture of controllability and of educational ambitions has developed and is still developing around those educational spaces. It will be shown that the presented late twentieth-century case is narrowly related to the long-term growth of educational space in history, in particular with its increasing educational ambitions and raising educational and developmental standards (Sect. 5.4). We start with a brief introduction into the meaning of the concept of educational space for the history of education (Sect. 5.2).

5.2 Educational Space, Educational Ambitions and Education and Childhood in History

Looking at the historical processes of education and childhood, the time dimension of educational spaces differs from educational places. While educational places could be considered as specific portions of spaces in a particular historical setting, for

P.R. Schreuder (✉) • J.J.H. Dekker
Faculteit Gedrags- en Maatschappijwetenschappen,
Rijksuniversiteit Groningen, The Netherlands
e-mail: p.r.schreuder@rug.nl

P. Smeyers et al. (eds.), *Educational Research: The Importance and Effects of Institutional Spaces*, Educational Research 7, DOI 10.1007/978-94-007-6247-3_5,
© Springer Science+Business Media Dordrecht 2013

example, the primary school of the Dutch reform pedagogue Jan Ligthart in 1885 at the Tullinghstraat in the city of The Hague, educational spaces are linked to the 'longue durée' time dimension of the historical process (Braudel, 1969). In this chapter, on the emergence of institutional educational of young children, those 'longue durée'-linked educational spaces are conceived in two ways: (1) they delineate the always restrictive and changing availability of education, and (2) they work as a series of historically changing conditions that enable educational ambitions (Dekker, 2010b). In approaching educational space in that way, compatibility is sought with the well-known and classic definition of culture that covers both the historically and culturally limited set of results of human activity, and a series of conditions that enable the producing of that set of results, in other words culture's potential for the future (Dekker, 1992, pp. 12–13, 2006, pp. 13–15, 2001a, 2001b, pp. 10–15; Dekker & Groenendijk, 1991; Frijhoff, 1983; Ginzburg, 1986; Grafton & Blair, 1990; Rogge, 1992; Siegel, 1996, pp. 28, 37–38; Steinmetz, 2008). Looking at the dimension of the limits and boundaries of culture—the first element of this definition of culture—allows us to approach educational ambition as a cultural phenomenon that is dependent on the educational space available. Looking at the dimension of the potential of culture—the second element of the definition—allows us to consider educational space as a set of conditions for educational ambitions. Educational space is a structural part of human history (Dekker & Groenendijk, 2012; Stearns, 2006/2011). Yet, it seems that the process of increasing educational space started in Europe in early modern times and accelerated in the late eighteenth century. As a result, a process of so-called 'pedagogisation' developed, a concept referring to an ever-growing societal and poli-tical interest in schooling, education and childhood, and expressed in ever-raising educational ambitions (Depaepe, 1998; cf. De Vroede, 1987; Dekker, 2010b; Dekker & Groenendijk, 2012; Smeyers & Depaepe, 2008).

The long-term dimension of educational space, with both its limits and its potential varying over time and across cultures, and with its continuity and change, is central in this contribution. As said above, educational space is different from educational place, that particular portion of space in a particular time and on a physically enclosed spot, such as a school (Burke, 2005, 2009; Grosvenor, 2007; Grosvenor & Watts 2003; Loughman & Montias, 2000; Richardson, 2000). Four elements of educational space seem to be essential to estimate its limits and potential in history: demographic space; socioeconomic and financial space; the relationship between private and public educational space; finally, mental space, or the space for acting educationally and for willing to map the child's world.

Demographic space does decisively limit educational space through infant and child mortality and through parental death (Stearns, 2006/2011; World Health Organisation). From early modern times until well into the nineteenth century—in the Netherlands until the 1870s (Dekker, Groenendijk, & Verberckmoes, 2000, pp. 43–60)—reaching adulthood remained an illusion for ca. fifty percent of the children due to high infant and child mortality.[1] This phenomenon sharply contrasted with the positive focus on education in the Enlightenment discourse and on the child in the Romantic discourse: demographic reality often destroyed educational illusions (Dekker, 2010b, chap. 1). Socioeconomic and financial spaces constituted the second form of limitation and potential, with private and public educational actors depending on the limits and potential of those spaces when considering investments in education. Thirdly, in the quest for educational power in facing, using and negotiating the available educational space, private and public agencies both cooperated and competed with each other, in particular when the national state became more powerful and educational ambitions rose (Steinmetz, 2008). Specific national situations resulted in various outcomes of this competition and cooperation between private and public agencies. Yet, all countries followed the same main trend: more education and more supervision of education by the state.

As a result, around 1900, more than 100 years after the birth of the Enlightenment idea of educational regulation and supervision by the state, compulsory education was introduced in almost all European countries. The state also started to deal with child-rearing problems. That ambition resulted, also around 1900, into legislative regulation of educational supervision of domestic child rearing by the introduction of Child Protection Acts in almost all European countries, as well as in North America (Dekker, 2001a, 2001b, pp. 41–55; Dupont-Bouchat et al., 2001). The educational threshold between the private and the public, supposed to be almost holy for many social groups, as for example the orthodox-protestants in the Netherlands and the Catholics in the Netherlands and Germany, was now crossed through the support of legislators and judges. This resulted in an increase of the public educational space and in a decrease of the private educational space. The mentioned three elements of educational space could serve as conditions for educational acting: children remain alive, the economy enables educational investments and public and private agencies develop their educational roles. But in order to make use of those conditions, a change of the mental educational space was necessary. That mental educational space, although never absent in history, changed in a decisive way by first an increasing focus on education in the Enlightenment discourse and by making the child the centre of attention in the Romantic discourse. This new focus on education and childhood was followed by the birth of child sciences and, at the end of the nineteenth century, justified by its emphasis on acting in the best interests of the child, by the introduction of Child Protection and Children's Rights Acts. The increase of this mental educational space with its growing educational ambitions became increasingly characterised by a pursuit of and a longing for supervision and controllability of childhood and education.

5.3 Supervision, Controllability and the Optimal Development of the Young

Educational spaces for young children are no recent invention. From the 1830s, those spaces are connected with the Fröbel-inspired way of approaching young children in an institutional environment. Through the nineteenth century, all over the world, educational spaces for the very young children, inspired by Fröbel's experiments, are founded (Fröbel, 1893; Heiland, 2006; Read, 2006; Wollons,

2000). In those times, child development was understood in educational theory as an individual track, and consequently, each child's development would naturally differ from that of another child. This way of looking at the development of children was not limited to Fröbel or Fröbel adherents, but consistent with main trend classical pedagogical theory. According to Jürgen Oelkers, "it is legitimate to cultivate freedom and at the same time put constraints on the child if we have in mind processes of liberal education…Knowledge forms the mind, but only in a free way; at the same time all forming of mind is a kind of bondage to cultural heritage. The result might be new knowledge, but all knowledge can only be educationally transmitted as a restriction of (personal) freedom. This restriction…cannot be called coercion if it serves the freedom of judgement. If not, education is illegitimate" (Oelkers, 1991, p. 81). Thus, according to Oelkers, all education that restricts personal freedom without serving freedom in the future is illegitimate.

Notwithstanding those then hardly contested ideas of classic pedagogical theory, the history of education and childhood often tells us another story. That story reveals that discipline, regulation and supervision were often used as strategies of educational ambition, in particular by educational agencies such as the state, the church, philanthropic organisations and by the school system itself (Ariès, 1960/1962; Dekker, 1996, 2010b, chap. 1; Dekker & Lechner, 1999; Foucault, 1975/1977). Philippe Ariès was probably the first historian to systematically make use of the concept of discipline in the history of education in his classic *L'enfant et la vie familiale sous l'ancien régime* (*Centuries of Childhood*) from 1960. Yet, Michel Foucault received 15 years later the credits for this through his analysis in *Surveiller et punir* (*Discipline and Punish*) from 1975. For the rest, Foucault was strongly influenced by Ariès's ideas on discipline.[2] While those ideas were inspired by his interpretation of seventeenth- and eighteenth-century French school history, Foucault's reflection on education and discipline became famous with his interpretation of the agrarian colony of Mettray near Tours, founded in 1839 for the re-education of delinquent boys, as the educational disciplinary institution *par excellence*. For the rest, Foucault, in relating the origins of the so-called carceral system, so clearly manifested in the example of Mettray, to the transformation of the sixteenth- and seventeenth-century European school system, again followed the ideas developed by Ariès (Ariès, 1960/1962, pp. 267 [1973, p. 295], 284 and 333 [1973, pp. 316 and 373]; Bec, Duprat, Luc, & Petit, 1994; Cunningham & Innes, 1998; Dekker, 2001a, 2001b, pp. 61–68; Dekker & Groenendijk, 2012; Dekker & Lechner, 1999; Dupont-Bouchat et al., 2001; Foucault, 1975/1977, p. 169 [1975, p. 171]).

Although discipline, regulation and supervision were part of the history of education, schooling and childhood for centuries, around 1900, a fundamental change took place. From then, state-directed educational regulation and supervision increased in almost all European countries, resulting in a remarkable increase of the public and a decrease of the private educational space. Moreover, educational standards, laid down in legal regulations and supervised by the state, started to rise. The introduction of Child Protection Acts around 1900 marked a fundamental change. These Acts made it mandatory for all parents to act according to the new educational standards. The ultimate consequence of not acting according to those standards could be dramatic, namely, the loss of parental power, or of all private educational space. This was the case for parents of hundreds of thousands of European children being taken from their families to be re-educated outside their family in 'their best interests', that being the legal justification (Dekker, 2010b, pp. 104–116; De Vries & Van Tricht, 1903/1910, vol. 1, 2; Dupont-Bouchat, 1996; Dupont-Bouchat et al., 2001, pp. 323–384). Parenting became 'a duty that implies a right, which can be lost when the duty is neglected', according to G. A. van Hamel, a Dutch professor of law at the University of Amsterdam, speeching in 1905 on the occasion of the coming into practice of the Dutch Child Acts (van Hamel et al., 1905). However, not all adherents of the new acts were that ambitious. The Dutch liberal Minister of Justice himself, P. W. A. Cort van der Linden, speaking in Parliament in 1901 in defending the acts, stated the basic idea behind them in the following way: 'Only reversing, not preventing is the responsibility of the state'. In other words, something would have to go wrong before intervention was possible according to the law, in the Minister's interpretation (Donker, 1955, p. 7).

However, this restrained attitude towards state intervention in the best interests of the child transformed slowly but steadily into a pursuit of more controllability. That process accelerated, at least in the Netherlands, after the Second World War, and it went together with a further raising of educational and developmental standards. In 1955, at the celebration for the fiftieth anniversary of the Child Acts, J. Overwater (1892–1958), president of The Dutch Association for Child Protection, a children's court magistrate and a leading figure in the world of child protection, emphasised the growing need for child protection. While child protection had initially been related to the 'major shortcomings of parents', it was, according to Overwater, now 'dominated by cases of various sorts of education problems and behavioural problems'. It was therefore no longer 'limited to one single social group', but was exercising a 'bad influence upon society as a whole'. This diagnosis of the need of child protection implied that now, despite the implementation and the good results of the Child Acts in the last 50 years, even more families and more children were at risk. The tackling of these risks required the streamlining and the professionalisation of the child protection system and also further supervision of child rearing (Overwater, 1955, pp. 15–23).

This growing demand of child protection according to Overwater—and he was not alone with his opinion, but the spokesman of a trend (Dekker, 2009)—was accompanied by an increasing emphasis on optimal development and optimal education of children, with as a consequence an increasing emphasis on at-risk children and risky parents, namely, those children who were not optimally developing and those parents who were not educating their children in that direction. The history of child maltreatment from the 1970s (Kempe et al., 1962) shows this emphasis on optimal development. The process of the broadening of the definition of child maltreatment, a process that started in the early 1970s, became increasingly related to the new focus on optimal development of the child (Dekker, 2010a; Giovannoni, 1990, pp. 9–16, 19–20; Jenny, 2008, pp. 2796–2797). As a result of the raising standards of development and of education, many at-risk categories saw increasing numbers, as Hermanns has recently made clear for the Dutch case.

Indeed, at first sight, the situation of Dutch children seems to be very serious with 491,290, or 14 % of the group aged 0–18, making use of a form of special care, an increase of about 10 % annually over the last 10 years, with about 20,000 being educated in a residential setting. However, recent epidemiological research on the welfare situation of Dutch children and youth seems to refute this impression. The results of that research make clear that the overwhelming majority seems to feel content, even happy (Rispens et al., 1996). This apparent inconsistency brings Hermanns to the conclusion that it must be the increasing availability of educational support and care that was mainly responsible for the increasing number of children at risk. This growth of educational support was connected to lowering trust in parental competences and an increasing trust in the competences of professionals, because of the belief that parenthood competences were not as a matter of fact part of the competencies of young parents, but should be learned by them, taught by educational professionals. According to Hermanns, however, the great majority of parents turned out to be competent at their task from the beginning because of their genetic and social background, with further parenthood capacities normally developing in their interaction with their children. For those parents, the great majority, there was, according to Hermanns, any need at all for professional support (Bullock, Gable, & Melloy, 2004; Conroy, 2004; Hermanns, 2009, pp. 7, 23, 24; Weijers, 2009).

Yet, it is much more a lowering trust in parental competences than the assumption of competent parents that dominated the new educational policy. In order to stimulate the optimal development of young children and to raise the controllability of professionals and of the state, a new instrument has recently been added to the machinery of the educational ambitions of the state and of the educational professionals, namely, the Electronic Child Dossier. This instrument was proposed by professionals and accepted eagerly by a government longing for more educational controllability. This innovation, approved by the Dutch Parliament and introduced for all children aged 0–18 and their parents from 1 July 2010, enables the supervision and controllability of all children, together with their parents, from birth—or even some months earlier—to adulthood. The intention behind the instrument is to reduce the number of children developing into risk-creating adults and to prevent parents from bad parenting (*Coalition Agreement*, 2007; *All Opportunities for All Children*, 2007). The report advising the introduction of the instrument, produced at the request of the government by a private organisation, the *Inventgroep*, consisting of professional pedagogues, psychologists and medical doctors, and published in 2005, was entitled 'Helping with growing up and educating: earlier, faster, and better'. With the Electronic Child Dossier bringing all children and their parents under the supervision of the state and professionals, the state, together with educational professionals, seemed to develop into an educational Big Brother (Hermanns, Ory, & Schrijvers, 2005, pp. 11, 28, 85).[3]

Although this policy was at first encouraged and strongly advised by several professional players in the field of children at risk, some of them changed their minds. J. Hermanns, one of the authors of the 2005 report, was one of them and the most prominent. Four years later, he turned out to become explicitly sceptical about the positive effects of the Electronic Child Dossier and critical about the dangers of perceiving all children as potentially at risk. According to him, 'there seems to exist a hunt for so-called at risk families that are not yet a problem, but may possibly become a problem in the future'. The Big Brother potential of the Electronic Child Dossier could according to Hermanns even increase by linking it to the so-called Reference Index Children at Risk. That index connects data on children at risk to the child's citizen service number, a unique number given by the state to each Dutch citizen from birth, thus enabling the combining of various sets of data (Hermanns, 2009).[4]

Altogether, this longing not only for mapping the child's world but also for increasing the standards of education and of child development, and for raising educational ambitions for both the public and the professionals, has resulted in a blurred and contested threshold between private and public educational space. In the following, we take a more in-depth look into a specific educational space for the education of young children, the recently developed institutions for day care, and how that space is increasingly characterised by the main elements of the above-sketched long-term trend into more controllability and raising standards.

5.4 The Development of New Educational Spaces for the Education of Young Children

The blurring and contesting threshold between the private and the public is clearly visible in most western countries, such as the Netherlands, not only for recently developed educational spaces for young children but also for the new controllability that is characteristic for modern mapping of the child's world. Examples of these developments can easily be found in everyday early childhood practice. Firstly, and most obviously, a large number of infants and toddlers now visit day-care centres when their parents go to work.[5] Thus, the upbringing and educating of young children has become a joint task for an increasing number of parents and professional caretakers. This is reflected in the pedagogical mission statement that day-care organisations are required to have: these statements put forward the upbringing and educating of young children as the core business of day care. Compared to the recent past, this is a profound change: until the year 2000, caring instead of educating children was understood as the principal function of day-care institutions. Both parents and caretakers agreed on this, as they now (sometimes openly, sometimes tacitly, from the part of the parents) agree on the importance of upbringing and education (Riksen-Walraven, 2000; Tavecchio, 2002).

Secondly, the discourse on professionally caring for and educating young children has undergone profound changes. Professionals working with young children are required to monitor and control children's development and progress by using standardised observation procedures and educational programmes, and by rigorous documentation and evaluation. This tendency can be found in countries all over the world (Dahlberg & Moss, 2005; Moss, 2007; Urban, 2008).

Some countries, such as England, have recently introduced a compulsory curriculum for early childhood education, in combination with a systematic series of tests to assess the child's progress and development. According to the website, this curriculum, the Early Years Foundation Stage (EYFS), "is a comprehensive statutory framework that sets the standards for the learning, development and care of children from birth to five. All providers are required to use the EYFS to ensure that whatever setting parents choose, they can be confident their child will receive a quality experience that supports their care, learning and development" (http://www. education.gov.uk/childrenandyoungpeople/earlylearningandchildcare/delivery/ education/a0068102/early-years-foundation-stage-eyfs). In several other countries, childcare institutions are strongly stimulated to implement early education programmes, some of which are oriented towards specific contents (e.g. the Dutch 'Pyramid' program) and some of which are more process oriented, with broadly defined ends, for example, giving the child a sense of belonging (the New Zealand 'Tē Whariki' curriculum).

Care workers react differently to working with programmes for early childhood education, but many of them embrace this development, as it is presented and understood as a boost for their professionalism. However, according to Mathias Urban (2008), more emphasis on working 'according to the book', and using prescribed programmes and tests, challenges our notion of professionalism, when this is understood as being able to make adequate judgements in changing situations. The value of professional knowledge, experience and judgement decreases as the emphasis on using standardised methods and guidelines increases. In this respect, the Belgian expert on childcare, Jan Peeters, uses the concept of deprofessionalisation, emphasising the paradox situation of personnel with much more educational training but not invited to use their knowledge and competencies fully (Peeters, 2008). The increased controllability of the education of young children affects the discourse or the mental space of pedagogical professionals working in day care. This mental space and the changes in mental space in turn affect the ways in which young children are addressed and understood, that is, the pedagogical relationship.

The pedagogical relationship has become a central issue in continental classic European philosophy of education, mostly by the work of Hermann Nohl (1933/ 1973). Other theorists of the *Geisteswissenschaftliche Pädagogik*, such as Theodor Litt, and the phenomenological approach, such as M. J. Langeveld (Bos, 2011), have elaborated on his theoretical work and have refined his central concepts (cf. Spiecker, 1984). The pedagogical relation can be described as an ongoing search for a balance that can never be reached satisfactorily. The necessity and impossibility of this balance is captured by the theoretical notion of 'antinomy'. For instance, the antinomy of the present and future as orientations for upbringing shows that when an educator is oriented towards the future, he neglects the present situation of the child; when he is oriented towards the present situation, he neglects the future. Yet, as an educator, he should be oriented to both present and future. This antinomy thus captures the impossibility and necessity of acting correctly in the education of children: there is no one clear and right way to do this. Next to a parent, a professional educator—be it a childcare worker or an early education teacher—can thus also be identified by his ability to make ethical, situational choices with regard to the best interest of the child. Interestingly, childcare workers have described their work in this way, when asked about the most fundamental aspects of their pedagogy (Schreuder, 2010; Schreuder & Timmerman, 2009).

Neither the choices of the educator nor the developmental and educational process of the child can or ought to be prescribed in advance as this would result in a loss of the personal and moral component of the pedagogical relation (Simons & Masschelein, 2008). Barrett expresses similar concerns in his article on current developments in teacher education, when he states that the focus on controllability results in an understanding of teachers as instrumental technicians, void of personal commitment (Barrett, 2009, p.1024). The inevitable unpredictability of the process of education is addressed by the existentially oriented German philosopher of education Otto Bollnow (1977) in an *avant la lettre* warning against controllability. He acknowledges that upbringing and educating children are undeniably disrupted by unforeseen circumstances. Therefore, educators can never fully control development and learning, nor should they want to. Some children need little time; others need more time before they understand something. Eventually, teachers and educators do not 'make' a pupil understand: this is something the pupil does, at a certain, unpredictable moment. Bollnow, in short, points out the importance of modesty on the part of educators.

In sum, in most of the twentieth century, philosophy and theory of education understood the pedagogical relationship between adults and children mainly in terms of mutual personal involvement towards an unpredictable future. Nowadays, however, the personal involvement is much more concerned with risk management: adults should enable and protect developmental opportunities, or optimal development, for each child. This shift in understanding the pedagogical relationship can be found in educational and pedagogical theories, in educational policy and in guidelines for educational and pedagogical practices, as for example, those for the very young.

5.4.1 A Shift in Educational Theories

One of the most dominant and hardly contested concepts in educational theory in the Netherlands today is the notion of an 'unbroken line of development'. This notion, grounded in a rather narrow interpretation of Vygotsky's theory of development, is strongly programmatic and prescriptive: education ought to be a process of ongoing and undisrupted development. Educators are called upon to choose their actions in such a way that the developmental course of the child is both steady and smooth. Ideally, the child's development has no setbacks, no periods of stagnation, no sudden jumps—in whatever direction. Therefore, all educational settings that a child attends ought to have a shared educational vision, shared educational goals and, preferably, shared educational programmes (Onderwijsraad, 2008). A child's development can thus be monitored, for example, by the Electronic Child Dossier, steered and checked all the way while protecting the child from unnecessary detours.

The popularity of the idea of the unbroken line of development can be understood from the experienced need for providing equal educational opportunities to children from disadvantaged backgrounds (Van Oenen & Hajer, 2004). As these children lack opportunities that are considered educationally valuable, schools ought to compensate by providing—or making accessible—such educational opportunities, for instance by organising cultural or sports activities after school hours. Many local communities have started so-called 'Broad Schools' (*brede scholen*) as a community service, combining primary education with playgroups and day care for young children, with medical facilities, a library, social clubs for various age groups and cultural organisations for music, dance and theatre. Thus, the idea of the unbroken line of development has become intimately connected with community services, especially in disadvantaged parts of towns or villages.

While education and learning are thus facilitated for a large group of children, the justification lies in a narrow interpretation of child development as a process that ought to be protected from disruptions as much as possible. In other words, the rationale does not lie in offering children more opportunities for learning, development and a pleasant way of spending free time but in offering educators more opportunities for control over children's life, resulting in a more instrumental pedagogical relationship.

5.4.2   Shift in Educational Policy

Changes in the understanding and the realisation of the pedagogical relationship can also be illustrated by recent examples from educational policy that strongly differed from the above cited Cort van der Linden's political maxim for retraining control and supervision in 1901: 'Only reversing, not preventing is the responsibility of the state'. The Dutch Programme Ministry for Youth and Family—established in 2007 and abolished in 2010—held another opinion of the educational responsibility of the state. Its programme for 2007–2011 under the ambitious title: "All opportunities for all children", embraced the new psychological and educational theory of optimal development. The educational ambitions written down in this programme consider the pedagogical relationship in a mainly technical, instead of a personal and moral, sense, as was the case in modernist educational and developmental psychological theories. In all educational domains, stretching from early childhood education to higher education, educational policy has seen a strong move towards systematic planning, documenting and testing. Schools, but also early childhood organisations, are prompted to use educational programmes that have been proven effective, are so-called 'evidence based', and do have a systematic approach to all relevant educational domains.

The reports of the Dutch Education Council (*Onderwijsraad*), an influential advisory board of the government, also show this policy focus on optimal development, recently resulting in an advice for formal education, starting at age three, *towards a new preschool phase* (2010). As almost all children start attending formal education at age four (though the law states that school is compulsory from age five), the Council sees no real problems in this proposal. They state that all children would profit more from a methodical and systematic education when they gradually get used to this from an early age. However, the Council warns that these very young children should be treated with a different pedagogy than older children; they are not yet ready for a more school-like pedagogy but should be given opportunities for learning in a variety of ways. Play, imagination and expression, as well as language development, ought to play a big part in a pedagogy for these children. Yet, according to the Council, the sooner the development of these children is assessed, the sooner we can provide them with appropriate materials for their development. This requires a careful documentation of the child's accomplishments and progress, thus leading to a portfolio with all relevant information for educators within or outside the educational environment.

With this report, the Dutch Education Council is consistent in its advices on policy since 2002. From then, the Council published a series of ever ongoing proposals for programmes, tests, curricula and other compulsory measurements with regard to the upbringing and education of young children. On the one hand, these advices reflect the blurred distinction between the private and the public in relation to young children; on the other hand, this distinction remains sharply in focus, as parents' role of critically choosing consumers is emphasised (Onderwijsraad, 2002, 2006, 2008, 2010). Parents are called upon to make informed choices on the (publicly or privately provided) types of day care, early education or playgroup they send their child to, while keeping the idea of an unbroken line of development in view. This places a heavy burden on parents, as they are told that the day-care centre they choose for their infant might seriously influence its developmental opportunities. But as the demand for day care is often larger than the supply, parents very often have little choice (Vandenbroeck, 2009). They are thus held hostage between the availability of day care and the best interest of their child, as it is presented to them. Thus, when it comes to deciding what is best in parents' and children's personal space, the influence of the public space has strongly increased.

5.4.3 Shift in Educational Practices in a New Institutional Space for Young Children

Thirdly and finally, the mentioned changes in the understanding of the pedagogical relationship affected the ways in which parents and professionals raise and teach children in practice. Both parents and professionals are supposed to be now 'more aware' of the young child's development and of possible disturbances of that development than earlier in history. One of the most popular books on Dutch parenting of the past 15 years is called in translation: 'Oops, I'm growing!' (Oei, ik groei; Van de Rijt & Plooij, 1992/2004). Its popularity can be illustrated by the fact that it has been reprinted at least 35 times since 1992, and some local health services provide young parents with this book as a standard for raising their children. In this book, parents are encouraged to observe several aspects of their infant's development in order to assess the stage the child is in. Each following stage will only be reached by a period of apparent stagnation, after which the child suddenly moves on to a new, higher stage. This process is called the 'little jump' between stages. When the expected 'jump' does not happen at the 'right' time, this can and does lead to concern or sometimes even panic on the part of the young parents. The popularity of the book had a big impact on the language that young parents used to describe their infants and toddlers, and parents who did not join in that discourse were immediately recognised as not having read the book in question. 'Oops, I'm growing' strongly changed the language and the discourse on parenting and upbringing,[6] but it also changed many parents' outlook on their children and on their own parenting behaviour, as shown on several web fora for parents.[7]

In a day-care setting, where professionals work with young children, a similar popularity has befallen the ideas of Marianne Riksen-Walraven, a professor in developmental psychology. In 2000, she formulated four pedagogical goals for day care, followed in 2002 by six competencies for childcare workers.[8] Together, these goals and competencies should enable professionals to reach and maintain a sufficient level of quality of their pedagogical work (Riksen-Walraven, 2004). The six competencies all have bearing on the pedagogical relationship, as they focus on appropriate ways of interaction and communication with young children. These competencies can be recognised in the Professional Competencies Profile (Van de Haterd & Lammersen, 2006) that describes the requirements for working professionally in day care. Reducing pedagogical qualities to competencies, however, carries the risk that the pedagogical relationship will be understood in a reduced sense—as a tick box instead of a personal and moral relationship that acknowledges uncertainty as an inescapable part of that relationship.

Nowadays, these competencies can be found in most mission statements of day-care centres, and they figure prominently in the recently published handbook—a novelty in this field—for professionals in day care (Singer & Kleerekooper, 2009). An optimal development of the child is understood as something that can and should be stimulated, monitored and discussed, both by professionals and parents. Even though parents are not required to be professional stimulators of development themselves, they are understood as critical customers who expect professionals to be experts. A folder of the Dutch 'Pyramid' program (http://www. cito.nl/onderwijs/vroeg%20en%20voorschoolse%20educatie/piramide/kieswijzer_ piramide.aspx) addresses day-care workers this way as it persuades them to use this program for early childhood education ("Parents expect a lot from you, these days, including playing a part in the stimulation of their child's development. Therefore, it is important to reflect on how you can provide this. What is best for the development of the youngest children").

In the new educational space of early childhood education and day care, the controllability of the optimal development of the young child now dominates theory, policy and practice. The influence of this shift on the role of parents and even more professionals is both strong and ubiquitous and leads to a new educational discourse.

5.5 Conclusion

Looking at the long-term perspective from the late nineteenth century onwards, the notion of 'the best interest of the child' has increasingly informed and shaped pedagogical practices, resulting for instance in specific laws that define criteria for what counts as 'good pedagogical' acting, or 'good parenting'. Since the 1970s, the best interest of the child has been understood in terms of 'optimal development': the new standard for judging the appropriateness of upbringing and education. Mental space and (practical) educational space changed over time, while the influence of national policy and laws continually contested the threshold between public and private space.

Over the past few decades, the newly emerging institutional educational spaces and their corresponding pedagogical professions for educating the very young have produced a new pedagogical discourse connecting the child's optimal development with the notion of its controllability. This discourse provides the rationale for shaping educational spaces in such a way that professionals—informed by governmental policy—have become a new type of authorities on child development, that is, authorities who can set new standards for the pedagogical relationship between parents and their children. Paradoxically, however, these professionals are required to rely less on their theoretical and practical knowledge and more on standardised programmes, methods and tests in order to meet the best interest and the optimal development of each individual child.

In sum, within the long-term growth of educational space in history, new pedagogical spaces with new controllability have emerged and developed, directed by new child development ambitions, laid down in new theories of education, in new mission statements of new educational spaces such as day-care centres and in new instruments of educational policy, such as the Electronic Child Dossier. As educational space has grown so have educational ambitions.

Notes

1. The parents' own vulnerability also limited the educational space and stimulated the foundation of orphanages (see Dankers & Verheul, 1991; Dekker, 2006; Gavitt, 1990; Groenveld, Dekker, Willemse, & Dane, 1997).
2. Foucault made only one reference to Ariès (Foucault, 1975/1977, pp. 141 [1975], 143, n. 3) but was praising Ariès at several occasions (Dekker, 2010a, 2010b, pp. 21–23).
3. The screening proposal was laid down in *All opportunities for all children*. See www.rijksoverheid.nl/onderwerpen/digitaal-dossier-jeugdgezondheidszorg-ekd
4. Earlier, critical comments were published by Dekker (2007) and by J. Lamé, director of the Diagnostic and Therapeutic Psychological Centre of Rotterdam-Rijnmond, who in an interview with the national newspaper *NRC Handelsblad* (Interview in *NRC Handelsblad*, February 9, 2008) sharply criticised the Electronic

Child Dossier, even calling it 'absurdist, Stalinist and an example of megalomania'. Cf. also Lamé (2011) and *Trouw*, 18 February 2010, 'Beware of the Youth Health Office'.

5. In 1989, approximately 35,000 children 0–4 years attended day care (about 5 % of this age group); in 2007, this number had increased to 255,000 children (32.5 % of this age group). The Education Council (Onderwijsraad, 2010) stated that in 2010, 90 % of all 3-year-olds attended some kind of day care or preschool.

6. After its first print in 1992, the book quickly became very popular and had its 35th print in 2004. While the ideas in the book were based upon empirical research, they were strongly criticized in a Ph.D. dissertation, also based on empirical research, by de Weerth (1997).

7. A short and simple web search generated several sites referring to this popular book and its specific ideas on development: www.vrouwenpower.nl, www.alles-overkinderen.nl, www.ikkeben.nl, www.overkinderen.nl, www.zwangerschapspa-gina.nl and (unsurprisingly) www.oeiikgroei.nl

8. The four basic aims are security and safety, personal development, social development and socialisation (basic rules of conduct and communication). The six professional competencies are: sensitivity and responsiveness, respect the child's autonomy, talk and explain, structure and rules, stimulate the child's development and guide and support children's interactions.

References

Alle kansen voor alle kinderen. Programma voor jeugd en gezin 2007–2011 (2007) [All opportunities for all children. Program for Youth and Family 2007–2011]. Proceedings of the Dutch Lower House into Den Haag: Programmaministerie voor Jeugd en Gezin.

Ariès, P. (1960). *L'Enfant et la vie familiale sous l'ancien régime*. Paris: Librairie Plon. [Centuries of childhood: A social history of family life. New York: Alfred A. Knopf, 1962].

Barrett, B. D. (2009). No child left behind and the assault on teachers' professional practices and identities. *Teaching and Teacher Education, 25*, 1018–1025.

Bec, C., Duprat, C., Luc, J. N., & Petit, J. P. (Eds.). (1994). *Philanthropies et politiques sociales en Europe (XVIIIe-XXe siècles)*. Paris: Anthropos.

Bollnow, O. F. (1977/1959). *Existenzphilosophie und Pädagogik*. Stuttgart: Kohlhammer.

Bos, J. (2011). *M.J. Langeveld. Pedagoog aan de hand van het kind*. Amsterdam: Boom.

Braudel, F. (1969). Histoire et sciences sociales. La longue durée. In F. Braudel (Ed.), *Écrits sur l'histoire* (pp. 41–83). Paris: Flammarion.

Bullock, L. M., Gable, R. A., & Melloy, K. J. (2004). Foreword. In M. A. Conroy (Ed.), *Prevention and early intervention for young children at risk for emotional or behavioral disorders* (pp. 1–2). Arlington, VA: The Council for Children with Behavioral Disorders.

Burke, C. (2005). Containing the school child: Architectures and pedagogies. *Paedagogica Historica: International Journal of the History of Education, 41*, 489–494.

Burke, C. (2009). "Inside out". A collaborative approach to designing schools in England. *Paedagogica Historica, 45*, 421–433.

Coalitieakkoord tussen de Tweede Kamerfracties van CDA, PvdA en ChristenUnie. Retrieved February 12, 2013, from http://www.rijksoverheid.nl/documenten-en-publicaties/rapporten/2007/02/07/coalitieakkoord-balkenende-iv.html

Conroy, M. A. (Ed.). (2004). *Prevention and early intervention for young children at risk for emotional or behavioral disorders*. Arlington, TX: The Council for Children with Behavioral Disorders.

Cunningham, H., & Innes, I. (Eds.). (1998). *Charity, philanthropy and reform. From the 1690s to 1850*. New York: Macmillan.

Dahlberg, G., & Moss, P. (2005). *Ethics and politics in early childhood education*. London/New York: Routledge Falmer.

Dankers, J. J., & Verheul, J. (1991). *Als een groot particulier huisgezin. Opvoeden in het Utrechtse Burgerweeshuis tussen caritas en staatszorg 1813–1991*. Zutphen, the Netherlands: Walburg Pers.

Dekker, J. J. H. (1992). *Het gezinsportret. Over de geschiedenis van opvoeding, cultuuroverdracht en identiteit*. Baarn, the Netherlands: Ambo.

Dekker, J. J. H. (1996). Éduquer et punir. *Michel Foucault et l'histoire de l'éducation surveillée. Sociétés et Représentations, 3*, 257–268.

Dekker, J. J. H. (2001a). *The will to change the child. Re-education homes for children at risk in nineteenth century western Europe*. Frankfurt am Main, Germany: Peter Lang.

Dekker, J. J. H. (2001b). Cultural transmission and inter-generational interaction. *International Review of Education, 47*, 77–95.

Dekker, J. J. H. (2006). *Het verlangen naar opvoeden. Over de groei van de pedagogische ruimte in Nederland sinds de Gouden Eeuw tot omstreeks 1900*. Amsterdam: Bert Bakker.

Dekker, J. J. H. (2007). Opvoeding onder toezicht. De Nederlandse kinderwetten in de eeuw van het kind. In: *Honderd jaar kinderwetten 1905–2005* (pp. 10–33). The Hague, the Netherlands: Ministerie van Justitie.

Dekker, J. J. H. (2009). Children at risk in history: A story of expansion. *Paedagogica Historica, 45*, 17–36.

Dekker, J. J. H. (2010a). Child maltreatment in the last fifty years: The use of statistics. In P. Smeyers & M. Depaepe (Eds.), *Educational research: The ethics and aesthetics of statistics* (pp. 43–57). Dordrecht, the Netherlands: Springer.

Dekker, J. J. H. (2010b). *Educational ambitions in history. Childhood and education in an expanding educational space from the seventeenth to the twentieth century*. Frankfurt am Main, Germany: Peter Lang.

Dekker, J. J. H., & Groenendijk, L. F. (1991). The republic of God or the republic of children? Childhood and childrearing after the reformation: an appraisal of Simon Schama's thesis about the uniqueness of the Dutch case. *Oxford Review of Education, 17*, 317–335.

Dekker, J. J. H., & Groenendijk, L. F. (2012). Philippe Ariès's discovery of childhood after fifty years: The impact of a classic study on educational research. *Oxford Review of Education, 38*, 133–147.

Dekker, J. J. H., Groenendijk, L. F., & Verberckmoes, J. (2000). Proudly raising vulnerable youngsters: The scope for education in the Netherlands. In J. B. Bedaux & R. E. O. Ekkart (Eds.), *Pride and joy: Children's portraits in the Netherlands 1500–1700* (pp. 43–60). Ghent, Belgium/Amsterdam/New York: Ludion and Abrams.

Dekker, J. J. H., & Lechner, D. M. (1999). Discipline and pedagogics in history. Foucault, Ariès, and the history of panoptical education. *The European Legacy, 4*, 37–49.

Depaepe, M. (1998). *De pedagogisering achterna. Aanzet tot een genealogie van de pedagogische mentaliteit in de voorbije 250 jaar*. Leuven, Belgium/Amersfoort, the Netherlands: Acco.

De Vries, A. D. W., & van Tricht, F. J. G. (Eds.). (1903–1910). *Geschiedenis der wet op de ouderlijke macht en de voogdij (6 februari 1901, Staatsblad no. 62). Verzameling van regeringsontwerpen, gewisselde stukken, gevoerde beraadslagingen, enz., met enkele korte kanttekeningen en register* (3 Vols.) Groningen, the Netherlands: Wolters.

De Vroede, M. (1987). Inleiding. In J. J. H. Dekker, M. D. Hoker, B. Kruithof, & M. De Vroede (Eds.), *Pedagogisch werk in de samenleving* (pp. 9–15). Leuven, Belgium: Acco.

de Weerth, C. (1997). *Emotion-related behavior in infants: A longitudinal study of patterns and variability*. PhD dissertation, University of Groningen. Wageningen, the Netherlands: Ponsen & Looijen.

Donker, L. A. (1955). Rede van de minister van justitie, mr. L.A. Donker. In *Toespraken gehouden ter herdenking van de gouden kinderwetten op 1 december 1955, in de Ridderzaal te 's-Gravenhage* (pp. 5–14). The Hague, the Netherlands: Ministry of Justice.

Dupont-Bouchat, M.-S. (1996). *De la prison à l'école. Les pénitenciers pour enfants en Belgique au XIXe siècle (1840–1914)*. Kortrijk-Heule, Belgium: UGA.

Dupont-Bouchat, M.-S., Pierre, E., Fecteau, J.-M., Trepanier, J., Petit, J.-G., Schnapper, B., et al. (2001). *Enfance et justice au XIXe siècle. Essais d'histoire comparée de la protection de l'enfance 1829–1914, France, Belgique, Pays-Bas, Canada.* Paris: Presses Universitaires de France.

Foucault, M. (1975). *Surveiller et punir. Naissance de la prison.* Paris : Gallimard. (Discipline and punish. The birth of the prison, 1977). Harmondsworth, UK/New York/Melbourne, Australia: Penguin Books.

Frijhoff, W. (1983). *Cultuur, mentaliteit: illusies van elites?* Nijmegen, the Netherlands: SUN.

Fröbel, F. (1893/1826). *The education of man.* New York: D. Appleton and Company.

Gavitt, P. (1990). *Charity and children in Renaissance Florence: The ospedale degli innocenti 1410–1536.* Ann Arbor, MI: The University of Michigan Press.

Ginzburg, C. (1986). *Miti emblemi spie. Morfologia e storia.* Turin, Italy: Einaudi.

Giovannoni, J. (1990). Definitional issues in child maltreatment. In D. Cicchetti & V. Carlson (Eds.), *Child maltreatment: Theory and research on the causes and consequences of child abuse and neglect* (pp. 3–37). Cambridge. England: Cambridge University Press.

Grafton, A., & Blair, A. (Eds.). (1990). *The transmission of culture in early modern Europe.* Philadelphia: University of Pennsylvania Press.

Groenveld, S., Dekker, J. J. H., Willemse, T., & Dane, J. (1997). *Wezen en boefjes. Zes eeuwen zorg in wees- en kinderhuizen.* Hilversum, the Netherlands: Verloren.

Grosvenor, I. (2007). "Seen but not heard". City childhoods from the past into the present. *Paedagogica Historica, 43*, 405–429.

Grosvenor, I., & Watts, R. (2003). Urbanisation and education: The city as a light and becaon? *Paedagogica Historica, 39*, 1–253.

Heiland, H. (2006). Fröbels 'Tageblätter'. *Paedagogica Historica, 42*, 325–343.

Hermanns, J. (2009). *Het opvoeden verleerd. Rede, uitgesproken bij de aanvaarding van het ambt van Bijzonder hoogleraar op de Kohnstammleerstoel aan de Universities van Amsterdam op dinsdag 9 juni 2009.* Amsterdam: Vossiuspers/UvA.

Hermanns, J., Ory, F., & Schrijvers, G. (2005). *Helpen bij opgroeien en opvoeden: eerder, sneller en beter. Een advies over vroegtijdige signalering en interventies bij opvoed- en opgroeiproblemen.* Utrecht, the Netherlands: Inventgroep.

Jenny, C. (2008). Medicine discovers child abuse. *The Journal of the American Medical Association, 300*, 2796–2797.

Kempe, C. H., Silverman, F. N., Steele, B. F., Droegemuller, W., & Silver, H. K. (1962). The battered-child syndrome. *The Journal of the American Medical Association, 181*, 17–24.

Lamé, J. (2011). *Spookrijders in de zorg.* Delft, the Netherlands: Eburon.

Loughman, J., & Montias, J. M. (2000). *Public and private spaces. Works of art in seventeenth century Dutch houses.* Zwolle, the Netherlands: Waanders.

Moss, P. (2007). Meetings across the paradigmatic divide. *Educational Philosophy and Theory, 39*, 229–245.

Nohl, H. (1973/1933). Der pädagogische Bezug und die Bildungsgemeinschaft. In N. Kluge (Ed.), *Das pädagogische Verhältnis* (pp. 35–45). Darmstadt: Wissenschaftliche Buchgesellschaft.

Oelkers, J. (1991). Freedom and learning: Some thoughts on liberal and progressive education. In B. Spiecker & R. Straughan (Eds.), *Freedom and indoctrination in education: International perspectives* (pp. 70–83). London: Cassell.

Onderwijsraad. (2002). *Spelenderwijs. Kindercentrum en basisschool hand in hand.* The Hague, the Netherlands: Onderwijsraad.

Onderwijsraad. (2006). *Een vlechtwerk van opvang en onderwijs.* The Hague, the Netherlands: Onderwijsraad.

Onderwijsraad. (2008). *Een rijk programma voor ieder kind. Advies.* The Hague, the Netherlands: Onderwijsraad.

Onderwijsraad. (2010). *Naar een nieuwe kleuterperiode in de basisschool.* The Hague, the Netherlands: Onderwijsraad.

Overwater, J. (1955). Rede van de voorzitter van de Nationale Federatie "De Nederlandse Bond tot Kinderbescherming. In *Toespraken gehouden ter herdenking van de gouden kinderwetten op 1 december 1955, in de Ridderzaal te 's-Gravenhage* (pp. 15–23). The Hague, the Netherlands: Ministry of Justice.

Peeters, J. (2008). *De warme professional: Begeleid(st)ers kinderopvang construeren profession-aliteit.* Ghent, Belgium: Academia Press.
Read, J. (2006). Free play with Froebel: Use and abuse of progressive pedagogy in London's infant schools, 1870-c. 1904. *Paedagogica Historica, 42,* 299–323.
Richardson, T. (2000). The home as educational space: Bayonne housing and the architecture of working class childhood, 1917–1940. *Paedagogica Historica, 36,* 299–337.
Riksen-Walraven, M. (2000). *Tijd voor kwaliteit in de kinderopvang.* Amsterdam: Vossius Pers.
Riksen-Walraven, M. (2004). Pedagogische kwaliteit in de kinderopvang: doelstellingen en kwaliteitscriteria. In R. van IJzendoorn, L. Tavecchio, & M. Riksen-Walraven (Eds.), *De kwaliteit van de Nederlandse kinderopvang* (pp. 100–123). Amsterdam: Boom.
Rispens, J., Hermanns, J. M. A., & Meeus, W. H. J. (Eds.). (1996). *Opvoeden in Nederland.* Assen, the Netherlands: Van Gorcum.
Rogge, J. (1992). *Der Weserraum zwischen 1500 und 1650.* Marburg, Germany: Jonas.
Schreuder, P. (2010). De pedagogische relatie in context: kinderopvang tussen nut en vrije tijd. In S. Ramaekers, T. Storme, P. Verstraete, & J. Vlieghe (Eds.), *De publieke betekenis van peda-gogisch denken en handelen* (pp. 103–111). Amsterdam: SWP.
Schreuder, P., & Timmerman, G. (2009). Het woord is aan de groepsleiding. In A. Minnaert, H. Lutje Spelberg, & H. Amsing (Eds.), *Het pedagogisch quotiënt; Pedagogische kwaliteit in opvoeding, hulpverlening, onderwijs en educatie* (pp. 61–82). Houten, the Netherlands: Bohn Stafleu van Loghum.
Siegel, H. (1996). Education and cultural transmission/transformation: Philosophical reflections on the historian's task. *Paedagogica Historica Supplementary Series, 2,* 25–46.
Simons, M., & Masschelein, J. (2008). From schools to learning environments: The dark side of being exceptional. *Journal of Philosophy of Education, 42,* 678–704.
Singer, E., & Kleerekooper, L. (2009). *Pedagogisch kader kindercentra 0–4 jaar.* Maarssen, the Netherlands: Elsevier gezondheidszorg.
Smeyers, P., & Depaepe, M. (Eds.). (2008). *Educational research: The educationalization of social problems.* Dordrecht, the Netherlands: Springer.
Spiecker, B. (1984). The pedagogical relationship. *Oxford Review of Education, 10,* 203–209.
Stearns, P. N. (2006/2011). *Childhood in world history.* New York & London: Routledge.
Steinmetz, G. (2008). Logics of history as a framework for an integrated social sciences. *Social Science History, 32,* 535–553.
Tavecchio, L. (2002). *Van opvang naar opvoeding.* Amsterdam: Vossius Pers.
Urban, M. (2008). Dealing with uncertainty: Challenges and possibilities for the early childhood profession. *European Early Childhood Education Research Journal, 16,* 135–152.
van de Haterd, J., & Lammersen, G. (2006). *Groepsleidster kinderopvang.* Utrecht, the Netherlands: NIZW Beroepsontwikkeling.
Van de Rijt, H., & Plooij, F. X. (1992/2004). *Oei, ik groei! De acht sprongen in de mentale ontwik-keling van je baby.* Utrecht, the Netherlands: Kosmos.
van Hamel, G. A., et al. (1905). Een woord bij het inwerkingtreden der kinderwetten. Verslag van de Openbare Vergadering op Zaterdag 2 December 1905 in het gebouw "Eensgezindheid" te Amsterdam. *Mededeelingen van de Nederlandschen Bond tot Kinderbescherming, 9,* 1–35.
van Oenen, S., & Hajer, F. (Eds.). (2004). *De school en het echte leven: leren binnen en buiten de school.* Amsterdam: SWP.
Vandenbroeck, M. (2009). *In verzekerde bewaring: Honderdvijftig jaar kinderen, ouders en kinderopvang.* Amsterdam: SWP.
Weijers, I. (2009). Het gaat niet slecht met de Nederlandse jeugd. *Justitiële Verkenningen, 34,* 38–48.
Wollons, R. (2000). *Kindergartens and cultures. The global diffusion of an idea.* New Haven, CT/London: Yale University Press.
http://www.cito.nl/onderwijs/vroeg%20en%20voorschoolse%20educatie/piramide/kieswijzer_piramide.aspx (retrieved October 15, 2011).
http://www.education.gov.uk/childrenandyoungpeople/earlylearningandchildcare/delivery/education/a0068102/early-years-foundation-stage-eyfs (retrieved October 15, 2011).
http://www.who.int/maternal_child_adolescent/epidemiology/en/ (retrieved February 12, 2013).

Chapter 6
A Different Training, a Different Practice: Infant Care in Belgium in the Interwar Years in the City and in the Countryside

Pieter Dhondt

6.1 Introduction: The Development of Infant Care as an Educational Space

Following the hygienic movement that was taking root in the whole of Western Europe and North America at the end of the nineteenth century (Bideau, Desjardins, & Perez Brignoli, 1997; Dwork, 1987; Fildes, Marks, & Marland, 1992; Meckel, 1990), the fight against infant and child mortality gradually also became an important policy objective in Belgium. In contrast to France, where the defeat of 1870 against Prussia particularly gave a crucial impulse to the developing initiatives of child protection, in Belgium it was the First World War which primarily functioned as a catalyst in this regard (Gourdon & Rollet, 2004, pp. 249–250), with the National Board of Child Welfare (*Oeuvre Nationale de l'Enfance*, ONE) being established immediately after the war. The ONE characterised itself as "un établissement public autonome (faisant) de la protection de l'enfance non un service administratif mais une oeuvre, avec tout ce que ce mot comprend de dévouement et de générosité" (Velge, 1940, p. 7). From the start, the ONE aimed to combine a medical goal (particularly in increasing child mortality) with an educational objective, viz. teaching best practices with regard to hygiene and childcare.

In result, infant care developed into a specific educational space due to the changing intention. Instead of being only focused on medical care, the education of the mothers explicitly became one of the main functions of the upcoming consultation centres for infants. Already a few decades earlier, this professionalisation of motherhood had begun through the introduction of a number of specific training courses for mothers, specialised journals (Bakker, 1987), and the establishment of

P. Dhondt (✉)
Department of Geographical and Historical Studies,
University of Eastern Finland, Joensuu, Finland
e-mail: pieter.dhondt@uef.fi

P. Smeyers et al. (eds.), *Educational Research: The Importance and Effects of Institutional Spaces*, Educational Research 7, DOI 10.1007/978-94-007-6247-3_6, © Springer Science+Business Media Dordrecht 2013

écoles de puériculture, which were intended for women who would be professionally in contact with mothers and their children (e.g. a professional school for
maternity nurses in Antwerp or a school connected to the maternity hospital in
Ghent) (Marissal, 2007–2008, pp. 395–396). However, the First World War made
the need for an improved (medical) education of the staff, active in these first works
of social welfare, very apparent. Already from its establishment in 1919, the ONE
wished to replace philanthropic volunteering ladies (who had been leading the
existing consultation centres up until then) as much as possible by specially
educated nurses. Making use of specialised staff offered two big advantages: firstly,
it obviously contributed to a qualitative improvement of the service in consultations and, at the same time, it formed an ideal opportunity for employment for
women, and this against the background of an increasing influence of feminist
groups and a great number of war widows (Marissal, 2007–2008, p. 393).

The inspiration for the introduction of specially educated (lay) nurses (in a sector
that previously had been monopolised completely by female religious congrega-
tions) mainly came from Anglo-Saxon countries (Arguello, 1995, pp. 63–66).
Shortly after the First World War, several Belgian physicians and nurses, actively
engaged either within the ONE or independently of the organisation, had visited the
United States to study in situ the way in which professional nurses were called forth
in initiatives in the educational space of child protection. In 1919, some representatives of the board of the ONE participated in the international conference for child
protection in Washington, and, in 1920, two qualified nurses, supported by the ONE,
left Belgium for a 6-month study trip through the United States. During these visits,
they paid special attention to the education of visiting nurses (who were responsible
for conducting home visits in order to guide and counsel working-class mothers
more personally and closely) and of hygiene nurses, with the hope of adopting some
of the American methods in Belgium (Marissal, 2007–2008, p. 233).

The struggle to make nursing into a recognised profession did not pass off without striking a blow. As will be shown in the first section, the establishment of special
nursing schools and the laying down in laws of the requirements of the education of
qualified nurses happened comparatively quickly from an international perspective.
However, in practice, during the interwar years, a great number of responsible
figures in the medical and political world considered nursing still a vocation, rather
than a profession. The discussion in Belgium resembled to a large extent to the
debate regarding this in neighbouring countries, e.g. in France. Particularly within
catholic circles, qualities like devotion and charity were ascribed to nurses, instead
of professionalism and the recognition of a profound scientific medical training.
The second and third sections will discuss how and to what extent the education of
(visiting) nurses and the resulting approach of infant care were pillarised along ideological lines, not only what concerns the institutional basis but also with regard to
the content of the education and the ideas on the work of the nurse.

The way in which the educational space of infant care took shape was thus
dependent to a large degree on the training of the nurses responsible for it. In this
chapter the catholic nursing school St. Elizabeth in Bruges and the liberal *École
belge d'Infirmières diplômées* in Brussels function as the typical examples of both
opposite views. Whereas graduates of the former institution were primarily active in

the countryside and rather gave a pedagogical interpretation to their vocation, most of the graduates from the school in Brussels were employed in the city itself and emphasised the medical function of the professionalised consultation centres. Therefore, not only infant care itself can be regarded as an educational space (characterised by different approaches), but also the nursing schools can be defined as institutional spaces of educational research. Both in the catholic school in Bruges and in the liberal school in Brussels, teachers were searching for the best way to take care of the infants and to educate the mothers.

Gradually, the more medicalised approach within liberal nursing schools clearly asserted its influence on catholic institutions. In that way, the education of, and the tasks ascribed to, visiting nurses confirms a general trend of increasing professionalisation and medicalisation. Of course, the concept of medicalisation has a history of its own, going back until the middle of the 1970s (Conrad, 1992; Nye, 2003; Velle, 1990). The sociologist Irving Zola was one of the first to introduce the term, defining medicine as 'an institution of social control' (Zola, 1972). Zola criticised the fact that medical practitioners passed moral judgements yet presented them as neutral facts. Medicalisers were depicted as the villains of the story, expanding the medical field into areas where it does not belong, allegedly in order to extend their power and control (Conrad, 1992, pp. 215–218). Ivan Illich and Michel Foucault, amongst others developed this idea of medical imperialism, the latter linking it to the concept of normalisation (Foucault, 1963; Illich, 1975, pp. 31–60). However, the role of the layman in this regard is not as passive as is sometimes suggested. Therefore, the Dutch sociologist Abram de Swaan introduced the concept of "reserved imperialism" on the one hand to confirm that the power of medical practitioners increased steadily indeed but on the other hand to indicate that this often happened on the request of others, who called upon physicians to solve specific social problems (De Swaan, 1988, p. 249). Often not the medical practitioners themselves took the initiative (Dekker, 1990, p. 112). The aim of this chapter in general, and more in particular in the fourth and last section, by way of conclusion, is to show that infant care as an educational space received a different interpretation in the countryside and in the city depending on the training of the nurses. And indeed, on the whole, an increasingly medical approach characterises the education of visiting nurses, yet indeed, this certainly cannot be considered a straight-lined process, unilaterally initiated by medical practitioners. Especially the differences between a catholic and a liberal approach will be thrown light upon.

6.2   The Training of Nurses as an Institutional Space of Educational Research

The first school that offered a special training for (lay) nurses was established in Great Britain in 1862. Before the First World War, the example was copied in Sweden, the Netherlands, New Zealand, Australia, Canada and the United States, yet the war of 1914–1918 contributed largely to the dissemination of the Anglo-Saxon methods on the European continent (Rollet-Echalier, 1990). In Belgium the foundation of specialised nursing schools dated already from before the First World War, but this had not yet resulted in the official recognition of nursing as a profession. One of the first successful attempts to create a nursing school was the establishment of the Higher Institute for Nursing Stuyvenberg in Antwerp of 1902. However, its contribution to Belgian nursing remained extremely modest, mainly because it only offered evening courses for a long time (Arguello, 1995, p. 69). Much more important was the establishment of three competing schools in Brussels in 1907: the *École Saint-Jean* founded by the Social Service of Brussels, in association with the city council; the *École belge d'Infirmières diplômées* established by liberal circles; and its catholic counterpart the *École Saint-Camille*.

When comparing the two last mentioned schools, one of the differences between a liberal and catholic approach of the education of nurses, which will be developed further, can already be seen. The *École belge d'Infirmières diplômées* was founded by the Brussels surgeon and professor, Antoine Depage. He wanted to connect his school to the Anglo-Saxon example even to the extent that he had put the direction of his school in the hands of the English nurse Edith Cavell. His aim was in the first place to provide for a scientific, medical training of lay nurses of a very high level, by which Depage explicitly set his face against the, in his opinion, dangerously low-educated religious sisters. Obviously, his combats against "clerical obscurantism, especially in medical matters", were far from appreciated in catholic circles (Gillard, 2004, p. 104). Therefore, to the day 1 month after the opening of the liberal-inspired school of Depage, there followed the opening of its catholic counterpart of *Saint-Camille*, intended to educate nurses of a religious disposition. In contrast to the *École belge d'Infirmières diplômées*, its ambition was only to offer the training that was strictly necessary, in order not to focus too much on the medical side of the vocation of nurses, to the possible cost of the neglect of their social function. Because of this, as well as because of its openness towards nuns, the school was much more popular than its liberal counterpart (Arguello, 1995, pp. 80–81).

Until the introduction of a degree in nursing in 1921 and the establishment of an educational programme for visiting nurses, these schools did not offer a special training for the latter, working in the pay of the ONE. The ONE (and more precisely its medical committee) decided completely autonomously on the conditions required for working as a nurse in the consultation centres for infants that were financially supported by them. One of these conditions was to have taken a course in one of the existing nursing schools, completed by a specialised education of 6 months in infant care. The knowledge of the latter was tested through an examination, made and organised by the medical committee itself. In contrast to some other European countries, celibacy was not required even though some societies, such as the Christian guild of female workers (KAV), imposed it for their own assistants and nurses (Marissal, 2007–2008, p. 397).

However, the medical committee increased its pressure on the government. This resulted in the declaration of a legal programme in 1921 which was decided on in consultation with, amongst other bodies, the *Association des infirmières visiteuses de Belgique* (that had been involved in the introduction of a special training course for visiting nurses in the liberal nursing school of Depage), but also with countess

Marie van den Steen de Jehay (who had been one of the founders of the catholic *École d'infirmières Saint-Camille*).[1] During the first 2 years, medical courses were mainly included in the programme (common for all future nurses, those working in the hospital as well as visiting nurses). These courses included anatomy, physiology, microbiology, parasitology and child hygiene, completed with a section of home economics and a course of deontology "qui leur inculquent que leur futur métier est une fonction de dévouement, d'altruisme, nécessitant une moralité irréprochable", as the Higher Council of Public Hygiene stated in its comments on the law (Première section, 1922, p. 53).

The third year, which was specific for visiting nurses, included courses on social legislation and on public and private welfare provisions, advanced courses in child hygiene and lessons on which measures to take in the fight against infant mortality and against social abuses (alcoholism, sexually transmissible diseases, depopulation, etc.). Moreover, the students had to gain some notion of paedagogics and to familiarise themselves with the organisation and function of provisions for the protection of children and mothers. On a practical level, they had to study the methodology of home visits (Marissal, 2007–2008, p. 314). During their training, all students had to board within the institution for a period of at least 6 months for obvious pedagogical and moral reasons. Dr. Van Langendonck nicely summarised the main argument for this decision. In line with the authors of the programme, he assumed that "les multiples petits heurts de la vie commune prépareront l'infirmière à la patience, à la résignation dont elle aura tant besoin au cours de sa carrière" (Van Langendonck, 1922).

Whereas in the early years the visiting nurses were almost only active at the consultation centres for infants, the decision was taken at the national conference of the ONE in 1927 to invest more in home visits, particularly in rural areas where it was more difficult to establish consultations for several reasons. Often the communities did not have enough means to support the consultations financially and, moreover, the scattered population made it not only difficult but from a financial viewpoint also not really expedient to begin separate consultations within every single community (*4me Congrès National*, 1927). Instead, specialised nurses (or in the lack of them, specially trained midwives) would visit the mothers at home to give them educational advice in their own environment and to control the children medically. With this initiative, the ONE clearly broke through the border between the public and private sphere, a development which had started at the end of the nineteenth century and which had resulted in Child Protection Acts and the introduction of compulsory education in almost all European countries (Dekker, 2001, pp. 41–55). Gradually, the almost inviolable paternal authority had to give way to the increasingly powerful governmental authority, characterised by a longing for supervision and controllability of childhood (see Chap. 5 by Schreuder and Dekker, this volume). In consequence of this transition, infant care as an educational space was no longer solely located within the consultation centres, yet slowly but surely, it transferred to the home (Richardson, 2000). Still this development was far from evident, neither for the families nor for the nurses or other social workers. Therefore, series of directions were passed on to them about how they could gain the confidence of the people they were going to visit (e.g. Rubbrecht, 1925).

When visiting the mothers at home, the nurses always proceeded from a subordinate position towards the physician (Massart, 1995, p. 136). Conflict on the distribution of duties between physicians, nurses and the still active philanthropic ladies occurred quite regularly, as is proven for instance by the frequency by which this topic is discussed in publications of the ONE, e.g. in the journals intended for the nurses themselves. Nevertheless, the comparatively limited enthusiasm of the general practitioners to engage in the consultation centres (because of, amongst other reasons, low wages and limited prestige) gradually resulted in increasing power of the visiting nurses. Therefore, the balance between the need for a strong medical education of visiting nurses and the risk that, on the basis of this education, they would present themselves as possible competitors of the physicians always stood under discussion during the interwar years. Moreover, the physicians certainly did not pull all in the same direction in this regard, as will be discussed further. Besides, even though the administration of the ONE in general adopted a positive attitude towards the calling in of midwives (especially after the introduction of a separate in-service training for them in 1924), many physicians also feared their competition and devoted themselves to fix the duties of the different practitioners very strictly (Marissal, 2007–2008, pp. 407–408, 414–437).

6.3 Nursing as a Vocation: The Social Nurse Offering Social Education in the Countryside

Still, the role of the midwife or the nurse during these home visits in the countryside was not limited to a medical function, and the midwives particularly were expected to be able to gain the confidence of the mothers much easier, something that would increase the chance that the well-intentioned educational advice being followed up more actively (*5me Congrès National*, 1928, p. 54). The catholic nursing school St. Elizabeth in Bruges, which the ophthalmologist Raphaël Rubbrecht had opened in 1919, attempted explicitly to pay more attention to this educational and social role, also in the nurse's training. This was criticised as being more than was required according to the legal programme, which was itself characterised too much exclusively by a medical approach, according to Rubbrecht himself (Rubbrecht, 1923, pp. 15–16). By emphasising the social and moral education of his students, Rubbrecht wanted to realise the catholic inspiration of his school, which in a short time grew into one of the most important nursing schools of the country, both in numbers and in prestige (Magnée, 1996–1997; Van den Bon, 1969). Courses in religion and ethics were compulsory for all the students,[2] and very regularly separate lessons were organised in art history and architecture to counter the emphasis on a scientific, medical education, "to keep in mind the general education" and "to take care of character building". "The formation of the mind is necessary to train the nurse in judging accurately and acting efficiently", according to August Van den Bon, in his reflections as a former teacher of the school (Rubbrecht, 1930, pp. 5–7; Van den Bon, 1969, p. 47).

The school in Bruges stated its intention clearly from the very beginning with the name of the function. Deliberately, Rubbrecht chose to talk about "social nurse" instead of "visiting nurse". Nursing the sick was considered a work of charity; "and the duty of charity is not performed by stacking up barren science" (Rubbrecht, 1923, p. 16). His lecture in 1923, on the occasion of the opening of the school at its new location, was devoted to the general direction that had to be given to the life of the nurse, viz. the example of St. Elizabeth of Hungary, patroness of the school. Like Rubbrecht indicated himself, this choice was not inspired by protest against the scientific background of nursing, but science could and should not be regarded as the ultimate goal of the nurse, yet only as a means to realise the work of charity (Rubbrecht, 1923, pp. 26–27). Of course, to a certain extent, Florence Nightingale could function as a role model too, but whereas her moral development had reached its peak during the Crimean War and thereafter no growing development could be seen anymore in this regard, the moral development of saints such as Vincent de Paul had increased until their ripe old age, according to Rubbrecht (1925, pp. 10–11). The thrust of Rubbrecht's lectures about the task of the social nurse is clearly visible in the lecture series 'Naar dienende liefde [Towards serving love]', with chapters such as 'About ethics', 'About self-sacrifice', 'About devotion', 'About taciturnity' and 'About tolerance' (Rubbrecht, 1937). More importantly, in his perception of controlling the children medically was the social (and moral) education of the mothers.

People from both the Catholic University of Leuven and the State University of Ghent supported Rubbrecht's specific approach. Particularly the generally respected gynaecologist Frans Daels from Ghent enforced Rubbrecht's plea to emphasise the social rather than the medical and scientific function of the nurse. Nowhere in Daels' 'Lecture series on nursing and social medicine' is mentioned the need of a medical training (even though obviously, its importance is not denied as such either), on the other hand, he points repeatedly to

> […] the socially educated lay nurse as the ideal visitor, who, on the basis of a profound knowledge and experience of real life and inspired by deep feelings of charity, will be able to gain the friendship and the confidence of the people, without losing her authority. […] The first and most wonderful task of the visitor is still the education of her people with regard to hygiene, and in result the edification of her people. (Daels, 1937, pp. 30–31)

To realise these goals, it was absolutely crucial that nurses could study in the language of the people, viz. Flemish, which was also one of Rubbrecht's underlying motivations when founding his school. Some years before, Daels had been striving very actively for the introduction of Dutch as the language of education at his own university, which had been realised in 1930 (Mantels & Vandevoorde, 2010).

Mothers were addressed in their own language also to gain their confidence more easily. But apart from that, particularly at the countryside, the nurse mainly had to show great patience and tactfulness to make the mothers listen to her well-intentioned advice on the importance of a more hygienic style of living, a better care of the children and the fight against all kinds of ingrained habits (e.g. children who were put to sleep much too warm), according to Henri Compernolle, one of the teachers in the nursing school of Bruges (Compernolle, 1943). A uniform or a pin could certainly help to increase the authority and the prestige of the nurse, but should not be misused. In Rubbrecht's opinion, it even imposed some extra duties: "The nurse in uniform should abstain from certain acts, which most probably would never be noticed at other people acting in the same way. All frivolity, exuberance and loudliness should be avoided" (Rubbrecht, 1925, p. 9). Moreover, the uniform did not relieve the nurse from the necessary modesty, as Compernolle confirmed: "It is a big mistake to present our opinions as indisputable. […] We may not believe that we are infallible. […] It is our duty to make clear to the parents that some of the principles which we are teaching them did not or only insufficiently stand the test" (Compernolle, 1943, pp. 21–22). A similar awareness of the limits of medical science could not be found in liberal institutions as the *École belge d'Infirmières diplômées*, as will be shown further.

One of the outcomes of this specific approach of the education and the role of the visiting/social nurse in the school in Bruges was that Rubbrecht and his colleagues characterised nursing as a vocation, rather than as a profession. Although they shared the opinion that the nurse deserved a fair allowance, "the wage should not be the direct aim of the nurse, but instead it should be considered the natural outcome of her work of charity. She does not work to earn a wage, but after she did her work, she deserves a wage of honour" (Rubbrecht, 1923, p. 27). Also in this regard, the predominant opinion within the catholic community conflicted with the one in liberal circles. For instance, Cécile Mechelynck, vice-president of the professional organisation *Fédération nationale des infirmières belges*, devoted herself to the recognition of nursing as a profession and to the improvement of the extremely hardworking conditions (Mechelynck, 1933, pp. 21–23).[3] Indeed, Mechelynck had studied at the catholic *École Saint-Camille*, yet afterwards, she was involved in the *Association des infirmières visiteuses*, and so in the liberal *École belge d'Infirmières diplômées*.

Of course, the discussion whether nursing should be considered a vocation or a profession had close links with the attitude of the Catholic Church towards women going to work in general. In 1920, several female labour unions together still had to convince the religious authorities to lend their support to the catholic nursing schools (Marissal, 2007–2008, pp. 10–12, 315). On the one hand, giving support to the profession of (visiting) nurse was far from evident because of the emancipatory aspect that was connected to it. Indeed, was the place of the woman not at home, taking care of her own children? On the other hand, it was impossible to ignore the fact that more women offered their services on the labour market and in that case, obviously, it was preferable that they chose a female profession in which they could develop their personality and their female qualities, instead of entering into competition with men. As such, from a feminist viewpoint, the profession of visiting nurse was almost a contradiction in terms. On the one hand, the visiting nurses indeed managed to emancipate themselves to a certain degree (e.g. towards the physicians in the consultations), but on the other hand, through the consultations and home visits, they spread the role model of the mother, exactly as it was propagated by the Catholic Church, particularly during the interwar years and particularly in the countryside (Knibiehler, 1984; Walkowitz, 1990).

6.4   Nursing as a Profession: The Visiting Nurse Offering Medical Care in the City

In France, visiting nurses were generally much more regarded as voluntary workers. The most important explanations for this were that even in 1930 almost half of the visiting nurses still only had a certificate of the Red Cross as a qualification, and those who had a diploma of one of the few nursing schools clearly had enjoyed a much less in-depth (medical) training than their Belgian counterparts (Dessertine, 1995; Henry, 2009). However, in Belgium several professional unions of physicians were concerned about the comprehensiveness of the educational programme for visiting nurses when it was elaborated in the beginning of the 1920s. Many general practitioners were astonished by the amount of courses and their complexity:

> En réalité, il aborde des sujets si complexes, si variés que nous nous demandons comment une femme de vingt ans, si douée soit-elle, pourra prendre une teinture de ces sciences d'ordre médical. [...] Nous estimons le programme d'examen par trop touffu, fait plutôt pour former des bas bleus et des manières d'officiers de santé, que de vraies infirmières. Le dévouement, l'abnégation doit être le *primum movens* d'une vocation exigeant de rares vertus. (*Les infirmières visiteuses*, 1920)

The programme was evaluated as being too complex for young girls who in the first place had to prove their capacities of domestic science. And even more, it was of that sort that on the basis of such a programme, the visiting nurse possibly could injure the authority of the general practitioner.

Striking in this regard was the difference of opinion about this also within the ONE itself, as it could be noticed at the national conference of the institution in 1925. Whereas Henri Velge, as being the general secretary, in his annual report fixed the attention particularly on the extension of the social character of their work and the idea of offering social assistance, the president of the higher medical committee of the ONE, F. Herman, pointed in his report to the need to give a more and more explicit medical character to the consultation centres, especially to those in an urban setting (*Congrès National*, 1925, pp. 63 and 70). In the light of what preceded, it is probably no coincidence that Herman had a liberal background, whereas Velge had a catholic persuasion.

Examples of the ONE (and especially its medical committee) trying to give a more medical interpretation to infant care and the education of the mothers are easy to find. The foundation of chairs in paediatrics at the universities in the 1920s, for instance, was aimed at primarily by members of the medical committee who were afterwards mostly promoted to this position (Dourlet & Couvreur, 1939), even though to a certain degree, it was logical that professors labour at their own discipline. More convincing are the courses that some of them, such as the professor of paediatrics in Liège, organised especially for physicians who were in charge of a consultation centre (*5me Congrès National*, 1928, p. 92). Another example was the fact that the plea was repeatedly uttered within the ONE for more medical supervision on the home visits. According to some of the people involved, the increasing medical pressure on the nurses had some immediate effects. In 1926, some catholic members within the *Fédération nationale des infirmières belges* declared that the lack of nurses could at least partly be explained by the fact that many women were scared off by the high medical-scientific standard of the training (Busiau & Héraut, 2009). Most probably, the hard-working conditions were very important in this regard as well. The absolute job security on which the visiting nurse could count was not enough to compensate for the unattractive terms of employment (Jacques, 1995; Massart, 1936, p. 13).[4]

In spite of all this, the liberal *École belge d'Infirmières diplômées* of Depage even wanted to go a step further, by incorporating itself in 1936 within the liberal *Université libre de Bruxelles* and renaming the school into *École universitaire d'infirmières*. The publication on the occasion of the opening of the new school is dominated by an almost unlimited faith in medical science and also in other publications of the school in which a certain degree of modesty is difficult to find (Depage, 1956; *Discours*, 1936). The reasons to connect the nursing school with the university forced themselves upon, according to the freemason René Sand, a famous hygienist and one of the teachers of the school:

> Devant ces tâches, devant ces responsabilités, s'étonnera-t-on d'entendre proclamer que la formation des infirmières doit relever de l'enseignement universitaire, au même titre que les études médicales? Seuls un corps professoral d'élite, des méthodes éprouvées, un milieu scientifique peuvent former des auxiliaires dignes de la mission qui leur est tracée, et capables de contribuer à l'avancement de leur profession. (*Discours*, 1936, p. 26; cf. Eilers, 2011)

For a long time, it was thought that to become a nurse, only qualities such as cleanliness, honesty, devotion and docility were needed; now it was increasingly acknowledged that a nurse had to be educated in a profound scientific way, he continued.

At the same time, the teachers within the new university school also realised the need of a social education of the people. Indeed, a human being could not be looked upon exclusively from a medical viewpoint yet had to be approached in his or her entirety with attention to his or her social condition and work and living conditions, they asserted (*Discours*, 1936, p. 36). Particularly in an urban setting where most of the graduates of the liberal nursing school of Depage started to be employed, the importance of taking into account the livings conditions could not be overlooked. However, in contrast to their catholic counterparts, they considered the education of the mothers in this regard in the first place the duty of a specific group of social workers. Most of the (liberal-minded) hygienists too (who had specialised themselves to the extent of having their own diploma from 1908) chose for a model in which the nurses were responsible for the medical care for the children and in which the social workers had to meet the social needs of the families, in order to promote together the medical and social supervision by the government (Schepers, 2002, pp. 207–210; Vanthemsche, 1994). At the end of the 1930s, in France it was opted for bringing together both tasks again by introducing the *Diplôme d'Etat d'Assistante Sociale*. The education consisted of medical studies during 1 year, completed by 2 years of social studies (Diebolt, 2001; Knibiehler, 1980). In Belgium, the call for social workers within the consultation centres of the ONE remained very limited during the interwar years. According to most of the local administrations, they lacked the advantage of a good medical training indeed.

Different motivations lay at the basis of this increasingly intensive medical training of visiting nurses, which was also aimed for by the medical committee of the

ONE: the lack of general practitioners who wanted to engage in the consultation centres, as mentioned before; the fight against social plagues such as tuberculosis and syphilis (again, especially in the cities) and against infant and child mortality, the latter still being the main point of departure of the ONE (Debuisson, 2001; Nys, 2003); and the increasing competition between consultation centres of a different ideological background. The expanded and improved medical treatment had the intention of convincing mothers to (keep on) come(ing) to the consultations at a time when, around the middle of the 1920s, the material advantages (which previously had been introduced to attract the mothers) were largely abolished (*4me Congrès National*, 1927, p. 164). Indeed, the consultations had become embedded increasingly in a pillarised structure and they now had to win over the mothers, in a spirit of competition. Moreover, they were not able to force the mothers into visiting the consultations for infants and, what is more, according to the foundation act of the ONE, the organising committees had the legal duty to show their respect for the religious and philosophical convictions of the families the children were living in (Velge, 1940, p. 21).

6.5 Conclusion: A Different Training, a Different Practice

If only because of this competitive spirit, the mothers far from undertook the consultations passively. Suggestions that the parents saw as useful were followed, whilst others were just ignored. And in addition to that, the mothers made use of the benefits on offer at the consultations with, amongst other considerations and advantages, the free medical care for their sick children (indeed, in principle the consultations were only intended for preventive medicine, but when it was clear that the social situation of the family would not allow it to consult a private doctor, many nurses and physicians could not find it in their heart to leave the child to fend for itself), distribution of material advantages and the use of the consultations as a social meeting place (Marissal, 2007–2008, pp. 330–334). In this way, it would be a very biased assessment to consider the mothers passive victims of a medicalisation offensive started by the ONE, which itself was established on the initiative of the government.

For many mothers at home, the consultations clearly functioned as an opportunity to come outside and to meet other women, mostly mothers. Of course, from time to time, the nurses intervened in the spontaneous conversations between the mothers about the care for and the education of their children, by passing on useful advice, trying to do so without taking a pedantic attitude. Also, during the home visits in the countryside, the nurses often acted rather as a social worker than as a nurse in the strict sense of the word, this mostly against the wish of the physician. When being confronted with the sorry living conditions in many of the working-class houses, out of necessity, they sometimes momentarily brushed aside all of the medical advice from the physicians and their whole theoretical training in order to pay attention first to the most urgent needs (Knibiehler, 1984, p. 154). Even though it is very difficult, if not impossible, to estimate as to what extent the efforts proved to be successful—the ONE itself likes to boast of the figures proving the decrease of infant mortality—Marissal concludes in her detailed study about *La protection sanitaire du jeune enfant en Belgique 1890–1940* that particularly the social function of the visiting nurses has proven its usefulness. According to her analysis, the visiting nurses have played a crucial role in referring those in need to the different welfare provisions that were established during the interwar years (Marissal, 2007–2008, p. 477). On the other hand, of course, one cannot deny that the figures of infant and child mortality decreased drastically in the interwar period, leading to the fading away of one of the limits to the educational space (see Chap. 5 by Schreuder and Dekker, this volume).

The circle is round in this way. Despite the signs that indicate an increasingly medical interpretation of the educational programme of the visiting nurses and their work in the consultation centres and during the home visits, the visiting nurses largely managed to keep up their irreplaceable moral and social duties. And still, if medicalisation is defined as medical imperialism—the physician who strives for a greater participation in public life, an increasing number of people that come into contact with the physician and an increasing number of domains that are appropriated by medicine—then the medical committee of the ONE only succeeded to a certain extent. The visiting nurses, for instance, preserved clearly their moral and social function, and, moreover, in many of the consultations, they gradually clearly took the lead. The general practitioners themselves did not pull all in the same direction, if only to defend their own position, as we have shown. On the other hand, one cannot deny that in the training of visiting nurses, the medical component became increasingly dominant, particularly in liberal institutions.

In contrast to that, a number of catholic nursing schools, the St. Elizabeth School in Bruges in the first place, attempted to counter the increasing medicalisation at least to some extent. Mainly out of a moral solicitude, towards the visiting nurses themselves as well as towards the mothers which the former would advise and assist, the administration and the teachers of the catholic school wanted to put a stronger emphasis on the moral and social duties of the nurses in their work for the ONE. In the end, this caused an increase in the difference between the predominating interpretation of childcare initiatives in rural areas and in the city. In any case, the home visits were intended in the first place for rural areas, where they were often done by catholic-trained nurses. On the other hand, in the city, the mothers were counselled primarily by the general practitioners in the consultations, where more lay nurses were active who had benefitted from a (medical) training, e.g. at the liberal-inspired nursing school of Depage. Future research is needed to examine how this tension between social education and medical care was dealt with after the Second World War. Whereas much research has been done already on the coming into existence of the social welfare state in Europe, for the time being, and especially in Belgium, its possible transformation from the 1950s has gained much less attention.

Notes

1. Brussels, Carhif, ONE, *Procès-verbal du Conseil supérieur des oeuvres de l'enfance*, 30-12-1919.
2. On the request of the government in 1934, to integrate the nursing school in Bruges in the new general structure of technical education, the main concern of the school governors was "whether the school could retain its confessional character? In our view it is absolutely crucial indeed (even more so in a nursing school than in another school), that the whole education is penetrated by a catholic philosophy of life". When they got the confirmation from the government that this would not be a problem, the school applied for and received its official recognition. Cf. Bruges, Archief van de hospitaalzusters van Sint-Jan, Verpleegstersschool St.-Elisabeth, O/4.2.1./1-a, *Verslagboek van den beheerraad*, 17-02-1935.
3. Besides, the pillarisation also left its traces in the professional nursery organisations. In 1924, a separate section for catholic nurses was established within the *Fédération nationale des infirmières belges*, which in 1932 led to the foundation of a completely separate *Association des infirmières catholiques de Belgique*.
4. Yvonne Knibiehler also points to French visiting nurses complaining about their extreme tiredness when talking about their professional life (Knibiehler, 1984, p. 157).

References

4me Congrès National des Oeuvres de l'Enfance. (1927). *Assemblée générale. Année 1927*. Brussels, Belgium: Office de Publicité.
5me Congrès National des Oeuvres de l'Enfance. (1928). *Assemblée générale. Année 1928*. Brussels, Belgium: Office de Publicité.
Arguello, J. (1995). L'introduction du nursing laïque en Belgique (1882–1914). D'une vocation à l'émergence d'une profession. *Sextant, 3*, 61–82.
Bakker, N. (1987). De wetenschap der moeders. De vrouwenbeweging en het streven naar professionalisering van het ouderschap aan het begin van de twintigste eeuw. In J. Dekker, M. D'hoker, & B. Kruithof (Eds.), *Pedagogisch werk in de samenleving. De ontwikkeling van professionele opvoeding in Nederland en België in de negentiende en twintigste eeuw* (pp. 47–61). Leuven, Belgium: Acco.
Bideau, A., Desjardins, B., & Perez Brignoli, H. (Eds.). (1997). *Infant and child mortality in the past*. Oxford, England: Clarendon.
Busiau, M., & Héraut, J. (2009). *Historique de la profession. 50 ans FNIB Régionale Tournai-Mons-Centre*. Retrieved October 18, 2011, from http://www.fnib-tmc.be/conference50emea/anniversaire-50-ans-fnib-tmc-final-2-.pdf
Compernolle, H. (1943). *De verpleegster in het raam van het nationaal werk voor kinderwelzijn*. Bruges, Belgium: Vereeniging voor katholieke verpleegsters en vroedvrouwen.
Congrès National des Oeuvres de l'Enfance. (1925). *Assemblée générale. Année 1925*. Brussels, Belgium: Office de Publicité.
Conrad, P. (1992). Medicalisation and social control. *Annual Review of Sociology, 18*, 209–232.

Daels, F. (1937). *Voordrachten over verpleegkunde en sociale geneeskunde*. Antwerpen, Belgium: De Sikkel.

Debuisson, M. (2001). The decline of infant mortality in the Belgian districts at the turn of the 20th century. *Belgisch Tijdschrift voor Nieuwste Geschiedenis, 31*(3–4), 497–527.

Dekker, J. J. H. (1990). Witte jassen en zwarte toga's. Medici, juristen en de opvoeding van verwaarloosde en achtergebleven kinderen in Nederland in de tweede helft van de negentiende eeuw. *Pedagogisch Tijdschrift, 15*(2), 111–121.

Dekker, J. J. H. (2001). *The will to change the child. Re-education homes for children at risk in nineteenth century Western Europe*. Frankfurt am Main, Germany: Peter Lang.

Depage, H. (1956). *La vie d'Antoine Depage*. Brussels, Belgium: La Renaissance du Livre.

Dessertine, D. (1995). Les infirmières-visiteuses de la lutte antituberculeuse en France (1900–1930). *Bulletin du Centre Pierre Léon d'histoire économique et sociale, 2–3*, 55–63.

De Swaan, A. (1988). *In care of the state: Health care, education and welfare in Europe and the USA in the modern era*. Oxford, UK: Oxford University Press.

Diebolt, E. (2001). *Les femmes dans l'action sanitaire, sociale et culturelle, 1901–2001: les associations face aux institutions*. Paris: Femmes et Associations.

Discours prononcés à l'occasion de l'Inauguration solennelle de l'École le 28 Mars 1936. (1936). Brussels, Belgium: Scripta.

Dourlet & Couvreur. (1939). L'enseignement de la puériculture en Belgique. Ce qu'il est et ce qu'il devrait être. In *XIIe Congrès National des Oeuvres de l'Enfance (Liège 1939)*. Brussels, Belgium: Office de Publicité.

Dwork, D. (1987). *War is good for babies and other young children: A history of the infant and child welfare movement in England 1898–1918*. London: Tavistock.

Eilers, K. (2011). *René Sand (1877–1953) – Weltbürger der internationalen Sozialen Arbeit*. Opladen, Germany: Verlag Barbara Budrich.

Fildes, V., Marks, L., & Marland, H. (Eds.). (1992). *Women and children first: International maternal and infant welfare, 1870–1945*. London: Routledge.

Foucault, M. (1963). *Naissance de la clinique*. Paris: Presses Universitaires de France.

Gillard, R. (2004). Antoine Depage (1862–1925). In L. Nefontaine (Ed.), *Illustres et francs-maçons* (pp. 99–106). Brussels, Belgium: Editions Labor.

Gourdon, V., & Rollet, C. (2004). Modèles français, modèles belges, un jeu de miroirs. In G. Masuy-Stroobant & P. C. Humblet (Eds.), *Mères et nourrissons: De la bienfaisance à la protection médico-sociale (1830–1945)* (pp. 223–250). Brussels, Belgium: Editions Labor.

Henry, S. (2009). Les infirmières-visiteuses pendant l'entre-deux-guerres en Haute-Normandie: entre professionalisme officiel et bénévolat officieux. *Genre & Histoire, 5*. Retrieved December 12, 2011, from http://genrehistoire.revues.org/index836.html

Illich, I. (1975). *Medical nemesis*. London: Calder & Boyars.

Jacques, C. (1995). Les infirmières dans l'entre-deux-guerres et l'action des "dames d'oeuvres". *Sextant, 3*, 107–126.

Knibiehler, Y. (1980). *Nous, les assistantes sociales: naissance d'une profession*. Paris: Aubier.

Knibiehler, Y. (Ed.). (1984). *Cornettes et blouses blanches. Les infirmières dans la société française (1880–1980)*. Paris: Hachette.

Les infirmières visiteuses. (1920). *Le Scalpel, 33*, 714–716.

Magnée, C. (1996–1997). *Les infirmières belges dans l'entre-deux-guerres, entre émancipation et soumission*. Unpublished master's dissertation, Université libre de Bruxelles, Brussels.

Mantels, R., & Vandevoorde, H. (2010). *Maar wat een wespennest! Het rectoraat van August Vermeylen en de vernederlandsing van de Gentse universiteit*. Ghent, Belgium: Academia Press.

Marissal, C. (2007–2008). *La protection sanitaire du jeune enfant en Belgique 1890–1940. Question sociale, enjeux politiques et dimension sexuée*. Unpublished doctoral dissertation, Université libre de Bruxelles, Brussels.

Massart, G. (1936). Le dévouement a des limites: pourquoi les infirmières échappent-elles à la loi des huit heures? *La Famille Prévoyante, 5*, 13.

Massart, B. (1995). Soigner la petite enfance. *Des femmes au service de l'Oeuvre Nationale de l'Enfance. Sextant, 3,* 127–147.

Mechelynck, C. (1933). L'infirmière visiteuse. *Egalité, 5*(18), 21–23.

Meckel, R. A. (1990). *Save the babies: American Public Health Reform and the prevention of infant mortality, 1850–1929.* Baltimore: Johns Hopkins University Press.

Nye, R. (2003). The evolution of the concept of medicalisation in late 20th century. *Journal of History of the Behavioral Sciences, 39*(20), 115–129.

Nys, L. (2003). De ruiters van de Apocalyps: 'alcoholisme, tuberculose, syfilis' en degeneratie in medische kringen, 1870–1940. In J. Tollebeek, G. Vanpaemel, & K. Wils (Eds.), *Degeneratie in België 1860–1940: een geschiedenis van ideeën en praktijken* (pp. 11–41). Leuven, Belgium: Universitaire Pers.

Première section. Hygiène des individus et des groupes. Séance du 3 avril 1922. Examens d'infirmières – programme des cours (1922). *Conseil supérieur d'hygiène publique. Recueil des rapports* (Vol. XXIII, p. 53). Brussels, Belgium: Guyot.

Richardson, T. (2000). The home as educational space: Bayonne housing and the architecture of working class childhood, 1917–1940. *Paedagogica Historica. International Journal for the History of Education, 36*(1), 299–337.

Rollet-Echalier, C. (1990). *La politique à l'égard de la petite enfance sous la IIIe république.* Paris: INED.

Rubbrecht, R. (1923). *Over verpleegkunde.* Bruges, Belgium: Excelsior.

Rubbrecht, R. (1925). *De sociale verpleegster. Maandblad van het Nationaal werk voor kinderwelzijn.*

Rubbrecht, R. (1930). *Levensgedachten.* Bruges, Belgium: Wiek Op.

Rubbrecht, R. (1937). *Naar dienende liefde.* Bruges, Belgium: Wiek Op.

Schepers, R., et al. (2002). Een wereld van belangen. Artsen en de ontwikkeling van de openbare gezondheidszorg. In L. Nys, H. De Smaele, & J. Tollebeek (Eds.), *De zieke natie. Over de medicalisering van de samenleving 1860–1914* (pp. 200–218). Groningen, the Netherlands: Historische Uitgeverij.

Van den Bon, A. (1969). *Geschiedenis van de Brugse verpleegsterschool. Vanaf de St.-Elisabethschool 1919 tot aan het St.-Jansinstituut voor verpleegkunde 1969.* Bruges, Belgium: Sint-Jansinstituut voor verpleegkunde.

Van Langendonck, D. (1922). La réorganisation des études d'infirmières. *Le Scalpel, 40,* 819.

Vanthemsche, G. (1994). *La sécurité sociale: les origines du système belge, le présent face à son passé.* Brussels, Belgium: De Boeck.

Velge, H. (1940). *L'activité de l'Oeuvre nationale de l'enfance pendant vingt-cinq ans (1915–1940).* Brussels, Belgium: Office de publicité.

Velle, K. (1990). Medikalisering in België in historisch perspectief: een inleiding. *Belgisch Tijdschrift voor Nieuwste Geschiedenis, 21*(1–2), 162–210.

Walkowitz, D. J. (1990). The making of a feminine professional identity: Social workers in the 1920s. *American Historical Review, 95,* 1051–1075.

Zola, I. (1972). Medicine as an institution of social control. *Sociological Review, 20*(4), 487–504.

Chapter 7
Disability, Rehabilitation and the Great War: Making Space for Silence in the History of Education

Pieter Verstraete

> *Le silence est fait de parole que l'on n'a pas dite*
>
> (Marguerite Yourcenar, 1929)

In this chapter, we will introduce the historian of education to a topic he/she for too long a time has neglected, namely, the rehabilitation of Belgian disabled soldiers from the First World War. We will do this in such a way that not only some of the educational processes encountered by the disabled soldiers during the war will be retraced, but also traditional interpretations of silence as being the mere opposite of language will become insufficient for any historian interested in the importance of silence for the history of education. In particular, we will pay attention to how space plays an important role in what we will call the *instrumentalization of silence*. Rather than being the mere acoustic quality of particular environments, we will think of silence as a meaningful quality of life and space that one can make use of in order to realize particular educational/political goals. To set the stage for this retracing of silences in the history of education, we'd like to start this contribution by introducing a rather unknown book by Max Picard, namely, *The World of Silence*.

In 1948, the Swiss writer and critical thinker Max Picard, who in a former life had studied medicine and up till the First World War quietly worked as a physician, collected his thoughts on silence in a publication entitled *Die Welt des Schweigens/The World of Silence* (1948). The book itself, written in a feverish and staccato style, was inspired and based on the fact that in the modern world silence was not being considered important anymore. On the contrary, for Picard, a pre-eminent and far-reaching consequence of the unstoppable modernization of the Western world was precisely the marginalization, not to say the destruction, of silence by huge and

P. Verstraete (✉)
Centre for the History of Education, KU Leuven, Leuven, Belgium
e-mail: Pieter.Verstraete@ppw.kuleuven.be

P. Smeyers et al. (eds.), *Educational Research: The Importance and Effects of Institutional Spaces*, Educational Research 7, DOI 10.1007/978-94-007-6247-3_7,
© Springer Science+Business Media Dordrecht 2013

unbearable soundscapes which now loomed all over Europe and the rest of the world. The two world wars that struck Europe in the first half of the twentieth century illustrated painfully this tendency to suppress all silence under a huge and cruel amount of sound produced by innumerable barrels, caused by the deadly explosion of shells or set in motion by the murderous activity of machine guns. The enormous amounts of noise produced by the machinery of war, for Picard, however, were not to be considered exceptions. On the contrary, these deadly soundscapes were to be seen as the self-evident and almost natural consequence of the industrialization of the modern world.

The machine that, for Picard, exemplified this intolerable approach of Western societies towards silence at its best was the radio: "Radio is a machine", Picard wrote, "producing absolute verbal noise. The content hardly matters any longer; the production of noise is the main concern. It is as though words were being ground down by radio, transformed into an amorphous mass [...] Radio has occupied the whole space of silence. There is no silence any longer. Even when the radio is turned off the radio-noise still seems to go on inaudibly". This all-encompassing presence of noise as exemplified by the radio was compared with the consequences of warfare itself for "The noise of the radio destroys man". And if, for Picard, this perhaps not had to be understood literally, he at least underlined some of the manifold detrimental effects of the radio—and sound in general—as follows: "Radio-noise is so amorphous that it seems to have no beginning and no end; it is limitless. And the type of man formed by the constant influence of this noise is the same: formless, undecided inwardly and externally, with no definite limits and standards" (Picard, 1948, p. 198).

Intimately connected to these amorphous men—which philosophers of education coming from a Deleuzian background nowadays probably would describe as postmodern or rhizomatic—was, according to Picard, the instrumentalization of almost everything. The modern world was characterized by a deep-grounded wish to fit all objects, human beings and sensations into an instrumental scheme that would support and promote the rise of capitalist society. Silence, for Picard, not only reminded of a different society but also had to be associated with a possible way out for: "Silence is the only phenomenon today that is 'useless'. It does not fit into the world of profit and utility; it simply *is*. It seems to have no other purpose; it cannot be exploited" (ibid., p. 18, emphasis in original). In the commercialized, rationalized and bureaucratized world, Picard said to be witness of, only sparks of silence were left, sparks which themselves witnessed of a different world, a world which could be discovered when one turned towards childhood for, according to Picard, "the child is like a little hill of silence [...]. Children are scattered about everywhere in the world of words [...] They are like a conspiracy against the all-too-dynamic world of the words of today" (ibid., pp. 119–121). Rather than the hard-working and machine-like labourers, it was these vestiges of silence that educators and the like had to bear in mind when thinking about how to rebuild and reconstruct Europe after the devastating effects of the Second World War. It was silence, not sound, which could bring about the new, idealized and religious world Picard had in mind when compiling his *World of Silence*.

In this chapter, we will take up Picard's interesting and thought-provoking association between space, silence and education from a history of education's perspective. After having highlighted some instrumental perspectives on silence within contemporary educational practices, we will show how scholars coming from divergent backgrounds have stressed the need of a political perspective on silence. This political approach will inspire us to examine how, in the context of the rehabilitation of Belgian disabled soldiers from the First World War, silence was considered a crucial component of the educational spaces that were constructed for the mutilated men and how, at the same time, silence was considered a powerful way for the disabled men themselves to resist the rehabilitative spaces constructed for them.

7.1 Spaces, Silence and Educational Research

Let us, however, for the time being, return a little to how Picard presented silence in his book *The World of Silence*. For Picard, silence was endangered by but also was one of the last things that resisted the modern tendency to approach everything from an instrumentalized point of view. There is something paradoxical in Picard's approach because the solution he offers for the decline of mankind is exactly the same as what is endangered by its existence, namely, silence. By transforming silence into the most important goal of any educational attempt that wants to curb the modern tendencies of instrumentalization, rationalization and performativity, Picard seems to undermine himself the critical potential of silence he had been referring to throughout the book.

If the instrumentalization of silence in Picard's *The World of Silence* only is a kind of undertone, recently, silence has been rediscovered as an important educational instrument and goal. In Flanders, at least two concrete examples have attracted increasingly the attention of educators, teachers and politicians. Within the context of philosophy for children, for example, 'silence' has been promoted as a meaningful and efficient instrument and goal that enabled teachers to raise important issues, discuss sensitive subjects and install dynamic subjectivities. But silence also has been associated literally to particular geographical spaces that consequently formed the stage for innovative ways to build up a community.

In 2007, an invitation to reflect upon 'the value of silence in education' was send to all educators and teachers working in Flanders and the Netherlands. Given the fact that all of us lead an increasingly hectic life, it was said, more and more teachers became convinced by the extraordinary importance of inner quietness and silence for education and instruction.[1] By means of more than 200 activities and based on the reactions teachers and educators send to the organizing committee, for one day long, libraries, schools and cultural institutions promoted silence as a powerful instrument which for sure deserved a place in the educator's toolbox. Since then, as can be derived from an article published in the Flemish newspaper *De Standaard* on July 3, 2009, the importance of silence has been taken up by almost all active ministries in Flanders.[2] Whether one now was responsible for developmental issues related to the countryside, engaged him/herself for issues of National Health or had to tackle environmental subjects, all in one way or another thought about silence as a way to move forward and attain the goals set out at the beginning of the legislature. The potential of silence in therapeutic settings is a widespread and fully accepted example of how silence might be considered an educational tool that solves particular social problems. The newspaper article, however, mentioned one other example where space, silence and community became related, namely, the so-called acknowledged and certified silence areas or *Stiltegebieden*.[3]

Since the very beginning of the twenty-first century, one can find at the border between East Flanders and Flemish Brabant Flanders' first officially recognized area of silence, namely, Dender-Mark. This area of silence not only refers to the particular geographical characteristics that make this area a place where one can find rest, peace and silence. It also has to do with the fact that in this area, one experiments with new ways of forming a community. Silence then not only has to do with the absence of sound or the esoteric longing for a world beyond the one wherein we on a daily basis live. Silence in this context also triggers notions of respect and tolerance; it bears in itself a longing for community and the establishment of respectful relationships among men themselves but also between men and the surrounding environment. Silence then is considered a part of our immaterial heritage that not only has to be preserved in one way or another but also has to be used in order to install communal ties between the inhabitants of an area of silence.[4]

Just as was the case in Picard's approach, silence here is approached from an instrumentalized perspective and has to be connected to the production of a particular kind of world-view. There is a considerable amount of literature dealing with the intersections of silence and education that shares the same assumptions and so to say educationalizes silence.[5] This educationalized approach of silence, however, is not the only possible perspective on silence. From the 1960s onwards, one also can see the emergence of a rather sceptical approach towards silence. For several authors, silence became connected to the suppressive and discriminatory power relations and had to be demythologized, not to say destructed. The best-known example taken from the history of educational theory probably is Paulo Freire's pioneering book *Pedagogy of the Oppressed* (1972). In contrast and as an answer to the installation of what was being called *Cultures of Silence*, Freire constructed his critical theory as a means to emancipate those who were caught by the sounds of the powerful. People from the Third World were silenced by the developed countries. Therefore, a critical education should then consist in giving them back 'the right to say their own words, to name the world'. If silence for Freire maybe not so much referred to the absence of sound but rather referred to the absence of language in particular places, his interpretation of silence nevertheless emphasized the fact that silence is never neutral and always should be seen in the light of particular power and knowledge relations.

Freire was not the only one who at the end of the 1960s/the beginnings of the 1970s pleaded for a critical approach of silence. Also on the European continent, voices were raised. In favour of a critical approach of silence, or as exemplified by, the French philosopher Michel Foucault tried to write critical histories by focussing on silence rather than language. In the preface to his doctoral dissertation *Histoire de la folie,* Foucault mentioned explicitly that the history of madness he wanted to write not so much would be directed towards the language of psychiatry, but rather would focus on the innumerable points of contact between reason and madness that throughout the seventeenth and eighteenth century were suppressed and silenced:

> The construction of madness as mental illness at the end of the eighteenth century, bears witness to a rupture in a dialogue, gives the separation as already enacted, and expels from the memory all those imperfect words of no fixed syntax, spoken falteringly, in which the exchange between madness and reason was carried out. The language of psychiatry, which is a monologue by reason about madness could only have come into existence in such a silence. My intention was not to write the history of that language, but rather draw up the archaeology of that silence. (Foucault, 2006, p. xxvii)

The critical and political approach of silence, as can be encountered both in the work of Foucault and Freire, has undoubtedly influenced the work undertaken by historians in general and historians of education in particular. In contrast to philosophers of education, however, historians of education up till now have not yet studied the history of education *from* the perspective of silence itself.[6] Within the current state of being, silence indeed has not yet been the lens through which the educational past was perceived, reconstructed or demythologized.[7] In the following paragraphs, this precisely is what we intend to do: first of all, to approach a particular fragment of the history of education, namely, the rehabilitation of Belgian disabled soldiers from the First World War, from the perspective of silence, and secondly, to see how and what kind of relationship in the context of this rehabilitation there is to be drawn between silence, space and the political.

7.2 Retracing Silence in the History of Rehabilitation, 1914–1918

At first sight, it seems a little awkward to approach the history of war from a perspective of silence for isn't war actually the very opposite of silence? Did not war in general and the Great War in particular—as this war has been recorded as an industrial and total war—result in the complete and merciless destruction of silence? According to Picard, this indeed was the case. For him war had to be put on a par with a huge rebellion of noise against silence (see Picard, 1948, p. 83). Recently, however, a couple of scholars have argued the opposite and pleaded for a revaluation of silence for the soldiers themselves as well as for scholars interested in the divergent ways warfare is commemorated. Alex Gadby, for example, who examined how silence was present in, but also problematized, soldier poetry of the First World War concluded that although silence is a "puzzlingly ignored area of study in the field of war poetry, [it] is actually a vital aspect of war and a significant barrier to the war poet, whose voice meets its match at the very limits of language" (see Gadby, 2007). For the soldiers at the front, silence was part of their everyday life, intimately associated to issues of life and death and for some an almost inevitable and visceral reaction towards the atrocities of warfare—as in the case of what would become known as shell-shocked soldiers.[8]

Besides the almost tangible reality of silence for those living in the trenches, Jay Winter also pointed recently towards the importance of silence for scholars interested in the commemoration of war-related events. The best-known example of this for sure is the one/two minute(s) of silence installed in both France and England in order to remember the end of the First World War on November 11, 1918.[9] According to Winter, however, the deployment of silence in practices of commemoration cannot be put on a par with the absence of language. On the contrary, for Winter:

> Silence … is a socially constructed space in which and about which subjects and words normally used in everyday life are not spoken. The circle around this space is described by groups of people who at one point in time deem it appropriate that there is a difference between the sayable and the unsayable, or the spoken and the unspoken, and that such a distinction can and should be maintained and observed over time. Such people codify and enforce norms which reinforce the injunction against breaking into the inner space of the circle of silence. (Winter, 2011, p. 4)

Just like Paulo Freire, although coming from a completely different field, Winter here points towards the political aspects closely connected to issues and practices of being silent. Silence should not be considered the mere absence of language. In a way silence speaks for itself or at least is the result of people speaking in one way or another, expressing their ideas on how history should be remembered and what should be remembered. It is precisely this political approach to silence which we in the next paragraphs would like to explore by turning towards the lived realities of Belgian disabled soldiers from the First World War.

7.2.1   Geographical Diaspora and the Breakdown of Communication

In order to trace back the importance of silence for the Belgian (disabled) soldiers who were enlisted or volunteered right after the outbreak of the War, we have to go back to the turbulent first months of the war.[10] On August 4, 1914, German troops led by General Von Kluck and Von Bulöw crossed the Belgian border in the neighbourhood of Liège. After the Belgian army resisted the German military supremacy in the neighbourhood of Liège and Namen, in the end, the Belgian force had to retreat to Antwerp until the situation became unbearable and all of the troops again had to be evacuated from the beleaguered town in October 1914. What was left of the Belgian army after the fall of Antwerp broke in several pieces, all of which, given the harsh bombardments and the heavy fighting in August and September, contained a number of wounded soldiers. Some mutilated men, who were still able to walk, could be found among the soldiers who were ordered to march immediately to the utter West of the country where they were said to set up a new line of defence together with the British and French troops. Others fled over the river Scheldt towards the Netherlands where they would be interned for the remainder of the war or tried after a while to rejoin illegally their fellow soldiers who continued the war in the trenches. Still others, those who could not walk any more but still were capable of being transported, were evacuated by train to Ostend where they were put on a boat and shipped off across the Channel or to the North of France. Finally, there were those soldiers whose situation prevented them of being transported and who stayed in the abandoned hospitals and were taken prisoners by the German authorities.

Official statistics indeed do not leave any doubt with regard to the human price also Belgium had to pay for its recovered independence on November 11, 1918. Léopold Mélis, for example, who was *Inspecteur Général du Service de Santé de l'Armée* during the war, stated in his 1932 published historical overview of the army's health services between 1914 and 1918 that at the end of the war, Belgian forces counted the loss of 41,111 men and stated that 5,273 Belgian soldiers became permanently disabled.[11]

At the end of October 1914 and given the military diaspora following upon the fall of Antwerp, a number of these 5,273 mutilated Belgian soldiers thus could be found in France, England, the Netherlands and the occupied home country. Except for those Belgian soldiers who had to face a life as a wounded soldier under the reign of the Germans in an occupied home country, all of the other mutilated soldiers, and those who still would become mutilated at the Western front in the remainder of the war, were more or less isolated from their previous family and professional life. Most of the soldiers to be found among the Belgian military forces were only very recently enlisted—compulsory military service for all young men only became operative in August 1913—and thus suddenly pulled away from their families and regular occupations. The fact that their home country was occupied, however, added largely to the feelings of isolation and homesickness that reigned among the Belgian forces while being relegated to the trenches in the West. Not only were they separated from their loved ones and colleagues, but German authorities also tried as much as possible to destroy all attempts of communication between the ones living at home and those fighting in the mud of the Yser or living abroad as a war refugee.[12]

Although of course all of the soldiers fighting at the Western front actually experienced being separated from their loved ones, those soldiers enlisted in the armies of the Commonwealth or the German emperor still were capable of visiting their families during military leave—an outlook Belgian soldiers could not profit from. The feelings of despair and solitude this breakdown of communication, or so to say communicative silence led to, were wonderfully described by Cypriaan Verhavert in his book *Zij die gingen … en zij die blijven*. The distributed book did not carry Verhavert's own name on the title page but was made public under the telling pseudonym 'I. Eenzame' (Eenzame, 1924). Translated into English, this would sound as 'I. Solitary'. In one of the literary compositions, Verhavert renders a touching depiction of the pain experienced by a fictitious soldier when being confronted once again with the often repeated question posed by the home front: 'And, how do you do?'. Despite its fictitious nature, the answer given seems to refer to the importance of silence for the Belgian soldiers of the Great War: "Man of my region, do you know what being land sick means? Spleen, homesickness, 'Le Cafard' they call it here! It actually is a huge pain, which is anchored above the belly button. Usually it seizes the sensitive, hypersensitive beings who, suddenly being chased away of their precious piece of land where they left everything behind, own possessions, own habits, own love".[13]

7.2.2   The Reactivation of Human Wrecks in Silent Places

Silence, however, was not only a meaningful quality of life for the soldiers in the trenches who continuously were confronted with the impossibility to communicate with the home front and the by times surrealistic scenes of absolute silence amidst the horrors of war. Silence also was turned into a meaningful component of the rehabilitation strategies that were developed for those soldiers who, due to the amputation of one or more limbs or the loss of eyesight. One has estimated that at the end of the First World War, the total number of disabled soldiers who in one way or another had to be integrated anew in the society was around 8 million.[14] Besides the 9.5 million men who died on the battlefield or to the consequences of the military activities between 1914 and 1918, these disabled men demonstrated literally to what extent this war could be considered a total and industrial war. The new and deadly weaponry that both sides developed and used during the hostilities—for example, the use of toxic gases, flame-throwers and machine guns—was extremely destructive for both the bodies and minds at war.[15] In contrast to what the historical silence, by which the existence of Belgian disabled soldiers is covered, seems to suggest, Belgium was one of the first countries to establish a couple of specialized institutes for the mutilated men.[16]

Although in all of the geographical areas where Belgian disabled men could be found during the war, educational initiatives are to be found which aimed at restoring the mutilated men to their pre-war labour capacity and human form,[17] we, in what follows, only will deal with one of the institutes which was founded in the North of France where the Belgium government had sought exile, namely, *L'Institut Militaire Belge de Rééducation Professionnelle de Port-Villez* (Fig. 7.1).

During the first couple of months of the war, the medical corps of the Belgian army, as well as many of the high-ranked officers, were convinced that the war quickly would come to an end. As a consequence, many of the Belgian soldiers who became disabled during the first months of the war were dismissed from the army and rambled around on the French soil in search of shelter and some food. At first these rambling bodies were considered symbols of the fierce resistance of the Belgian army and sometimes one described the impairments as 'badges of honour'. But as time went by and all became convinced that the war would end much longer than one initially had foreseen, the representation of these mutilated Belgian men, who even could be encountered in the South of France, radically changed. In November 1914, while being confronted with a shortage of men power at the front—due to the loss of many Belgian soldiers and the imprisonment of a considerable

Fig. 7.1 Main entrance of the Belgian Military Institute for professional re-education at Port-Villez (Taken from De Paeuw (1917) © Private collection)

number in Dutch camps for the remainder of the war—and the fact that the mutilated bodies actually were threatening the pugnacious moral of the French population, the military authorities recalled their previous decision to reform the men and again put them under military authority. The sight of limbless men, it was said, would result in a decrease in the will of the French population to enlist in the army. Moreover, the Belgium authorities were in need of all the power that could be reassembled after the defeat and diaspora of Antwerp.

If the foundation of the Belgian institute for the disabled soldiers in the North of France of course also had something to do with the fact that the Belgian government in a sense felt responsible for its disabled 'civilians', the most important reasons for its establishment were considered to be its capacity to make the disabled men disappear from the public arena as well as the possibility of turning human wrecks into useful labourers again.[18] Intimately bound to the widespread concern with fatigue and energy at that time (see Rabinbach 1992), politicians, pedagogues and military officers alike promoted the idea of rehabilitation for it strongly held the promise of transforming wasted bodies into productive and useful elements. The objective of rehabilitation indeed time and again was summarized in phrases like 'to make the men 100 % fit again', 'to restore the men to the best physical shape possible' and 'to re-turn the men to their former industrial capacities'. From the very moment a soldier entered a field hospital, he was caught in a continuous succession of moral talks, therapeutic initiatives and educational programmes, all of which tried to reinstall the level of energy that he possessed before being injured on the battlefield.

This recovered amount of energy was considered indispensable. Not only could the disabled soldier be taught a new trade and so, for example, produce military goods that could sustain the ongoing warfare, but in some cases the soldier might even be restored completely to active service and thus send back to the front. Re-educating disabled soldiers, moreover, was also thought important from the perspective of Belgium's post-war reconstruction. If the disabled soldiers indeed became economically independent, the state would not only have to pay fewer pensions but also would be able to rely on their working capacities in order to restore its soil to its pre-war prosperity.[19]

It is precisely in this rational and calculative approach of human restoration and re-education that, at least for the Belgian case of Port-Villez, silence would be considered an important ingredient of the rehabilitative atmosphere which, from November 1914, the disabled soldiers were send to. In contrast to the noisy environment of the front as well as the modern city, the founders of the Institute of Port-Villez had chosen for a location that directly reconnected the soldiers with the quiet and silent life on the countryside without isolating them too much from the inspirational view of peasants at work:

> Le plateau boisé où s'élève l'École ne comprend qu'une petite agglomération bâtie, où quelques paysans vivent tranquillement de la culture des champs voisins. Un grand calme y pénètre l'âme. Mais le va-et-vient continuel des trains, qui roulent vers Paris ou Le Havre, et l'animation incessante qui règne sur le fleuve, donnent aux homes l'impression salutaire que, malgré leur isolement apparent, ils vivent au milieu d'un people au travail.[20]

The quietness of the environment, the calming effects of the countryside and the peaceful sight of peasants working at the border of the Seine all in one way or another added to the realization of the educational goal of the institute, namely, to restore the men—bodily as well as mentally—to a kind of lifestyle where one as much as possible tried to economize energies. Intimately connected to the demand of a quiet but inspiring environment was the fact that the internal organization, the educational procedures as well as the overall philosophy that reigned in the institute were all inspired by Taylorian theory. One of the most important ideas of this predominant economic approach of the world was, so to say, the spatial understanding of mankind. All human beings were considered to have a particular amount of qualities and capacities which made him/her more suitable for particular jobs and educational pathways. Given this belief in optimal matches between men, their education and the profession they will practise, one of the most crucial steps in this rationalized approach of human beings was to pinpoint at a very early stage for what kind of job and by means of what kind of education a particular person had to be instructed. At the heart of Taylorism, one indeed could find the belief of 'The right man at the right place'.

If the particular location of the institute already silently tried to steer the disabled men again into the direction of becoming useful citizens who being allocated to the right profession would enormously contribute to the ongoing warfare as well as the post-war reconstruction of the homeland, also the internal organization in divergent ways wanted to install a spatialized working ethos. After being relegated from the battlefield and after their wounds had been healed, those soldiers who were not able anymore to rejoin their fellow comrades in the trenches were sent to the Port-Villez Institute where they

Fig. 7.2   New tools for a new trade. Soldiers disabled in Belgium's defence at work in the machine shop of Port-Villez and the Belgian re-educational school established in French soil (Taken from McMurtrie (1919), p. 30)

immediately had to undergo a medical, pedagogical and technical examination. These conversations were intended to reveal the inclinations of the disabled men, his level of energy, the capacities he still possessed, etc., in order to direct him to this or that profession which fitted perfectly with his newly acquired bodily state.

Moreover, after being admitted to this or that atelier where the disabled soldier would be learned a new trade or would be reskilled in the profession he practised before the outbreak of the war, he continuously was confronted with some appropriate proverbs written on signboard which were hang all over the institute. The following proverbs subtly had to lead the soldier away from a way of life wherein he was not preoccupied with the right use of energy and human power: 'Stel niet uit tot morgen wat gij heden doen kunt' and 'En temps de paix le gaspillage est une faute, en temps de guerre c'est une crime'. But the proverb reflecting the Taylorian course steered by the Belgian institute in Port-Villez towards a spatialized world-view probably was the one that hang in the machine shop and stated: 'Een plaats voor elk voorwerp, Elk voorwerp op zijn plaats/A place for each object, Every object on its own place' (Fig. 7.2).

Within the particular context of war and the hard-felt need of manpower by the Belgian authorities, it was in particular these Taylorian ideas which among other things triggered two processes which are closely connected to each other, namely, the educationalization of silence and the spatialization of learning. Inspired by an economic theory which heavily relied upon the belief that all human beings had to be educated for a seemingly predestined place in professional life, the case of the rehabilitation of disabled soldiers at Port-Villez shows us how both silence and space were instrumentalized in order to create a learning environment where the 'right man' was steered towards the 'right place'.

7.2.3   Silence, Resistance and the Disabled Soldier's Voice

Given the authoritarian military context, it seems tempting to presuppose that all of the Belgian disabled soldiers merely underwent the rehabilitative programmes and that the envisioned educational goals of energetic lifestyle and spatialized identities did not meet any resistance from the side of the mutilated bodies.[21] However, considering the archival records we discovered at the *Royal Museum of the Armed Forces and Military History* in Brussels, this hypothesis does not hold true.[22] A couple of sources make abundantly clear that not all the soldiers were pleased with the rehabilitative efforts nor that they believed in the personal advantages sketched out for them by those in charge of the rehabilitative programmes. Moreover, the disabled soldiers actually sometimes made use of silence as an important tool by which they could raise their voice against the preconceived programmes and envisioned educational goals of energy management and restoration. In the following paragraphs, three examples will be given of how Belgian disabled soldiers tried to counter the particular world-views closely connected to the rehabilitative initiatives and actually at times put forward an alternative definition and meaning of restoration.

First of all, we can recall the first contingent of 50 disabled Belgian soldiers destined to be rehabilitated in Port-Villez. These men clearly were not that anxious to start their re-educational journey due to a persistent rumour according to which soldiers would get a smaller pension after the war when they would be able to earn their own livelihood.[23] If this hold true, then it was undeniably better not to be re-educated, and this attitude was precisely what the authorities of Port-Villez had to face right after the men were admitted to the institution. If there are no documents left that enable us to get an insight into how the authorities dealt with this particular moment of resistance, there are, however, a couple of pamphlets that show us how the same belief was countered in the case of those disabled soldiers living across the pond. If the rehabilitation itself would not lead to smaller pensions, it was said, the disabled soldiers staying in England who resisted the invitation to become rehabilitated had to be aware of the fact that if they would not follow the vocational training, their post-war position on the labour market would be inferior to those of mutilated men who were willing to be restored to economic independence. In one pamphlet, for example, which was distributed in England to persuade the Belgian disabled soldiers living there to come to France in order to be rehabilitated, one clearly could read:

> The public administrations, of course, will reserve a huge place for those disabled by war when choosing their personnel. However, because they have to assure the daily routine, they will give preference to those mutilated men who in wartime already courageously prepared themselves for their new occupations. Those who give preference to lead an easy and idle life in Britain and who live at the expense of Britain's charity will have to wait. And that is rightly so.[24]

A second example of how Belgian disabled soldiers at time resisted the educational programmes installed for their restoration to military service and post-war professional life can be found when one takes a closer look at what happened with the Belgian soldiers who were blinded during the war. In first instance, the Belgian government had decided to leave the care of those blinded soldiers to the operational institute for the congenitally French blind at Amiens.[25] Here, however, not everything went according to plan. A report of Corporal Bonnet, for example, mentions that

> our blind soldiers felt too weak to start a firm and immediate new battle against their blindness. They remained unconscious about the strengths a man finds within himself while undergoing terrible ordeals and they veiled themselves in a mute and even savage melancholy. They spend their days stretched out on their beds or abandoned in a certain corner completely overwhelmed by their fears, by their doubts.[26]

If silence had been integrated by the founders of the Port-Villez Institute as an active and crucial element of the environment adding largely to the (re-)establishment of a productive, energy-like and rationalized working ethos, the blinded Belgian soldiers made use of silence in a completely opposite way. The silence they veiled themselves in, the melancholy that made them not to leave their beds for days and the inactivity resulting from their doubts and fears all stood in contrast with the energetic future envisioned by the rehabilitative programmes developed for the Belgian disabled soldier. Instead of being educated towards the leading Taylorian principle of the 'right man on the right place', these blinded soldiers confronted with an all-encompassing darkness and the outlook of not seeing their wives, relatives and children anymore did not recognize the advantages sketched out by the rehabilitative programmes and decided not to insert themselves in the increasingly dominant instrumentalization of time, body and space. Actually, the sources show us that the disabled soldiers themselves formulated alternative definitions of what rehabilitation could consist of. This at least if what can be found in the letter written by a Belgian soldier named Rousseau towards the end of the war.

On June 4, 1919, soldier Rousseau, whose right arm had been amputated during the war and who at that time still was waiting in exile (Fig. 7.3) to be allowed to go home and finally see his loved ones again, wrote:

> We are here with some hundreds of invalids who experience a huge cafard due to the fact that already seven months ago the armistice was signed and we are still exiled, far away from our homeland, from our parents, wives and children. An observer would be rendered a sad spectacle when casting an eye on the hospital where the mutilated men walk around like troubled minds not knowing what else to do with their time than dreaming about their relatives while sitting on a wooden bench [...].[27]

Following his description and critique of the ongoing rehabilitative initiatives in the French institutes, Rousseau gives his own definition of re-education and added that simply sending them home would lead to the following result: "Instead of watching all those mutilated men with sad and melancholic faces, one would see them all smiling, enjoying the familial life, born again to life and taking up their small occupations (which would be the best rehabilitation)".[28]

Fig. 7.3 Samuel De Vriendt, *La toute petite amie/Het vriendinnetje/Making friends* (Taken from De Vriendt (1920), p. S.l. – © Private collection)

7.3 Space, Silence and History of Education

Historians of education traditionally have predominantly included silence in an indirect way into their research agenda. Silence then not so much was considered an educational object/tool in itself but rather was seen as the starting point for doing research with regard to particular subject which for a very long time had been covered up by silence. The main task for the historian of education then consisted in replacing the historical neglect by an exploratory narrative. Although this of course is well needed and rightly can function as a legitimation for the work undertaken by historians of education, we, in this chapter, have tried to show how silence in addition to the more traditional approaches also can be considered as, so to say, having a language of its own. The task of the historian of education then not so much consists in replacing silences by reconstructed languages but can be described as revealing the particular places taken in by silence in the history of education. If we, in this chapter, of course, also have pointed towards the historical silence that, in the course of the twentieth century, came to cover up the existence and experiences of disabled soldiers, we, however, also have tried to make clear that in the case of the rehabilitation of Belgian disabled soldiers at Port-Villez, silence also was considered an important educational tool in the hands of those responsible for the realization of rehabilitation as well as a political mean for the disabled soldiers themselves who were submitted to the re-educational initiatives. Up till this very moment, school teachers on a daily basis make use of silence to stress particular elements of their talks or become silent in order to reprimand a noisy classroom. It is precisely this instrumentalized use of silence which we have sought to lay bare by examining what happened with the Belgian disabled soldiers during the First World War. By revealing, on the one hand, how this educationalized approach of silence was intimately bound with a spatialized view on mankind—the right man on the right place—and, on the other hand, how silence at the same time was being used by the disabled soldiers themselves in order not to move towards the envisioned world-view and rehabilitative definitions, we hope to have succeeded in making clear that for historians of education, silence itself can be considered a place where historical research is necessary.

Notes

1. Anon. (2007). *Uitnodiging aan alle leerkrachten en opvoeders in Vlaanderen en Nederland. De waarde van stilte in het onderwijs. Stilte en eenvoud Thema van Gedichtendag*. S.l.; For the Dutch-speaking countries, two websites are of particular interest in this context: www.stilte-educatie.nl and www.stilte.org. One also can turn towards the book *Met kinderen stilte ontdekken* of Gerda and Rüdiger Maschwitz which originally was published in German as *Mit Kindern Stille entdecken*.
2. Bormans, L. et al. (2009). Stilstaan om vooruit te gaan: Stilte en rust waarderen in een actief Vlaanderen. *De Standaard*, 3 juli, p. 22.
3. The idea and concepts behind the so-called *Stilte-gebieden* are promoted by the Waerbeke Centre [See www.waerbeke.be]. In a couple of publications, this non-profit organization has made explicit the value of silence for contemporary society and community formation: *Monumenten van stilte/Over fotografie van stilte* (2005) and *Stilte werkt* (2003).
4. Capenberghs, J. & Sturtewagen, D. (2003). Het verbindende vermogen van stilte als erfgoed. Centrum Waerbeke en stiltegebied Dender-Mark, twee grensoverschrijdende pilootprojecten. In: Centrum Waerbeke (2003). *Stilte Werkt*. Centrum Waerbeke.
5. Helen Lees, for example,, of Stirling's Laboratory of Educational Theory states that "In areas of better learning outcomes, better interpersonal relationships, better self-esteem and wellbeing measures, silence in a person's life and

an individual's education is shown throughout the relevant research literature to be a benefit" (Quoted in Graeme, P. (2011). Silence is golden: How keeping quiet in the classroom can boost results. *The Telegraph*, 7 December). See also Lees' book *Silence in Schools* (in press) or the older but still readable *Perspectives on silence* which was edited by Deborah Tannen and Murielle Saville-Troike in 1985.

6. Philosophers of education have, when being compared to historians of education, already included silence as a subject worth of inquiry in their scholarly agenda. See, for example, Zembylas, M. & Michaelides, P. (2004). The sound of silence in pedagogy. *Educational Theory* 54 (2), 193–210; Byron, H. (2003). A rhetoric/pedagogy of silences: Sub-version in Paul Kameen's writing/teaching. *Pedagogy* 3 (3), 377–397 and Smith, R. (2009). Half a language: Listening in the city of words. In: P. Smeyers & M. Depaepe (Eds.), *Educational research: Proofs, arguments, and other reasonings*. Amsterdam: Springer.

7. Although the title of the book might suggest otherwise, silence actually was not the real object of the edited volume *Silences & Images: The Social History of the Classroom* of Ian Grosvenor, Martin Lawn and Kate Rousmanier (New York: Peter Lang, 1999), rather, their "silent partner was an unspoken set of questions about the social construction of classrooms as places of learning and places of work" (p. 2). Silence then within the existing educational historiography refers to a suppressed group of people or a neglected set of research questions. As a case in point, one can turn towards the introduction in Myers, K. (2001). The hidden history of refugee schooling in Britain: The case of the Belgians, 1914–1918. *History of Education* 30 (2), 153–162.

8. A close reading of the diaries of Henri Barbusse, Louis Barthas, Ernst Jünger and Erich Maria Remarque, for example, reveals immediately to what extent silence became both a precious as well as an alarming aspect of everyday reality at the front. In Remarque's anti-militaristic diary-like novel *Nothing new on the Western front*, for example, silence is being presented as a strong expression of communality when the main characters are sitting on a couple of boxes and recall the dangerous moments they just overcame: Remarque, E. F. (1929). *Van het Westelijke front geen nieuws*. Utrecht: Erven, J. Bijleveld, p. 14.

9. See, for example, the article 'The silence in Manchester' that appeared in *The Guardian* on November 12, 1919: "It may be doubted whether the great central streets of Manchester have ever before been so silent as they were for two minutes yesterday morning. Even during the dead hours of the night there is ordinarily some little stir of traffic, and on Sundays silence never completely falls": Anon. (1919). The silence in Manchester. *The Guardian*, November 12.

10. Up till now, the best study devoted to the events that lead to and happened during the First World War in Belgium remains: Sophie de Schaepdrijver (1997). *De Groote Oorlog: Het Koninkrijk België tijdens de Eerste Wereldoorlog*. Amsterdam: Atlas.

11. Mélis, L. (1932). *Contribution à l'histoire du Service de Santé de l'armée au cours de la guerre 1914–1918*. Bruxelles : Institut Cartographique Militaire, pp. 532–533. See also Lefevre, P. & Lorette, J. (Eds.) (1987). *La Belgique et la*

Première Guerre mondiale—Bibliographie; België en de Eerste Wereldoorlog : Bibliografie. Bruxelles: Musée Royal de l'Armee, p. 118 [Footnote 1] & Van Der Beken, B. & Van Der Beken, H. (s.d.). *La première Bataille belge. Rabosée 5–6 août 1914*. Bruxelles: Ferd. Wellens-Ray.

12. See, for example, Van San, P. (Ed.). (1999). *De Belgen en hun briefwisseling gedurende de Eerste Wereldoorlog*. Brussels: Algemeen Rijksarchief and Hemelaers, J., Ludwig, G. & Plovie, L. (Ed.). (1999). *De briefwisseling van de Belgen tijdens de Eerste Wereldoorlog*. Brussels: Algemeen Rijksarchief.

13. Eenzame, 1924, p. 14 [Translation PV].

14. On casualty statistics and the numbers of disabled men, see Whalen, R.W. (1984). *Bitter wounds: German victims of the Great War*. New York: Ithaca, pp. 40–41 and Cohen, D. (2001). *The war come home: Disabled veterans in Britain and Germany, 1914–1939*, pp. 1–2.

15. For some of the existing literature on the history of disabled soldiers, see Anderson, J. & Pemberton, N. (2007). Walking alone: Aiding the war and civilian blind in the inter-war period. *European Review of History* 14 (4), 459–479; Bourke, J. (1996). *Dismembering the male. Men's bodies, Britain and the Great War*. London: Reaktion Books; Cohen, D. (2001). *The war come home: Disabled veterans in Britain and Germany, 1914–1939*. Berkeley: University of California Press; Gelber, S. (2005). A 'Hard boiled order'. The reeducation of WWI veterans in New York city. *Journal of Social History* Fall, 161–180; Hickel, K. W. (2000). Medicine, bureaucracy, and social welfare: The politics of disability compensation for American veterans of World War I. In: P. Longmore & L. Umansky (Eds.), *The new disability history: American perspectives*. New York: New York University Press; Koven, S. (1994). Remembering and dismemberment: Cripples children, wounded soldiers and the Great War in Great Britain. *American Historical Review* October, 1167–1202; Gerber, D. A. (Ed.). (2000). *Disabled Veterans in History*. Ann Arbor: University of Michigan Press. Prost, A. (1977). *Les anciens combattants 1914–1940*. Paris: Gallimard; Reznick, J. (2005). *Healing the nation: Soldiers and the culture of caregiving in Britain during the Great War*. Manchester: Manchester University Press; Larsson, M. (2004). Restoring the spirit. The rehabilitation of disabled soldiers in Australia after the Great War. *Health and History,* 6 (2), 45–59.

16. Garrard Harris, for example, who wrote a comparative historical overview of what happened with the disabled soldiers during the war, entitled chapter six of his work, which was devoted to Belgium, as follows: "Belgium: The pioneer in restoration work". Harris, G. (1919). *The redemption of the disabled. A study of programmes of rehabilitation for the disabled of war and of industry*. New York: D. Appleton and Company, p. 64 and further.

17. For all of these wounded and mutilated soldiers (educational), initiatives were set up. In occupied Belgium, the disabled soldiers were taken care of by private organizations like *Aide et apprentissage aux invalides de la guerre* [See, e.g. Cloquet, J. (s.d.). *Aide et apprentissage aux invalides de guerre. Renseignements, notes et commentaires sur l'activité de l'oeuvre durant l'occupation dans la région des Etapes de la IV. Armée Allemande*. Gand : Comité National de

Secours et Alimentation]. In the Netherlands, an institute for Belgian disabled soldiers was founded at Katwijk-sur-Mer [See, e.g. Anon. (s.d.). *Oeuvre des mutilés & invalides de guerre en Hollande. Le Phalanstère Belge de Katwijk-sur-Mer, 1915–1918.* La Haye : Comité Central]. Information with regard to the existence of Belgian disabled soldiers in Britain can be found in the Moscow archives at the *Royal Museum of the Armed Forces and Military History.*

18. This actually was a widespread and commonly accepted view among those who in one way or another were responsible for the realization of rehabilitative initiatives during as well as rightly after the war. One only has to take a look at important publications as McMurtie, D. (1919). *The disabled soldier.* New York: The Macmillan Company; Harris, G. (1919). *The redemption of the disabled. A study of programmes of rehabilitation for the disabled of war and of injury.* London: D. Appleton & Company and (1917). *Report on the Inter-Allied conference for the study of professional re-education, and other questions of interests to soldiers and sailors disabled by the war held at Paris 8ᵗʰ till 12ᵗʰ May 1917.* London: His Majesty's Stationery Office.

19. An example of this link between Belgium's post-war reconstruction and the rehabilitation of disabled soldiers during the war can be found in the foreword to De Paeuw's book written by Henry Carton de Wiart: De Paeuw, *La rééducation professionnelle*, pp. XIII and further.

20. See Note 19, ibid., p. 60.

21. This is at least what disability historian Henri-Jacques Stiker suggested in his pioneering book: *A history of disability* (pp. 124–126).

22. The archival documents related to the foundation, organization and transfer of the Port-Villez Institute and Sainte-Adresse belong to the so-called Moscow archive of the *Royal Museum of the Armed Forces and Military History* [Box 1814 185-14-4441; Box 5341 185-14a-6850; Box 5047 185-14a-5753].

23. See De Paeuw, L. (s.d.). *La rééducation professionnelle des grands blessés de guerre*—The same argument can be encountered in a lecture given by the Captain-Commandant Pieters on November 26, 1916: Anon. (s.d.). *Conférence donnée par le Capitaine-Commandant Pieters aux invalides de la Guerre, le 26 Novembre 1916 à l'école Coloniale et Commerciale sous la présidence de Madame la Comtesse Jean de Mérode [pendant l'occupation ennemie].* Bruxelles : Société Anonyme Belge d'Imprimerie.

24. See Anon. (s.d.). *Gestichten van Port-Villez en Mortain. Aan de belgische soldaten die voor den militairen dienst ongeschikt werden verklaard en in Engeland verblijven.* Port-Villez: Belgisch Militair Gesticht van Vak-heropleiding.

25. See Note 11, Mélis, 1932, pp. 204–213.

26. Royal Museum of the Armed Forces and Military History—Moscow Archive— Box 5047 185-14a-5723.

27. Letter of G. Rousseau, Rouen—le 4 juin 1919: Royal Museum of the Armed Forces and Military History—Moscow Archive Box 5047 185-14a-5753.

28. See Note 27, ibid.

References

De Paeuw, L. (1917). *La re-education professionnelle des soldats mutilés & estropiés*. Port-Villez, France: Imprimerie de l'Ecole Nationale belge des Mutilés de la Guerre.

De Vriendt, S. (1920). *Aveugles de la guerre, Oorlogsblinden, The blind of war—Croquis, Schetsen, Sketches*. Boitsfort, Belgium: Institut des Aveugles de Guerre.

Eenzame, I. (1924). *Zij die gingen … en zij die blijven*. Brussels, Belgium: 't Spaeverke.

Foucault, M. (2006). *History of madness*. Oxon, UK: Routledge.

Freire, P. (1972). *Pedagogy of the oppressed*. London: Sheed and Ward.

Gadby, A. (2007). *"I have no words to speak of war": The problem of silence in the soldier poetry of the First World War and the present day*. Master's thesis, University of Stirling.

McMurtrie, D. (1919). *The disabled soldier*. New York: The Macmillan Company.

Picard, M. (1948). *The world of silence* (S. Godman, Trans.). London: The Harvill Press.

Rabinbach, A. (1992). *The human motor: Energy, fatigue and the origins of modernity*. Berkeley, CA: University of California Press.

Winter, J. (2011). Thinking about silence. In E. Ben-Ze'ev, R. Ginio, & J. Winter (Eds.), *Shadows of war. A social history of silence in the twentieth century* (pp. 3–31). Cambridge, UK: Cambridge University Press.

Yourcenar, M. (1929). *Alexis ou le traité du vieux combat*. Paris: Au Sans Pareil.

Chapter 8
Interpretation: The Space of Text

Richard Smith

We have to translate while suspending our belief in an original... The aim of psychoanalysis would be to free people to translate and be translated, rather than to acquire a definitive, convincing version of themselves.

(Adam Phillips, 2000, *Promises, Promises*, p. 147)

Above all it is when the pressure to understand is taken off that the most valuable words are spoken or written.

(Adam Phillips, 2002, *Equals*, p. 105)

8.1 Architects and Rhetoricians

One of Descartes's first thoughts, secluded with his stove in the midst of the wars in Germany, was that

> often there is not so much perfection in works created from several pieces and made by the hands of various masters as there is in those which one person has worked on alone. Thus, we see that the buildings which a single architect has undertaken and completed are usually more beautiful and better ordered than those which several people have tried to refurbish by making use of old walls built for other purposes. That is why those ancient cities which were only small villages at the start and became large towns over time are ordinarily so badly laid out, compared to the regular places which an engineer has designed freely on level ground. Even though, considering the buildings in each of them separately, we often find as much beauty in the former town as in the latter, or more, nonetheless, looking at them as they are arranged—here a large one, there a small one—and the way they make the streets crooked and unequal, we would say that chance rather than the will of some men using their reason designed them this way. (Descartes, 2000, *Discourse*, Part II, Trans. Clarke, 2000)

R. Smith (✉)
School of Education, University of Durham, Durham, UK
e-mail: r.d.smith@durham.ac.uk

P. Smeyers et al. (eds.), *Educational Research: The Importance and Effects of Institutional Spaces*, Educational Research 7, DOI 10.1007/978-94-007-6247-3_8,
© Springer Science+Business Media Dordrecht 2013

There is, we might say, something indisputable and conclusive about the architect-designed town. We can inspect the plan and infer the architect's intention. We can ask him, or her, if we are uncertain (and if he or she is still alive, of course). We cannot understand the organic town in the same way. Its meanings, we might say, are more subtle and perhaps more obscure. There is no authority to appeal to, and this perhaps disturbs us. The architect, in the image I take from Descartes, is that reassuring authority, a father-figure. He releases us from ambiguity and from the effort of interpretation. Here there is a kind of relief, achieved at the cost of univocity, of reducing all meanings to a single one. By contrast there are ways of making sense of the town—here taking on the status of a metaphor for reading a text—that challenge authority. The architect may signal his or her clear intentions, but those who live in the town or visit it see things otherwise. They incline to the view that the town is inhuman in its scale or its layout or that there is something uncomfortable about its overwide avenues and imposing buildings; or, in the case of another town, the very playfulness of the mixing of styles suggests a self-absorption on the part of the architect, an indifference to the lives of the people who will be its citizens.

Given that knowledge is largely transmitted and received as text, there is a strange lack of attention to the nature of text and how we read it in the literature (one must use this word, with its implications of sophisticated textuality) of educational research. Text is a site or place of research, and one that we contrive largely to ignore. The ideal text, it seems, is like the good referee in a game of football: you do not notice he is there. An article or research report conveys some truths about a good way of teaching science in primary schools (a way that *works*, of course), and it does so economically and effectively, almost self-effacingly. As a text it should make minimal claims on the reader and should undoubtedly not draw attention to itself as a piece of writing. Ideally it is transparent, allowing the reader to see straight through, without distortion or distraction, to the realities beneath. We praise writing for its clarity, seldom noticing that this innocent word is itself heavily metaphorical (as if language were a glass window which we peer through to what is real or water beneath which reality can be discerned) and implies a whole theory of meaning. That theory is in essence Augustinian, critically discussed by Wittgenstein at the beginning of the *Philosophical Investigations*, and rendered further problematic by the body of theory that we have come to call poststructuralism.

To foreground the textuality of educational research and writing is to be reminded, among other things, that education is heavily coloured by rhetoric. The history of the decline of the study of rhetoric from its position in the mediaeval trivium is complex and interesting (see, e.g. Booth, 2004). Rhetoric has suffered from its association with the Greek sophists, portrayed in the Platonic tradition as purveyors of tricks of persuasion. (I do not say by Plato: his dialogues show the relationship between rhetoric and philosophy as less than clear-cut.) In the context of education, rhetoric has been cast as frivolous and irrelevant by the general assumption that education is an intensely practical business (of course such assumptions themselves tend to be expressed in highly rhetorical ways) and by the proliferating tendency to cast educational research in scientific or quasi-scientific terms and to conclude that the arts and humanities have nothing to contribute to understanding it. It seems to me however that to expose the rhetoric of educational discourse is immediately to demonstrate that it is not quite what it claims to be, and that this on its own has a valuable role to play in opening up space for thought that undetected rhetoric threatens to close down. I offer the following reading of the rhetoric of an educational document as an illustration.

8.2   White Paper

The UK's Coalition Government published in June 2011 a White Paper on the future of universities: *Students at the Heart of the System*. The cover text appears below, as nearly as I have been able to reproduce it: in the original the lettering is in white against a black background, which is itself set against the deep blue of the whole page.

BIS	Department for Business Innovation & Skills

HIGHER EDUCATION
Students at the Heart of the
System

JUNE 2011

We might notice immediately that this bears the imprint of **BIS**, glossed as Department for Business Innovation & Skills. There is much to remark here, not least the oddity that UK universities fall under the remit of such a government department, its business-like qualities signalled by the abbreviation to 'BIS', as if its ministers and civil servants were too busy and energetic to waste time on the full title. This suggestion of no-nonsense briskness seems to be confirmed by the absence of a comma between 'Business' and 'Innovation', as well as by the use of the ampersand for 'and'. The demands of business and the economy seem to be too pressing for the niceties of punctuation and other conventions.

So much for the front page. The first chapter of the document is titled 'Sustainable and Fair Funding'. There is a widespread tendency to call anything you are in favour of 'sustainable', as if longevity trumped all other values, though no doubt we could go on doing bad things badly for a long time just as much as we could go on doing good things well; and no doubt the implicit nod to environmentalism helps to lull the reader's critical faculties. Here are the first two paragraphs:

1.1 English higher education has a high reputation for scholarship and research, which have a fundamental value in themselves, and for turning these into valuable innovation which can change the world. We have world-class research universities as well as universities which are excellent in other ways such as through their contribution to their local economy or the opportunities they provide for mature students. They are not part of the public sector and their staff are not public sector employees. They depend, however, on grants from the Exchequer and with these have come an ever more intrusive burden of regulation, notably quotas specifying exactly how many students each institution should recruit each year.

1.2 The Coalition is taking a bold approach to reform which places students at the heart of the system. We inherited an enormous deficit which created significant spending pressures.

We could have responded by reducing student numbers or the level of spending per student. But this would have deprived people of the opportunity to go to university or jeopardised the quality of their education. Instead our proposals for graduate contributions mean that good institutions will be well funded into the future, if they respond to student choices. They must focus on the quality of the academic experience and the efficiency with which it is provided. We are also leading a new drive to ensure people from low-income families without a history of going to university have a fair opportunity to do so. That includes more generous help for living costs whilst at university.

The first sentence seems to assert that scholarship and research have both intrinsic value and value in generating useful innovation. However, the grammatical structure casts the intrinsic value as parenthetical: the sentence works perfectly if 'which have a fundamental value in themselves' is omitted, which quietly suggests that the idea of the fundamental intrinsic value of the university might be redundant. The second sentence suggests that the excellence of a university, if it does not consist in doing the high-quality research that generates innovation—and we should by now have become attuned, by the connection between Business and Innovation, too close to allow for a comma, to the assumption that innovation means new and marketable products and ideas—consists in 'contribution to the local economy'. The opportunities provided for mature students are not explained but can only, in this kind of climate, be opportunities for paid employment. Universities are 'not part of the public sector' but the title of the White Paper casts them as part of the 'system' that students are to be at the heart of. Is this a case of central government extending its powers over universities that had previously been semi-autonomous and protected by bodies such as the University Grants Committee (abolished in 1989) or the Higher Education Funding Council (that move from university to higher education again)? We are reminded ('They depend… on grants from the Exchequer') that he who pays the piper calls the tune. There then follows a clear implication that this White Paper intends to *free* higher education from government regulation, an implication so breathtaking (not least because a new quango, the Office for Fair Access—OFFA—has been set up to monitor the setting of fees and bursaries) that the parliamentary draftsman seems to have suffered a loss of grammar. 'With these have come an ever more intrusive burden of regulation': a burden may be heavy but can hardly be 'intrusive', and it is not plural ('have') but singular ('has').

The second paragraph makes it clear that it is 'the market' that will resolve the contradictions and tensions. Government spending—the villainous inherited deficit—is to be replaced largely, though this is not explained at this point, by fees that students will repay later in their lives. They will thus become consumers exercising choices to which universities are going to have to respond. Universities will need to focus on 'the quality of the academic experience and the efficiency with which it is provided'. I pass over the way in which talk of the quality of university education on the one hand and 'the efficiency with which it is provided' on the other comes from different worlds, as though we were to talk of dedicated, caring doctors and nurses working in an environment that prioritises driving down costs or of child protection officers guided by the need to improve the input-output ratio. Already some universities have warned that much small-group teaching will have to be replaced by large-group lectures; in my own university several seminar rooms, with chairs set out in a style to encourage discussion, have been re-equipped recently with chairs and desks in rows facing the front. They are new desks and chairs, so no doubt the quality of the 'academic experience' is protected, even if its older meanings are consigned to oblivion. Lastly, these two paragraphs of the White Paper are 1.1 and 1.2. Decimal notation is precise and scientific. In itself it constitutes a rhetoric that carries all before it.

Now my own text here, it might be said, is itself written in a particular style, perhaps even a rhetorical style. While I accept responsibility for it, I would not say that I consciously intended to achieve any stylistic effects. The sentences just seemed to emerge as they did in response to what demanded to be said. This may sound disingenuous and give rise to the suspicion that the author is not altogether to be trusted here. At any rate, it serves to make the point that an astute reader might well be better equipped to comment on it than the author. If she found there—the astute reader, responding sensitively and perceptively—things I did not think I put there, it would be no kind of answer if I were to say, 'But that is not what I meant'. These might however be the opening exchanges in a discussion that took things forward, as might be the question (which I find is a common response) 'Don't you think you are reading too much into this?' if it was asked in the spirit of a desire to explore and test my reading rather than in exasperation with the very idea that text can be interpreted.

8.3 Interpreters and Listeners

A biographical documentary about Jacques Derrida (Dick & Kofman, 2002) includes a famous sequence in which at one point, impressed by the size of Derrida's library, one of the film-makers asks him: "Did you read all these?" Derrida replies, "I was given them… I haven't read all these books here". "But you've read most of them?" insists the film-maker, to which Derrida responds, "No, three or four. But I read those really, really well". How would we estimate this as an answer to the question, 'How do you know?' or 'What are your grounds?' My grounds for saying that I can justify my interpretation of the poem by Thomas Hardy or the novel by Jane Austen are partly that I have read them very carefully and more than once. Of course I do not expect you to take my word for what I say about the poem or the novel, but it is why I have confidence when I suggest you read the third line with a different emphasis. Similarly, the psychoanalyst's or psychotherapist's grounds for saying that she thinks it is your mother who is the problem here, and not your father, is that she has been listening to you as sensitively as she can for some time… and listening to, scrutinising, her own responses to you. We have more confidence in such an interpreter or analyst than one we suspect of cursory readings, whether of poems or people. Might we take interpretation as paradigmatic of understanding, even of knowing, rather than science, explanation and *erklärung* with its picture of turning on the light and revealing what is definitely and really there?

In a seminar in the Department of English Literature, they are trying to make sense of, and reach a measured evaluation of, a particular novel, play, or poem. It is immediately clear that our confidence in an interpretation of a poem does not increase insofar as it is 'robust', a term currently favoured in social science research: talk of robustness in fact carries a suggestion of insensitivity, a sense that somebody is being altogether too brisk with the complexity of the text. We may require the interpretation to be 'rigorous', but only in the sense that we expect the interpreters to be properly thorough rather than slapdash. There is something alarming in talk of 'rigour' when we recall its literal meaning of stiffness and inflexibility. Aristotle's various remarks on precision in the *Nicomachean Ethics* are salutary. "Our discussion will be adequate if it has as much clearness as the subject-matter admits of, for precision is not to be sought for alike in all discussions" (Aristotle, 1980, I. 3, trans. Ross, 2000). Flexibility is needed rather than iron precision. An architect would go wrong in using a straight ruler on the indentations of a fluted column: he does better to employ "the leaden rule used in making the Lesbian moulding; the rule adapts itself to the shape of the stone and is not rigid" (ibid., V. 10: this is in modern times called a 'builder's comb'). We expect our literary critics to attend to the full text, and not just those features of it that support their preferred interpretation; to take account of other interpretations that have been offered in the past and those that are being made by other participants in this seminar. We are impressed by an interpretation that is rich, subtle and reflective and perhaps by one that stimulates further readings and further thought. In other words, we do not expect a good interpretation to be the last word: it may by contrast give rise to new debate and new ideas about the text. The good interpretation is one that we can engage with, argue with and develop in turn. Nobody imagines that the hallmark of a good seminar of this sort is the reaching of a point where everyone agrees 'We've got it—that's what the poem is all about!'—after which this particular poem can finally be laid aside. In similar terms the psychoanalyst Adam Phillips, in the first epigraph to this chapter, writes of 'translating' a person, the endless matter of exchanging interpretations and in the process creating possible meanings and even ways of living. This is as different as it could be from spotting when the interpretation has 'got it right', with the implication that we can now stop.

This way of thinking of things, I find, creates deep unease in some people. 'On your own account of it, this business could go on forever! Who is to say what makes for a good interpretation rather than a bad one?' Here is the germ of the idea that such readings are purely subjective. But of course they are not: the good reader locates her reading firmly in the text, rather than, for instance, in what the literary theorist I.A. Richards (1929) called 'mnemonic irrelevances', such as that the poem reminds you of a romantic evening you spent in Barcelona; she can relate it helpfully to other poems by the same author; she knows how to read it so that the music of the poem can be heard and so on. This is a long way from the one, right and conclusive interpretation, but it is a long way from mere subjectivity too. We might note four further points here. First, the good reader shows good judgement. She is alert to the features of *this* text. (She responds to *it* rather than to something she vaguely or lazily thinks is there). I.A. Richards, again (ibid.), showed how often even a relatively sophisticated reader (Cambridge undergraduates at least) misquoted the poem they were analysing. She attunes herself to it rather than bringing to bear a rigid (and in this sense rigorous) model for interpreting all poems indifferently, as though there could be a method for such things. She brings *herself* to it, being prepared to be moved emotionally by the poem as well as being prepared to be shown that she has got parts of it—perhaps all of it—wrong. Secondly, although readers may not converge on a single, authoritative interpretation, nevertheless, literary criticism displays progress. Certain ways of reading a Shakespeare poem ('How many children had Lady Macbeth?' the critic L.C. Knights famously asked in a publication of 1933, in order to point up the absurdity of one approach) have disappeared in the face of devastating criticism and are unlikely to re-emerge (Knights, 1979). Third, being now liberated from the idea that a good seminar is one that reaches 'the right answer', we can contemplate the possibility that a good seminar has what might be called 'internal goods'. It is one where the participants listen to each other respectfully, where nuances of language are cultivated, where the text under consideration is given, so to speak, a fair hearing. Patience, receptivity and irony are among the virtues here. Finally, the kind of seminar that we are imagining *brings into being* the text to which it responds. (I put this with deliberate paradox. To make the point briefly: no-one imagines that Emily Dickinson—say—set out to write a 'deconstructive' poem. But a 'deconstructive' reading is not for that reason ruled out.)

It is not only texts that we read. You read a friend's behaviour as indicative of depression, perhaps. Your interpretation is properly tentative, offered with some care, even anxiety: 'You seem depressed; is that right?' Or: 'if I said I thought you were feeling depressed, I wonder how you would respond to that'. Your friend may reject your suggestion, and his account of why he is behaving the way he is may give you further food for thought. Have you been thoughtless and simply misread him? By contrast, might his rejection of your diagnosis actually be a further symptom of his withdrawal into depression; is this an example of denial? Just as in the case of the literature seminar, you must respond to *this* person, rather than bringing to bear general diagnostic skills. You must put yourself into this relationship, rather than hiding behind the deployment of skills, and there are risks involved here. Your friend's depression will not leave you untouched. You must be attentive to yourself as well as to him (for instance, am I projecting my own state of mind onto him? Am I in danger of being overimpressed by my own sensitivity?). Judgement is central. Diagnosis here is very different from the doctor's diagnosis that someone is suffering from, say, diabetes: a diagnosis to be confirmed (or otherwise) authoritatively by tests of blood and urine samples. There is no authoritative confirmation, no certainty to be reached here, no point at which it can be concluded this is definitely depression, rather than, say, a simple desire to be alone. Nevertheless, there is progress: we move beyond particular ways of thinking about depression and similar conditions; we are unlikely to return to the mediaeval theory of the humours, according to which melancholy is a biological given, caused by a preponderance of black bile. And just as in the case of the poetry seminar there are 'internal goods', so in your conversation with your friend, the very process of listening sympathetically, of taking him seriously, of being non-judgemental and so on is at least as important as reaching any kind of 'diagnosis'. Perhaps it is the process itself that is the crucial thing: the thought, perhaps, behind Simone Weil's famous remark that "Those who are unhappy have no need for anything in this world but people capable of giving them their attention" (Weil, 1951) and behind some understandings of psychoanalysis as a 'talking cure' (more accurately a 'listening cure', as Adam Phillips several times remarks). The distinction between discovery and creation is far from clear here too: even if your friend agrees that you've seen into his heart (perhaps particularly if he does), it is possible that you have brought into being a new view of himself, on his part, rather than seen something that was already there. (Thus, users of the mental health services can be persuaded that they are 'episodic psychotics', rather than simply prone to getting into a bit of a state from time to time: much more could be said here.)

A third example is more conventionally part of 'social science research'. Imagine that we are investigating why in a particular area of the UK an unusually high number of girls between the ages of 12 and 16 years become pregnant and choose to continue with their pregnancies and keep their babies when they are born. We might hypothesise, after many interviews and other discussions, that (by contrast with a discourse that treats these girls as 'irresponsible') choosing to keep and bring up their babies is, for these girls in an area of deep economic and social deprivation where they have few opportunities for satisfying work, the most responsible thing they can do. Nothing else will give them the same sense that what they are doing is meaningful or confer upon them the status of adulthood in the eyes of their peers. Only a great deal of careful listening would justify reaching such a hypothesis, and there is every danger that in formulating a generalisation we do an injustice to particular individuals. Our testing of our hypothesis will have to be careful: it will need to be delicately phrased with much use of such expressions as 'I think what I hear you saying is…', 'I wonder if I am right in getting the impression that….' Hard evidence, of the sort attractive to those impressed by science and the model of 'what works', is barely available here. (Nevertheless, the attraction of scientific evidence persists, shown in the explanation that the girls don't know the techniques of contraception—an explanation repeated almost as often as it is shown to be false.) Once again, our attempts to interpret may begin to change what we are interpreting: when the response to an interpretation is 'You're right: *I'd never thought of it like that before*', we seem to have brought an idea, a possibility, into being. Now perhaps all the girls in the group begin to share the new idea and talk, with a defiance not seen before, of how bringing up their babies gives meaning to their lives—perhaps a meaning that they now see limited educational opportunities and low-skilled jobs could not begin to offer them. Have we, the researchers, brought to the surface an idea that was always there, though latent? Have we helped them to see the world differently— taught them something? Have we even encouraged a species of false consciousness? Finally, somewhat as in the case of a depressed friend, taking these girls seriously, treating them as adults and fully capable of insight into their own lives—the 'internal goods' of the investigation—may do at least as much good as any 'intervention' designed on the basis of what we think we have learned.

To ask these questions is to shift our thoughts about research decisively away from considerations of 'hard evidence' to those of interpretation, from *erklärung* to *verstehen*. But in the realm of *verstehen,* one element, that of listening, is under-theorised and has seldom been given its due. Gemma Corradi Fiumara (1990, p. 85) rightly notes that "we are the inhabitants of a culture hierarchised by a logos that knows how to speak but not how to listen and thus constantly avoids genuine dialogue". This is of course not simply a matter of not being able to identify appropriate 'listening skills'. It is worse than that: it is not clear that we have anything but a thin and debased notion of listening in our contemporary (western) world, in which it is seen principally as the poor relation of speaking, mute and passive by contrast to the active, dynamic creativity of speech. In philosophy in particular the foregrounding of *argument* (and there are gendered elements here, as well as a flavour of aggression) has pushed the importance of listening—a matter of, *inter alia*, openness, receptivity, attunedness, sensitivity—to the margins.[1]

8.4 Confidence and Certainty

The following passage from Plato's dialogue *Phaedrus* is well known but can perhaps be interpreted here in a distinctive way:

> Now in those days the god Thamus was the king of the whole country of Egypt; and he dwelt in that great city of Upper Egypt which the Hellenes call Egyptian Thebes, and the god himself is called by them Ammon. To him came Theuth and showed his inventions, desiring that the other Egyptians might be allowed to have the benefit of them; he enumerated them, and Thamus enquired about their several uses, and praised some of them and censured others, as he approved or disapproved of them. It would take a long time to repeat all that Thamus said to Theuth in praise or blame of the various arts. But when they came to letters, This, said Theuth, will make the Egyptians wiser and give them better memories; it is a specific both for the memory and for the wit. Thamus replied: O most ingenious Theuth, the parent or inventor of an art is not always the best judge of the utility or inutility of his own inventions to the users of them. And in this instance, you who are the father of letters, from a paternal love of your own children have been led to attribute to them a quality which they cannot have; for this discovery of yours will create forgetfulness in the learners' souls, because they will not use their memories; they will trust to the external written characters and not remember of themselves. The specific which you have discovered is an aid not to memory, but to reminiscence, and you give your disciples not truth, but only the semblance of truth; they will be hearers of many things and will have learned nothing; they will appear to be omniscient and will generally know nothing; they will be tiresome company, having the show of wisdom without the reality... I cannot help feeling, Phaedrus, that writing is unfortunately like painting; for the creations of the painter have the attitude of life, and yet if you ask them a question they preserve a solemn silence. And the same may be said of speeches. You would imagine that they had intelligence, but if you want to know anything and put a question to one of them, the speaker always gives one unvarying answer. And when they have been once written down they are tumbled about anywhere among those who may or may not understand them, and know not to whom they should reply, to whom not: and, if they are maltreated or abused, they have no parent to protect them; and they cannot protect or defend themselves. (Plato, *Phaedrus*, 274d–275b, Jowett's translation, 1971)

Writing, it thus appears, is inferior to speech: of course the context in this dialogue is that the young, impressionable Phaedrus has written out a speech by the sophist Lysias and learned it by heart. It is not further exposure to writing that shows him the error of his ways but live conversation with Socrates, dialectic with its familiar elements of elenchus and maieutic. It is easy, despite subtle treatments of the passage by Derrida (Derrida, 1981, 'Plato's pharmacy', 1981), among others, to fall in with the assumptions that seem to be being made here: that texts 'preserve a solemn silence' in the face of questions, when in fact they are open to the conversation of interpretation; that they 'always give one unvarying answer', when in fact texts often yield many interpretations or meanings; that the problem is that the author is not there to defend the text, when in fact the author's presence would solve little because she cannot be authoritative about what she has written.

My defence of interpretation here, such as it is, would not meet universal approval. John Guillory, for instance, in a long and searching discussion of the 'History of Criticism' (2002), writes of the way in which, in what he calls the "epistemic hierarchy of the disciplines" (ibid., p. 498), interpretation has come to be seen as a methodology of criticism rather than a methodology of the production of knowledge, i.e. of the sciences. Thus, its status is less that of any kind of secure or respectable knowledge, *episteme*, than of mere opinion, *doxa* (Guillory does not use these terms but this is clearly the distinction he intends). He writes of how "it has been notoriously difficult to give an account of the knowledge produced by interpretation that would not immediately invite invidious comparison with the sciences" (ibid.). He offers a complex narrative of how a kind of "interpretive holism generalised from the instance of the literary text" (ibid., p. 507) has emerged from the stance of opposition to science adopted by cultural criticism and the humanities to the detriment of the latter's ability to be taken seriously as producers of knowledge, with the result that the potential of an interpretive social science has never been fulfilled.

It will be clear that my own sense of the power and range of interpretation is very different: I see interpretation as able, under certain conditions, to produce statements in which we can have *confidence*, albeit always of a provisional kind, such that we do not have to crave the certainty that we have come to expect 'science' to provide. In fact I think of the problem with writing less as its *openness* to interpretation than as the expectation that interpretation will in the end yield one, true meaning: a problem less of polysemy than of univocity. The two quotations from Adam Phillips that preface this chapter point us to the thought that interpretation, whether of people or texts, is misconceived if it is thought of as the quest for 'definitive versions'. Phillips writes of "our consoling myth of interpretation" (2002, p. 104): one day we will offer the patient an accurate interpretation, she will accept it and all will be well; one day the seminar in the Department of English Literature will come to an end, having agreed on its readings of the canonical texts (and of course having agreed on just which texts are canonical). If the purpose of interpretation is not given by such possibilities, unlikely or even absurd as they are, how else can we think of its purpose?

Phillips further writes that "The words that matter most are the words we don't understand" (*ibid*. p. 105), and I end with this thought: that there is a kind of negative hermeneutics of keeping meaning in play, of "orientation towards openness" (Gadamer, 1979, p. 330), of practising a Weilian (see Weil, 1951) "waiting on" texts as on people, tolerating ambiguity, the kind of unusually attuned listening that

I alluded to above and that is part of the meaning of *Tiefenhermeneutik* or deep interpretation. At least we might think of interpretation as a continuum or long line: at one end, the right-hand one perhaps, interpretation yields meanings that while not conclusive are more than tentative. At the other end is the cultivation of listening, the quietening of the voice of what Iris Murdoch calls the 'relentless dinning ego' in the faith that things so far unheard will begin to make their presence known to us. Here we resist for as long as we can the call of the other end of the spectrum, where authors and architects can be questioned about their intentions, a degree of certainty and relief can be achieved, publications published and examination essays written.

This would be a space to dwell in, requiring time, patience and silence: almost as if it was a kind of spiritual exercise. Once, and not so very long ago, we talked of students 'reading for a degree', and the mediaeval university combined the spiritual with the academic in ways that we now tend to find uncomfortable. 'The academic experience' now suggests other goods, including those bright new tables and chairs facing the front, a state of the art Visual Learning Environment and the acquisition of employability skills. I do not mention these simply in order to denigrate them. Learning space however has other dimensions too, and the space of text is a dimension of learning that we need to recover and explore.

Note

1. This section draws in part on my unpublished paper, 'Philosophy of education as listening: the confidence to interpret', *European Conference on Educational Research*, Vienna, September 2009.

References

Aristotle. (1980). *The Nicomachean ethics* (D. Ross, Trans.). Oxford/New York: Oxford University Press.
Booth, W. C. (2004). *The rhetoric of rhetoric*. Oxford: Blackwell.
Department for Business Information & Skills. (2011). *Students at the heart of the system*. http://c561635.r35.cf2.rackcdn.com/11-944-WP-students-at-heart.pdf. Accessed 28 Oct 2011.
Derrida, J. (1981). Plato's pharmacy. In *Dissemination* (B. Johnson, Trans.). Chicago: Chicago University Press.
Descartes, R. (2000). *Discourse on method and related writings* (D. M. Clarke, Trans.). London: Penguin.
Dick, K., & Kofman, A. Z. (2002). *Derrida*. London, ICA Projects: Jane Doe Films.
Fiumara, G. C. (1990). *The other side of language: A philosophy of listening*. London: Routledge.
Gadamer, H.-G. (1979). *Truth and method*. London: Sheed and Ward.
Guillory, J. (2002). The Sokal affair and the history of criticism. *Critical Inquiry, 28*(2), 470–508.

Knights, L. C. (1979). *How many children had Lady Macbeth? An essay in the theory and practice of Shakespeare criticism. In 'Hamlet' and other Shakespearean essays*. Cambridge, England: Cambridge University Press.

Phillips, A. (2000). *Promises, promises*. London: Faber and Faber.

Phillips, A. (2002). *Equals*. London: Faber and Faber.

Plato. Phaedrus (B. Jowett, Trans., 1871). In *The dialogues of Plato*, 4 Vols. Oxford, UK: Oxford University Press

Richards, I. A. (1929). *Practical criticism*. London: Kegan Paul.

Weil, S. (1951). *Waiting on God* (E. Crauford, Trans.). New York: G.P. Putnam's Sons.

Chapter 9
Exploring Educational Research as a Multilayered Discursive Space

Stijn Mus

In this chapter I would like to use a spatial metaphor to describe the pursuit of educational research. I will conceive educational research as a discursive space and explore how this space is to be conceived. I will argue that the meaning of educational research is best understood by focusing upon multiple discursive layers.

In the heydays of positivist hegemony, the researcher approached (or did not approach) the field from a distant hill, carrying a set of binoculars. His invisibility safeguarded the grand ideal of scientific objectivity. His binoculars drew the reality under investigation close to his distant eye, while his scientific sourcebook provided the means to distil general claims from his meticulous observations.

This stance towards the field was criticised from different angles. The researcher on the hill could perhaps claim to avoid any interference in his field of study; a steadily increasing part of his audience began to question the suitability of his toolbox. Not only where certain area of the field persistently blocked from view—despite the fact that he moved to another hill from time to time—the lenses of his binoculars also seemed to deform the aspects of reality that were in his view. And although the researcher could provide us with a view on the subject's behaviour, the subject's voice did not reach to the top of the hill and was—subsequently—absent from the research. Finally, questions were raised about the appropriateness to treat the subject like this. The researcher began to appear as an indecent voyeur.

Confronted with both the ethical dubiousness of the research methodology and the growing concerns about the blind spots on the maps that were drawn on the hill, a new generation of researchers began to approach the field differently. Convinced that the subject should have a say in the research process, these researchers left their high altitude positions and descended into the muddy field itself. This change of place involved a change of the rules of the game as well. The old ideal of detachment was exchanged for the new ideal of subjective agency. Encouraged to restore the gap

S. Mus (✉)
Faculty of Psychology and Educational Sciences, Ghent University, Ghent, Belgium
e-mail: stijn.mus@ugent.be

P. Smeyers et al. (eds.), *Educational Research: The Importance and Effects of Institutional Spaces*, Educational Research 7, DOI 10.1007/978-94-007-6247-3_9,
© Springer Science+Business Media Dordrecht 2013

created by behaviourist technocrats between the social scientific subject and its representation, these qualitative researchers urged to let the subject speak for herself, to refrain from abstraction and to make an effort to fix, preserve and transmit the alleged initial meaning of the social situation under investigation. Thus, qualitative research sets itself the aim to save the subject and her meanings from the reductionism characteristic of quantitative social science. This ambition was marked by a move back to the 'rough ground' of social reality itself, with the ambition, we could say, to 'make the stone feel stony'—as Shklovsky once marked the modernist project (cited in Beaumont, 2007, p. 98). Truthfulness was to be found as close as possible to the subject itself. Faithful, vivid and accurate recording of the subject's words and its context of acquisition were the pathways to the meaningful dimension of the subject, previously left aside in the name of objectivity. Thus, this newly conceived research space was marked by the twofold engine of excessive empiricism—to ensure qualitative research of its truth-value—combined with the adoption of the discursive mode of Realism to fix and preserve the regained territory of authenticity.

The irony of this situation lies in the fact that the realist mode—which is here brought in as the salvation operation to restore the link between subject and object—signifies precisely the opposite in the world of literature, from which the realist mode has been derived. Within the world of literary theory, literary realism is generally regarded as the most rhetorical and seductive form of discourse in the literary landscape.

The sharpest critique on realism was staged by Roland Barthes. As Eagleton paraphrased it:

> In Barthes's view, […]. Realist literature tends to conceal the socially relative or constructed nature of language: it helps to confirm the prejudice that there is a form of 'ordinary' language which is somehow natural. This natural language gives us reality 'as it is': it does not — like Romanticism or Symbolism - distort it into subjective shapes, but represents the world to us as God himself might know it. […] In the ideology of realism or representation, words are felt to link up with their thoughts or objects in essentially right and incontrovertible ways: the word becomes the only proper way of viewing this object or expressing this thought. (Eagleton, 2008, p. 117)

What Barthes' critique suggests is that the idea that realism enables us to bypass interpretation, mediation, text and researcher, to look straight through it to behold the object in its authenticity, is nothing more than a powerful textual illusion. In short, it looks like he criticised the realist mode for wrongfully picturing those qualities which scientific realism seems to adhere to. And while his critique is more than four decades old, it still characterises much of the general feeling towards Realism in the domain of literary theory today.[1] Interestingly, within literary theory, the lack of truthfulness is not attributed to the absence of empirical correspondence, but precisely to the feature which scientific realism employs as truth's safeguard. So the eagerness to shake off the lifeless conventions of quantification and the longing for a reality behind the sterility of scientific abstraction apparently made the qualitative researcher blind for the conventionalism of the newly adopted mode.

From this point, we can move in two directions. We might either shield ourselves by postulating a fundamental difference between the Realist mode in science and in literature, reiterating the common story that science and the arts are fundamentally separate realms. Or, we might accept that by venturing out into a territory traditionally occupied by literary theorists, their insights may apply to social scientific accounts tributary to Realist discourse as well. In what follows, I will take the second option, as I think that an elaboration of this view may enable us to understand the question of meaning in educational research in relation to the way the field operates. In order to do so, I will consider qualitative research as a multilayered discursive space. That is, I will try to analyse the origin of meaning in qualitative inquiry by focussing back from the reality behind the text to the discursive spaces opened up by the text.

The metaphor I wish to develop then is to conceive of educational research texts as multistoried-buildings (with the semantic connotation to multistory as a welcome coincidence). Educational research, then, moves in different discursive spaces simultaneously. I argue that it is the *reception* of the interaction between these different levels which are the determinants for its meaning.

Let me first give some examples of different discursive levels which are often 'present' in research texts (without the ambition to be exhaustive). In pointing these out, I might sometimes appear a bit speculative, but for the purpose of this chapter, it suffices that the images I project are somehow recognisable:

- At the most visible level, we can identify the discourse *of* the subject, made present in the form of interview answers or testimonial, either through direct representation of speech or in paraphrases; this is—along with the next level—the narrative sublevel the meaning is often asserted to stem from.
- Second, within the framing of the research, the subject is assigned a subject position; a space is created for the subject to occupy, or, if you like, the subject is created, written into existence. Thus, the subject appears as a motivated student, a timid child, a silenced woman, etc.
- Related, but slightly different, is the space the subject is assigned *as subject of social scientific research*. This space consists of certain dispositions—like innocence or authenticity, to give some familiar examples, which reflect some of the prevailing presuppositions of qualitative research—and are themselves subject to the swings of intellectual fashion that also shape the self-conception of the researcher.
- Next, there are different similes to conceptualise the research site and—subsequently—the researcher's identity. To point out just two examples, I can mention the research space as archaeological site (which posits the researcher as excavator) or the research space as political arena—in which the researcher might appear as emancipator. This demonstrates that the researcher does create a subject position not just for the participants she works with but also for herself. In this sense, it also shows that the researcher is an interested party in the research; her identity is *quite literally* at stake.
- Other than that, it goes without saying that research in the social sciences somehow relates to other discourses which structure society, either in accordance or in opposition. I assume that the most obvious example here would be the Marxist critique often tacitly present in social scientific analysis, but another example might be the implicit endorsement of meritocracy or, conversely, its 'exposure' as a myth.

Obviously, all of these levels—and I am sure there are many more—are interconnected, and each discursive level's presuppositions and tropes carry consequences for the meaning of other levels, which can be either conflicting or mutually reinforcing. Thus, the understanding of the researcher's role and how he moves in the field will suggest a certain reading of the subject's voice or will reveal or suggest a stance towards certain cultural master-narratives. For example, the staging of the subject's voice as 'authentic' often finds its expression in specific written representation of speech—the excessive use of direct discourse, verbatim quotation, the use of slang, etc.—yet this formal feature might acquire other meanings in, for example, the metanarratives which structure society, in which certain speech representations signify a certain social class. So the tropes which are employed in one level of the text have consequences for the 'reading'—and evoked meanings—of the other levels too.

Yet sometimes, I presume this 'play of meaning' is used (semi)consciously, when certain tropes are employed for their effect on one level of the text, while they are being legitimised by another. This is, for instance, the case with the use of 'direct discourse' of the subject, which is explained or presented as an epistemological device, while it actually serves a differed purpose—by supporting other meanings—such as the underscoring of the researcher's emancipatory intentions, the endorsement of the discourse of authenticity or the attribution of certain interpretations to the subject, even when there is no real epistemic ground for these matters.

Of course, the space of qualitative research itself carries its own set of conventions and tropes too. We work with 'subjects' rather than speaking about the 'object of research', thereby evoking and postulating an equal relationship within the research process. Hedging strategies, like the delimitation of the scope of an interpretive claim, has the—I dare say sometimes intended—effect of evoking an image of modesty and trustworthiness and thus to ward of suspicion or pacify possible reader hesitation. Might it be possible then to explain something of the popularity of the Realist mode in qualitative research through these intricate balances of meanings and connotations? Might it be that the realist mode proves so valuable on these matters that it outbalances the critique which is staged on the literary front?

In order to bridge this analysis with the implications of the diffuse nature of meaning in qualitative research, I would like to focus on the discourse along which the researcher understands himself. I argued that through this discourse, the researcher acquires a subject position in the text. I also argued that this site is subject to what I called 'the swings of intellectual fashion'. This is to say that there are institutional ready-made patterns of subjectivity—or subject positions—which the (young) researcher is invited to assume or occupy.

I content that the default image of the educational researcher today (more questioned than in earlier times but still the default image) is the researcher as excavator. This image depicts the researcher as independent from the constraints of culture, power and god, only tributary to Truth itself, who proves his right by an appeal to incontestable proof and evidence. In its iconic form, it is the image, of Galileo and Copernicus. So, on top of the tailor-made set of methods and procedures that come along with the image of the researcher as excavator—a 'possible identity' in which researchers are being socialised at university departments and scientific institutions—the appeal of an empirical ground for interpretations thus also springs from the morally loaded connotations with whom this image is infused. In the scope of this contribution, it would lead us too far to illustrate this in detail, but the tenor of some of the warnings for the relativist abyss post-modern or constructivist theories would allegedly lead up to is testimony to this moral dimension.[2] When the intellectual battle against postmodernist conceptions sometimes reveals traces of moral outrage, I believe it often has to do with the strain it puts on this scientific self-image. Now, if the previous analysis on the nature of meaning in qualitative research has some bearing, meaning is too elusive, too fluid and, especially, too scattered to retrace its origin to the confines of the dataset, to authorial intentions or to subjective agency, I argue, therefore, that the image of the researcher as excavator is fundamentally at odds with the commitment to make meaning the primary focus of qualitative educational research. To illuminate this claim, I shall now look a bit closer to the issue of meaning and its specific nature and try to open up a space for a possible alternative.

As my brief analysis suggested, the analysis of the different discursive spaces might prove more useful to grasp the advent of meaning in educational research. In what follows, then, I argue that research which takes the issue of meaning seriously would benefit from rebuilding its legitimacy along these lines. Doing so would imply that it restates its aim to the disclosure of new areas of possible subjectivity, rather than extolling the prestige that is attached to the traditional role of research to 'mirror reality'. The metaphor which characterises the researcher, then, is not the excavator, but the artist, the novelist or the poet.

Let me try to envisage, then, what the conduct of educational research along these lines would imply. As my previous analysis illustrates, meaning emerges against the backdrop of broader structures of cultural signification. I assume that research which makes the question of meaning its primary object cannot but make this structure part of its analysis and aims to articulate, defend and legitimise a meaning which somehow departs from, or critically engages with, traditional categories and common-sense meanings. It cannot just appeal to the everyday meanings or explanations of educational events by default as doing so would obviously result in the production of mere tautologies—and would subsequently beg the very thing which is in dispute. Thus conceived, research acquires the form of a cultural discussion, in which the task of the researcher is to open up a public space to contemplate the possible meanings of its object in a broader context. In this regard, Ricoeur states that "the meaning of the text is not behind the text, but in front of it. It is not something hidden, but something disclosed" (Ricoeur, 1974, p. 106). What Ricoeur's claim suggests, then, is that research which takes the issue of meaning seriously is not driven by the question "what does it mean?" but rather poses the question "what *could* it mean?" Research, then, is the pursuit to construct possible meanings and to give them an intersubjective—that is, a shared, public—character by gaining them legitimacy and recognition on the cultural forum. This suggests that for educational research to exceed the character of truisms and commonplaces, it ought to take an active, performative role in this process.

This conceptualisation of qualitative research as a revitalisation of public meaning might also reveal one of its paradoxes. For how can we make something subject to investigation when it is part of our doxic structure, and therefore, 'beyond interrogation'? It is precisely at this point that the adoption of the metaphor of the literary artist might prove most useful. Parallel to what the poet does, we could reconceptualise the task of social scientific research as to make reality susceptible to change through *poetic reconfiguration*. In order to do so, the researcher must both develop a refined intuition for the spirit of the age and develop the skill to articulate it accurately, two things which are clearly intertwined. Thus, the paradoxical challenge that awaits the qualitative researcher is to find words to capture a new meaning that is in a sense 'waiting', just beyond reach of our present expressive capacities, for articulation (Hagberg, 2008, p. 210). As such, qualitative research, as a cultural moment, can be conceived as a recursive process (Iser, 2007, p. 324), caught in a permanent cycle of feedback loops between cultural description and cultural performance. From the acknowledgement of the primacy of meaning, then, follows the epistemic priority of the imagination over empiricism to bridge the seemingly natural and the not yet conceivable.

Another consequence of the primacy of meaning in qualitative research, follows from its fluid, temporal and shifting nature, which ought to be taken into account and, I would say, cherished, for such research must acknowledge that its object is in permanent flux, susceptible to change through the meanderings of living culture and the 'life of language' (Eldridge, 1996, p. 4). Foremost, it must take into account that its final product will undergo yet another hermeneutic circle—enter yet another space—before its meaning will materialise. This also means that the research text will inevitably start to live a life of its own and evoke different interpretations by different readers. Rather than making an effort to contain and steer this interpretive moment, educational researchers could stimulate this contribution to the cultural conversation for which they provide the ground. Doing so implies that qualitative research refrains from proclaiming fixed truths or revealing some sort of didactic message. Educational research, in this outlook, takes up the task to enrich and fertilise practice but eschews the task of prescribing it as some (more or less hidden) sort of moral guidebook.

The space of educational research, then, becomes a public arena in which common-sense meanings can be challenged and possible meanings can be discussed. This public character of the space of educational research needs to be defended not just in the face of the threat of the hegemony of a reductive scientific ethos but also from adopting a ghetto mentality under the seductive appeals of authenticity. In order for the educational research space to remain an inclusive one, its borders should be neither essential nor ontological, but imaginative.

Notes

1. Though literary theory has in recent years seen some efforts to 'reclaim' realism (see Matthew Beaumont's *'Adventures in Realism'*, James Wood's *How Fiction Works*), *and thus to grant it a more positive connotation*, the authors who engage

in this project depart from the naïve realist conception that text mirrors nature 'as it is'. This does not mean that realism is always exerted—and this certainly goes for its use outside the domain of literature.

2. Surely I am exaggerating? Let us listen then to Richard Pring: "If only the self-styled radicals of educational research, who subscribe to the equal validity of each person's socially constructed reality, would realize the justification they are providing to the Orwellian managers who seek to transform our understanding of education to their own image and likeness" (Pring, 2004, p. 212).

References

Beaumont, M. (2007). *Adventures in realism*. Malden, MA/Oxford: Blackwell.
Eagleton, T. (2008). *Literary theory: An introduction*. Minneapolis, MN: University of Minnesota Press.
Eldridge, R. (Ed.). (1996). *Beyond representation: Philosophy and poetic imagination*. Cambridge, UK: Cambridge University Press.
Hagberg, G. (2008). *Describing ourselves: Wittgenstein and autobiographical consciousness*. Oxford, England: Clarendon.
Iser, W. (2007). Culture: A recursive process. In J. Gibson & W. Huemer (Eds.), *A sense of the world: Essays on fiction, narrative, and knowledge* (pp. 318–331). London/New York: Routledge.
Pring, R. (2004). *Philosophy of education: Aims, theory, common sense and research*. London: Continuum.
Ricoeur, P. (1974). Metaphor and the main problem of hermeneutics. *New Literary History, 6,* 95–110.

Chapter 10
The Spaces of Mathematics: Dynamic Encounters Between Local and Universal

Karen François, Kathleen Coessens, and Jean Paul Van Bendegem

10.1 Introduction: To Be Situated or Not

> *... there is no activity that is not situated.*
>
> (Lave & Wenger, 1991, p. 33)

There is a lot of research activity around the notion of 'situatedness' in knowledge and learning theories: from 'situated cognition' (Clancey, 1997; Lave & Wenger, 1991) over 'situated knowledge' (Haraway, 1991) to 'situated learning' (e.g. Lang, 2011; Wilson & Myers, 2000). These are but some of the notions and authors that represent a, most often, social constructivist view on knowledge.

On the one hand, these inquiries open up new fields for education as well as for the sociology of scientific knowledge, recognising cultural, social, political and economical differences. On the other hand, stressing too much a relativistic and local view prevents creative and human processes that could transgress situatedness. For example, certain processes inherent to specific ways of transmission of theories and all sorts of knowledge as well as concerning the flexibility and possibilities of adaptation of the human being can challenge the local. Indeed, we do share after all with one another common biological roots that largely determine a set of basic behaviours, for example, to express power relations in a community. Moreover, the local is not fixed as societies change over generations due to new knowledge, techniques or by way of human mobility and migration. And finally, every 'local' has a periphery which is in connection with another 'local' and as such subject to neighbour influences.

K. François (✉) • K. Coessens • J.P. Van Bendegem
Centre for Logic and Philosophy of Science (CLWF), Vrije Universiteit Brussel (VUB),
Brussels, Belgium
e-mail: Karen.Francois@vub.ac.be

P. Smeyers et al. (eds.), *Educational Research: The Importance and Effects*
of Institutional Spaces, Educational Research 7, DOI 10.1007/978-94-007-6247-3_10,
© Springer Science+Business Media Dordrecht 2013

However, the notion of situatedness itself suggests closure: when something is 'situated', it is embedded in a specific 'situation' which refers to a rather closed, unique position in time and space. All situated acts are then part of different unique situations, and it becomes difficult to interact with another, even more difficult to encounter the other. Moreover, by labelling all epistemic action as 'situated', such a view, contrary to its own aims, supports/sustains a rather static institutional way of fixing theories and educational curricula concerning knowledge and education. If something is 'situated', it is defined, limited and fixed and as such can be filled in by way of local institutionally defined aims, embedded in some long (conservative) tradition of knowledge and know-how. Using 'situatedness' then becomes another way of classifying experiences and contexts—with all the danger the notion 'classification' bears when it comes to human experience and action.

This contrasts with the ephemeral character of the experience of 'situatedness': like the experience of 'now', every situation is always shifting and dynamic, impossible to delineate once and forever. While theories and representations are artificially 'immobilised' in a certain sense, there is a danger of talking about 'situating' and as such an underestimation of the process-like evolution of all actions and activities. Theories, practices and humans are always part of diverse 'situations', and situations overlap with other situations, evolve into other situations. This urges us to deconstruct the polarity between local and global and consider epistemic activities in a more dynamic framework of multiple shifting and interacting 'situations'.

The tension between the necessary recognition of the notion of situatedness in mathematical contexts and an informed view of math's possibilities to overcome situatedness, lurking at a notion of universality—and as such between the local and the global—is at the heart of this article. We will argue that mathematics is part of diverse situated contexts, temporarily 'fixed' by institutions and scientific communities. At the same time, to evolve, it tries to escape contextual centres, opening new trajectories and addressing in a plural way the human being.

After this introduction, the second section will address briefly the notion of situatedness of knowledge and of the knower. By way of a framework mapping epistemic, social-cultural and ecological parameters concerning context of origin and context of use (or reception) as ongoing processes, we will explore the complexity and difficulty of defining 'situatedness'.

In the third section, we will bring to the fore, by way of a philosophical dialogue, how to escape polarities between local and global, between situated and universal, making the nuance for both oppositions. Therefore, we present Husserl's analysis of the construction of objectivity as a move from the individual local knowledge— the original being-itself-there—towards the universal space of objective knowledge with geometry as the example *par excellence*. By introducing the work of Haraway, we explain the situatedness of objectivity itself and the richness of the conglomerate of diverse situated knowledges. Especially the situatedness of the 'strangers' becomes now a condition sine qua non for the construction of 'embodied' objectivity.

In the fourth and final section, we come back to the case of mathematics to consider the situatedness inside mathematical practice. A first example will develop an academic mathematical research case on the Coxeter system. The second example will explain the situatedness of mathematical practices as such being academic mathematical practices or local 'nonliterate' mathematical practices. With this final example we consider the conditions of learning mathematics and its institutionalisation in math classes expressed in terms of background and foreground of the learners.

10.2   A Tentative Framework of Situatedness

The theory of situated cognition…claims that every human thought is adapted to the environment, that is, situated, because what people perceive, how they conceive of their activity, and what they physically do develop together.

(Clancey, 1997, pp. 1–2)

Every activity involving knowledge is embedded in a specific epistemic, social and ecological situation: bound to local environments, cultural contexts and scientific expertise as well as to the biological cognitive and perceptual specificity of the human species (Baird, 2003; Knuuttila & Honkela, 2005). Practices and theories of knowledge are both part of specific settings in time and space, of particular scientific and social communities and cultural world views. While developing a coherent proper system of knowledge, these practices and theories seldom develop in total autarky, as autonomous closed systems: they share and exchange knowledge with other communities and world views over time and space, by way of transmission and interaction—by marriage, economic or power relations. But transmission of knowledge implies a space of communication where two different contexts meet: the context of origin referring to the creation of the representation and the context of use where the knowledge representation is received.

The context of origin or initiative is the initial situation in which a community or individual, having discovered or developed some knowledge, describes and represents it: it is the primary context of encoding—or re-encoding in the case of a revision of older knowledge. This context contains the how and why of a knowledge fact or theory, surrounded by traces of the own specific epistemic, social-cultural and ecological situation. In this process of construction the choice, the form, the design, the content and the purpose of the knowledge are permeated by this specific triple context. This process originates in a web of agent-based or community-based parameters as well as broader external context-based parameters. The available epistemic and material artefacts as well as the projections, interpretations and expectations of scientific communities and knowledge contexts orient the new knowledge output. A fine example from the mathematical world is the development in different cultures across the globe of counting systems (see, e.g., the classic Menninger, 1969). Even in those cases where parts of the human body are used as labels, the variety from culture to culture is enormous. Even a restriction to the use of the fingers of the hands, does not lead to a unique choice. This shows by the way that the argument that base 10 for numerals is somehow 'natural' because of our 10 digits is invalid.

The initial content of knowledge is outlined by the ontological and epistemic commitments of the knower and his or her scientific community: intentions and urgent questions, background knowledge and expertise. The development of this knowledge will be transmitted by way of a mode of representation which is dependent upon the prevailing level of symbolic and representational structures. The modes of transmission of knowledge all incorporate different levels of abstraction depending on the level of technological and knowledge expertise and the available possibilities of semiotic translation. Moreover, the space and modes of the transmission in itself are also subject to dynamics on the epistemic, social-cultural and ecological level and as such influence the context of use. This means, for example, that relativity theory in physics has been received differently in the 1950s than in the 1990s, not only because of a different context of use, but also because of evolving ways of transmission—for example, evolving status of the body of knowledge, new technologies, different conventions and communicative strategies.

Knowledge activities are embedded in a broader context containing a double contingency. On one hand these are dependent of the contingent context of science, knowledge and technology—the prevailing state of the art, social and intra-disciplinary conventions and human-made rules. The body of available knowledge decides which questions and answers and which translations and representational structures can emerge and which others remain undiscovered or unacceptable (Rescher, 1999). The same knowledge, object or theory, can be developed and represented differently in different times, by different communities of practice, inside different disciplinary and intellectual niches. On the other hand, scientific and intellectual communities are not closed upon themselves and their activities are overwhelmed by the contingency and complexity of the world and constrained by the available affordances—natural, epistemic and material resources. Earth-bound laws, processes, materials and dimensions have a strong impact on human discovery and understanding: matter constrains. This means that ecologically available models flirt with socially accepted ontological characteristics, merging in imperceptible ways—at least for the culture at hand—social and ecological constraints. Choices in the community on the level of policy, be it economic, educational or social, and its resulting administrative applications too restrain, or at least orient, possible developments. This complex actor-community-environment interaction influences knowledge development and representation, interferes with the choice over relevance and importance and obstructs every 'view from nowhere'.

What is launched from a certain context of origin always meets another reality in the space of its audience. Once an object of knowledge is launched into the world, it is met by other situations, where it is received, transformed and differently represented following different modes of transmission (see Fig. 10.1). Carefully created inside a particular context of initiative, it encounters other contexts of reception. Here it is received by a user or community with a certain, possibly different, amount

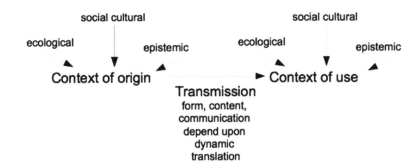

Fig. 10.1 Dynamic frame of context of origin and context of use

or kind of knowledge, skills and competences, in a specific intellectual, social and technological culture. Possibilities or incompatibilities of translation and meaning, levels of abstraction and competence at the side of reception as well as the specific content, design, form and inherent purpose of the knowledge itself—depending on the context of origin—have to be compatible to a high degree, if the matching between context of origin and context of use will be fruitful. Gaps between both contexts will be inherent to the competence of the user, the complexity and situatedness of the representation, and, more broadly, cultural lags (Coessens & Van Bendegem, 2006).

With the example of Husserl, in the next section, we will explain how originally Husserl analysed the move from the context of discovery to the context of the universal claim of objectivity of (ideal) objects, from the initial context of origin or initiative to the view from nowhere.

10.3   Situated Mathematics in Process: Moving Local Spaces

10.3.1   Towards Objectivity: Husserl

> *Clearly, then, geometry must have arisen out of a* first *acquisition, out of first creative activities.*
>
> (Husserl, 1962/1970b, p. 355)

In his search for a robust foundation of mathematics Husserl became aware of the 'situatedness' of human's search for a universal and objective knowledge of which mathematics is a perfect example. Husserl explains it with the example of the Pythagorean theorem: this theorem is and remains the Pythagorean theorem no matter the time or place and irrespective of what language it is expressed in (Husserl, 1962/1970b, p. 357). He analyses the process of how the individual knowing subject is floating away from its 'context of discovery'—in Husserl's terms its 'original being itself there'—towards a universal time and space.

Objectivity is often thought as the very opposite of subjectivity in the sense that both concepts have nothing to do with each other. At the same time the notion of objectivity is discussed in terms of the possibility of its 'pure' and transcendental existence. Both interpretations of objectivity have to do with a conception of objectivity as if objectivity has fallen from the sky. The question remains how the subjective situated subject can enter a (more) universal realm where (ideal or real) objects exist no matter the time or place and irrespective of what language it is expressed in. This ultimate surpass of the local space is the constitution of objectivity as Husserl (1962/1970b) explains in his 'The origin of geometry'. With the example of geometry par excellence, he argues how a local, internal, personal and psychological process of consciousness evolves into the universality of the objectivity of objects. Through the constitution of objectivity, one surpasses the local space and place to enter the universal one, though not without any concession, viz. the loss of the real world and the disconnection from the lifeworld—to speak in Husserl's words.

Husserl analysed the way in which objectivity is constructed and thus is characterised as a human practice. In this sense, it was Husserl who gave a humanised interpretation of the growth of objectivity and its construction founded in the real subjectivity or in the context of origin as we introduced this concept in the introduction. From now on, objectivity and subjectivity cannot longer be seen as discrete opposite concepts. Both concepts, objectivity and subjectivity, are indissolubly connected in a dynamic process of the construction of a universal meaning. Husserl describes the process in which a local subjective impression becomes the founding ground of the growth of objectivity, not only in relation to ideal objects, but also connected to the so-called material or real objects. In his analysis, Husserl takes geometrical objects (which are ideal mathematical objects) as the examples par excellence. However, the topic of the constitution of objectivity is also applicable to real objects insofar objective sciences studying those real objects—like physics and later on human sciences—found there objectivity through the application of mathematics.

Husserl formulates his initial question concerning the transformation of the local, psychic and subjective construction to the intersubjective universal objectivity as follows:

> But the question arises again: How does the latter [the primally establishing geometer], in its "ideality", thereby become objective? [...] But how does the intrapsychically constituted structure arrive at an intersubjective being of its own as an ideal object which, as "geometrical," is anything but a real psychic object, even though it has arisen psychically? Let us reflect. (Husserl, 1962/1970b, p. 359)

Husserl's solution to transcend subjectivity and to constitute the objectivity of objects consists of a transformation from the subjective and original being-itself-there of the objects to the intersubjective ideal objectivity (François, 2011a). This process passes off different layers by which the intersubjectivity increases and whereby objectivity is gradually produced. Objectivity as a product of human practice is not a monolithic, one-dimensional and discrete entity. It is a property of an object which is based on a local, intra-subjective and creative activity that evolves by way of an intersubjective to an objective status. In Husserl's analysis, the constitution of objectivity passes

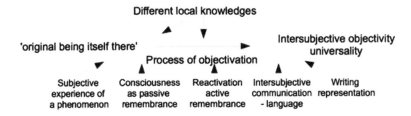

Fig. 10.2 Husserl's frame of the process of objectivation

through five phases. (1) The first phase is a first creative activity. It consists of the individual subjection to an original being-itself-there by which the subjection originates from the experience of a phenomenon. It is the stage of the first evidence, "the self-evidence". (2) During the second phase, the original being-itself-there which appears to the individual shall fade away into the passivity of consciousness. As time passes, the original being-itself-there by which the individual is confronted shall turn into the passivity of the flowingly fading consciousness. It is the stage of the passive remembrance and of the condition of "retention". (3) In the third phase, the passive remembrance can be reactivated by which the passive remembrance becomes an active remembrance. It is the stage of the possibility of remembrance and of the "reawakening". (4) An individual with an active remembrance has the possibility to communicate with another one. It is the intersubjective stage of communication where language becomes a central instrument of the construction of objectivity. (5) Finally, we enter the possibility to put the communication in writing, to establish the communication by which it becomes entrenched. This final phase of the process of constitution is the stage of sedimentation. Through this final step of sedimentation, a definite transformation is realised from a material to an ideal reality by the use of symbols and of language. Local spaces have made way for universal spaces of ideal objects such as mathematical objects (Fig. 10.2).

With this phenomenological meaning of the concept of objectivity, both objectivity and subjectivity are no longer seen as the very opposite of each other. Instead, both concepts are indissolubly connected with each other in one and the same process of building up a universal realm. It is within the bounds of human capacities and of human consciousness to constitute an objective and universal world by manipulating local and situated knowledges. It is precisely through the option of objectivity that we can change the 'situated' world which is the only world we can enter by its appearances. This process is not without any price. To Husserl (1962/1970a) the objective world is not the 'real' world. The 'real' world presents itself as a multidimensional plurality of local knowledges instead of the objective world which is only one world, a unique world and at the same time a universal world because it is always the same world for everyone. The objective world is indeed a product of the human subjective constitution. The objective world is an utmost product of subjectivity where local and universal places and spaces are connected in one constitutional process.

10.3.2   By Situatedness: Haraway

> Objectivity is not about dis-engagement, but about mutual and *usually unequal structuring,*
> *about taking risks in a world where 'we' are permanently mortal, that is, not in 'final'*
> *control.*

(Haraway, 1991, p. 201)

In her 'Situated knowledges', Haraway (1991) aims to reconsider objectivity. Therefore, she exceeds the ancient opposition between objectivity and subjectivity and hence follows in the footsteps of Husserl who connected both poles, the universal (objectivity) and the local (subjectivity), into one process of the construction of objective knowledge. The meaning of 'situated knowledge' in the work of Haraway links up with the ephemeral character of the experience of 'situatedness' as described in the introduction, being that knowledge is shifting and dynamic. Haraway emphasises the way knowledge is always situated and structured by privileged positions such as gender, race, nation and class. It is this situated knowledge that is the only possible way to negotiate objective knowledge. Haraway formulates an alternative to the (pre)dominant epistemological scientific ideal of transcendental objectivity, a concept she describes as "the standpoint of the master, the Man, the God, whose Eye produces, appropriates, and orders all differences" (Haraway, p. 193). She rewrites the objectivity criterion in terms of *situated knowledges* and argues in favour of an *embodied objectivity* as opposed to objectivism (Francois, 2011b). In *objectivism* the so-called variables have been stripped as much as possible so as to acquire knowledge about an object that is stripped as much as possible of the living environmental factors. In contrast to this view, *embodied objectivity* is a negotiated knowledge from different locations. It is a way of constructing and reconstructing meaning from diverse dimensions. The idea of negotiation here is far away from agonistic games to achieve an 'agreement', preferably at the own advantage. It is ideally partaking in what Haraway calls

> a critical practice for recognizing our own 'semiotic technologies' for making meanings, and a no-nonsense commitment to faithful accounts of a 'real' world, one that can be partially shared and friendly to earth-wide projects of finite freedom, adequate material abundance, modest meaning in suffering, and limited happiness. (Haraway, 1991, p. 187)

This process is a never-ending story that keeps all positions open. The topography of subjectivity is multidimensional, it is a 'vision' as Haraway calls it, and the knowing self is partial. Meaning is always constructed by this kind of negotiation and it is stitched together imperfectly. It is a never finished process. Rational knowledge is a process of critical interpretations from different 'fields', different locations, different power blocks, different so-called categories and different 'decoders' which are situated within the locality of the lifeworld (Fig. 10.3).

Haraway allots a special place to individuals on the fringes of social institutions, because of the surplus value of their dual view. The knowing subject is able

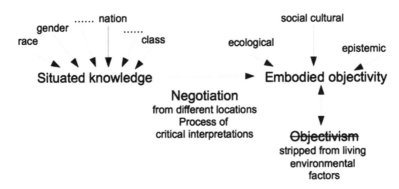

Fig. 10.3 Haraway's frame of knowledge negotiation

to enter into partial and prejudiced agreements that are at the real basis of all produced knowledge practice. It is a process of never-ending knowledge acquisition and it cannot claim any kind of universalism whatsoever. Completed knowledge practices that raise themselves to universal knowledge are autarchic and hence oppressive, and they are closed and static. Only partial perspectives preserve the promise of an objective perception (Haraway, 1991, p. 190). In line with critical philosophers such as Habermas, Foucault and Latour, Haraway puts into perspective the truth presumptions of Western science. Latour was mostly inspired by Reviel Netz's (2003) book on the shaping of deduction in Greek mathematics to illustrate "the first systematic non-formalist description of formalism at its early historical stage" (Latour, 2008, p. 441). The work of Netz is the most important work to argue how abstraction and deduction have to be seen as empirical, contingent developments. Haraway draws attention to both the historical specificity of scientific knowledge claims and the way that knowledge acquisition and science are interwoven with interests and power. These views offer an insight into how ethnomathematics is analysing academic mathematics as a (special) kind of situated mathematics. Let us consider the case of (academic) mathematics and its context of learning.

10.4   Ideal/Ideological Confrontations with Situated Mathematics

In this section, mathematical spaces are explored with the explicit aim to maximise contrasts. First, we have a look at mathematics as it is practised in an academic, Western, present-day setting and then at mathematics outside of this rather specific environment.

10.4.1 What Is This Knowledge Called 'Mathematics'? About Math's Epistemic Space

Ha Inq Hb: ?x 2x = 5
Hb Inq Ha: 5/2
Ha Inq Hb: Ben.

(Freudenthal, 1960, p. 92).

Rather than to present a theoretical framework for understanding academic mathematics, as practised today in the West, we prefer to start with a concrete case that might, so we believe, play the part of an exemplar in the Kuhnian sense. Or consider what follows as a thought experiment.

Consider an arbitrary mathematical journal, published by a European editor (de Gruyter, although now located in the USA), such as the *Journal of Group Theory*. Take an arbitrary issue, say the issue of volume 13, published in 2010. Take an arbitrary paper in that issue, for example, the paper written by Matthew J. Dyer (and communicated by G. Malle), entitled "Elementary roots and admissible subsets of Coxeter groups" (pp. 95–107). The paper opens, as it is customary now in academic publishing, with an abstract:

> Admissibility of a subset S' of a Coxeter system (W, S) is a condition implying that S' is the set of Coxeter generators of a Coxeter subgroup W' of W, in such a way that the root system of W', as permutation set, abstractly embeds in that of W. We give an algorithm determining whether a subset S' is admissible, in terms of a (previously known) finite state automaton which is constructed using the set of elementary roots of Brink and Howlett. (Dyer, 2010, p. 95)

It is safe to assume that one must be a specialist in group theory in order (a) to be able to simply read the paper and (b) to estimate the importance of the results reproduced in this paper. Even a trained mathematician in another area than group theory will hardly understand what is going on here. It is therefore also safe to say that a contribution such as this one is meant for a highly specialised group (!) of specialists. They form a close-knitted community and conferences they attend are meant only for them. What we have here is indeed a closed community of researchers with its proper agenda, including problems to solve, methods to use and proofs to convince.

At the same time it is not the case that this closure is a permanent situation. It must extend over at least one generation as present-day active mathematicians in the field must train the next generation to continue their work but it does not extend over an arbitrary range of generations. Let us list some arguments to support this thesis:

(a) A trivial observation to start with: before Coxeter there were no Coxeter systems or Coxeter groups. True, they could have been labelled otherwise but labels are not innocent at all. They suggest that objects are classified according to different schemes and that is definitely so in this case (as will be explained below).

(b) When one traces the origins of the concepts that occur in the abstract above, it becomes obvious that one rapidly leaves the micro-community and ends up with a form of mathematics that is available to us all. Let us look at one example in some more detail. The abstract refers to Coxeter systems. What are they? As stated in the abstract, a Coxeter system consists of two elements W and S. Let us focus on W, which is a Coxeter group. A group is a well-known mathematical structure that arises in a number of mathematical contexts. A group W is a set of (arbitrary) elements and an operation * such that four properties are satisfied:

(i) Closure (although now in the mathematical sense): for all a and b in W, a * b is also in W.
(ii) Associativity (or the order has no importance): for all a, b, c in W, a * (b * c) = (a * b) * c.
(iii) Neutral element: there is a special element e such that for all a in W, a * e = e * a = a.
(iv) Inverse element: for every element a, there is an element a-1, such that a * a^{-1} = a^{-1} * a = e.

As is often said, groups are everywhere. Addition on integers forms a group, permutations on a finite set can be expressed as permutation groups, corresponding to swapping elements around, and Coxeter groups are related to geometry. In fact a Coxeter group is a generalisation of a reflection group in classical Euclidean space. And there we are. Take the Euclidean plane, known to all of us, as it was often called in school: the blackboard. Draw a line A. Draw a figure and mirror that figure as if A were a mirror. If we call this operation R, then it is clear that the reverse operation R^{-1}, which is of course the same as R, brings you back to the original, so what we have here is a group with two elements, viz. R and E (for the neutral element = "do not do anything"). Obviously since $R = R^{-1}$, it follows that $R \times R = E$ (the reflection of the reflection is the original). What this shows is that it is rather easy to connect this highly abstract piece of mathematics to something familiar (at least in countries with educational systems that involve basic elements of mathematics) to all of us. We dare to suggest the hypothesis that this holds in general for any piece of mathematics.

(c) Part of the mystery in (b) disappears once we tell the story in the correct chronological order. We started out, long time ago, with Euclidean geometry (at least in this particular part of the world) and repetition is an important element, often associated with aesthetical pleasure, so we find repetition in ornaments. One such form of repetition is reflection. Gradually, and this process has taken a considerable amount of time, different geometries were developed (think of the geometry of perspective, which is something else than Euclidean geometry but can be drawn on the blackboard nevertheless) and it became evident that some form of classification was necessary and it turned out that it was more interesting to look at operations such as reflection and not at the geometric objects themselves. So now the structure of the operations became important and that led to group theory. In short, to generalise has been the mathematicians' aim for always, so the idea of a reflection group was generalised and that leads exactly to Coxeter groups. It sounds almost contradictory that the process of generalisation upon generalisation leads to such highly specialised communities. It suffices however to realise that, given any specific structure, it is almost never the case that one and only one generalisation is possible or available. The multitude of generalisations necessitates specialisation.

(d) The above considerations should be contrasted with the fact that it is possible for any mathematician to recognise a piece of text as mathematical. The common origins referred to in (c) and the fact that generalisations tend to make a language more uniform as the same terms and concepts are used to describe wildly different things create this idea of universality, of 'being a mathematician' without any further qualifications needed.

So, curiously enough, there is a large-scale global recognition of belonging to the same macro-community—'us, mathematicians', so to speak—but without any profound understanding and the belonging to a micro-community where understanding is high but closure an unavoidable consequence. Or, why not use mathematical terms to describe this situation? We have a macro-community M that falls apart in a set of disjoint parts M', such that for every pair M' and M'', there is a similarity relation R, that is, R expresses that members of M' recognise members of M'' and vice versa as mathematicians. In other words, R produces a quotient structure over M in separate communities. However, within each subcommunity M', members of M', say m_1 and m_2, are interchangeable as, mathematically speaking, they share the same mathematical knowledge. So each subcommunity M' is a permutation group. So consider a relation $U\left(m_i, \mathrm{pr}(A)\right)$ meaning that member m_i understands the proof of the statement A. Interchangeability here means that, if there is a m_i such that U holds, then it holds for all members of M'. We are allowed to make the transition from the existence of one member to all members and that indeed is as close to a universal property as one will ever get. However, at the same time, for any member m_j from another community, the relation U will not hold. Unless one expresses the counterfactual statement: were m_j to become a member of M', then U would also hold for m_j. As indeed it would, but then m_j is no longer an exclusive member of his or her original community. There is therefore nothing really contradictory in the statement that mathematics as we know it today can be best described as a community where universality is a local phenomenon everywhere in that community.

We already discussed in Sect. 3.1 the importance of Husserl for the understanding of the idea of objectivity, especially as it occurs in mathematics. The approach we have sketched in this section suggests another name that should be included: Ludwig Wittgenstein. More specifically, not the author of the *Tractatus Logico-Philosophicus* but the 'later' Wittgenstein who developed a conceptual toolkit for understanding the processes we are dealing with here, such as language games, forms of life, rule following and, to phrase it in terms of an equation that has acquired almost magical status, "meaning=use". This needs to be elaborated further but this single quote from Wittgenstein (1956) shows that the 'spirit' is the same:

> To say mathematics is a game is supposed to mean: in proving, we need never appeal to the meaning of the signs, that is to their extra-mathematical application [Can this be read as his version of what closure can be?, *our addition*]. But then what does appealing to this mean at all? How can such an appeal be of any avail?

Does it mean passing out of mathematics and returning to it again, or does it mean passing from *one* method of mathematical inference to another? (Wittgenstein, 1956, p. 259)

As a side remark, though an important one, we wish to emphasise the fact that one should not be amazed to find the names of Husserl and Wittgenstein together in a single article and, of course, not as opposites but as mutually inspiring sources. If Michael Friedman's thesis, see Friedman (2000), has some validity, as we believe it does, then the original philosophical problem 'agendas' of what were to become the phenomenological and analytical tradition were more similar than dissimilar. As we too believe that 'the parting of the ways', to use Friedman's expression, has not necessarily been an overall success story, this contribution can also be read as a support for 'the rejoining of the ways'.

10.4.2   What Is This Thing Called 'Mathematics'? About Math's Conceptual Space

A says to B: "What is the x, such that 2x = 5?"
B says to A: "5/2"
A says to B: "Good!".

(Freudenthal, 1960, p. 92)

The mathematical practice and theory as elaborated on by the experts on a Coxeter system is a nice example of a local mathematical practice and knowledge of a micro-community of mathematicians. Imagine that this specialised mathematical knowledge became a very important instrument in daily life, the challenge then should be how to communicate or educate this local, micro-community knowledge so that every individual should be able to use this basic mathematical knowledge.

This is exactly the challenge that mathematics education is dealing with. How to make abstract academic mathematics understandable and available for all students since abstract academic mathematics is of growing importance for the needs of the market and of university education at the international level. Not only the experts of a Coxeter system are a micro-community dealing with local mathematical practices and knowledge, also the pupils who enter the institutional space—which is called the math class—are a micro-community dealing with local mathematical practices they bring from there background. How can we now define a similarity relation R so that members of micro-community M′ recognise and understand members of M″ and vice versa as mathematicians. In what follows we will elaborate on the notion of ethnomathematics proposing that it would be the generic category which allows for a more systematic and comparative study of the whole domain of mathematical practices.

Ethnomathematics is the best situated concept to understand the 'situatedness' of mathematics. The meaning of the concept ethnomathematics shifted over the years as a result of the growing understanding that (subdisciplines of) academic mathematics itself is a situated knowledge (cf. the above mentioned example of the Coxeter experts). We will examine the shifted meaning of ethnomathematics and show how an initial meaning of the term with an 'exotic' connotation became a generic term for mathematical practices in general (Pinxten & François, 2011). This means that the initial local reference became a more general and global one.

The inspiring work of Alan Bishop (1988, 1997) distinguished between Mathematics with a capital M and mathematics with a small m. The capital M refers to the discipline of mathematics, especially as it was developed in the Western tradition. Leaving aside the questions on other cultural influences (from India to Egypt), this discipline can be identified in the learned societies and courses at our universities. Moreover, M refers to the knowledge about space, proportions, numbers and so on in this learned tradition and its institutional spaces of mathematics. The small m then refers to the actual practices, procedures and concepts which are developed and used in counting, designing, explaining, locating, measuring and playing in different (if not all) cultures around the world. The number of small m's is vast: every cultural tradition has some particular way of counting, eventually bookkeeping, and the ways spatial notions are shaped in different languages and cultures are varied. The many books and articles on what is now called 'ethnomathematics' offer an intriguing set of insights in this source of knowledge: Ascher, 1998, 2002; D'Ambrosio, 2001; Powell & Frankenstein, 1997; and many others (for a recent overview, see François & Van Kerkhove, 2010; François & Pinxten, 2011).

One major question was and is: what is the meaning and the status of ethnomathematics? In an oversimplified way, there are two major answers. The minimalistic view holds that ethnomathematics documents the mathematical notions and procedures of the so-called nonliterate peoples (Ascher & Ascher, 1997). The mere documentation 'challenges Eurocentric historical and logical concerns' (idem). A more ambitious view attacks the universality of the academic mathematics. Ubiratan D'Ambrosio (1997) makes the point that engineers, shopkeepers and lots of other people (street kids, ICT nerds, architects and so on) use a form of mathematics "which does not respond to the concept of rigor and formalism…in academic courses…" (1997, p. 7). All of this should be included in ethnomathematics. That is to say, the distinction is then defined as one between an academic format on the one hand (the M of mathematicians) and the many uses of correct, workable but 'unorthodox' mathematics in the work of people living their lives on the other hand. These people can be literate or not, Western or non-Western.

Borba (1997) is most outspoken in political terms on the issue: he defines ethnomathematics as all mathematical knowledge expressed in the language code of a given sociocultural group (1997, pp. 264–265). He voices this as an attack on the imperialism of academic mathematics. The way he approaches the issue is innovative. His point is that we should not be primarily focused on the mathematics as such, but rather on the educational aspects. Education, then, is not a uniform process. It deals with the identification of a problem and the consecutive learning of problem solving ways and procedures. Now, the identification of what is a problem is not universal, but is dependent on the context, the need of the moment, the lifestyle, etc. in one word: it differs according to cultural context. Our suggestion is to say that the relevance criteria will vary from culture to culture and hence that thematising a particular point will depend on the context, the survival needs and the traditional knowledge of each particular group. However, there is more than mere survival. It was Vithal and Skovsmose (1997) who introduced the concept of *foreground*—besides the notion of background. Where the background means what pupils bring to the classroom, *foreground* is to be understood as 'the set of opportunities that the learner's social context makes accessible to the learner to perceive as his or her possibilities for the future' (Vithal & Skovsmose, p. 147). Also the political and cultural situation is an important aspect of the foreground since they provide the opportunities for the learner (Skovsmose, 2005). The notion of foreground makes the political nature of the learning process explicit. It has to do with the student's possibilities in future life, not the objective possibilities as formulated by an external institution but the possibilities as the student perceives them. Mathematical literacy is one of the capabilities Martha Nussbaum (2011) mentions in her list of 'central capabilities'. Here mathematical literacy becomes part of human rights. A decent political order must secure to all citizens at least a threshold level of these central capabilities.

Looking at pupils' background experience, the academic mathematics curriculum is not directly of relevance since they have not direct survival value for them (François & Van Bendegem, 2007). A general anti-imperialistic view on ethnomathematics is that from an educational point of view, pupils' concepts and procedures should be the primary focus, and not those of the academic mathematician.

10.5   Afterthought: To Be Situated or Not

Dividing knowledge in the aforementioned polarity impedes all possibility of developing a decent *foreground*, a set of tools which affords students from all places to engage with useful knowledge in a broad sense. As long as we focus on our situated practices, backgrounds and subjective approaches of all objects of knowledge, or, the other way round, as long as we take the ideal of the universal as real or the notion of objectivism—knowledge stripped from living environments—as the obligatory aim, we may think we have ad hoc solutions for knowledge and institutions, but definitely not for critical citizens (in the future).

A first lesson from the trajectory we proposed is that knowledge starts as 'ethnoknowledge' or as knowledge inside a micro-community. This was shown by the Coxeter theory as well as by the generation and recent development of the notion of 'mathematics' where Mathematical theory with a capital M was confronted with mathematics with a small m. Knowledge originates in a certain context, inside a micro-community, and it will be transmitted over time and generations in other contexts, to members of other micro-communities.

A second lesson is that the process of being transmitted and understood is a complex but not impossible one. In the three models we proposed—the context of origin and use, the creation of intersubjective universality of Husserl and the negotiation of an embodied objectivity of Haraway—the space and place of transmission and accessibility of knowledge is a dynamic process, where different situations encounter each other, different interpretations are criticised, knowledge is negotiated from different locations and closed languages become more open. These processes are never completed. As we mentioned with the Coxeter theory, the closure of its situatedness—inside a micro-community—is not permanent. It must extend over time and space to become embedded, by way of transmission, negotiation and processes of objectivation, in a broader generalised framework of mathematics, accessible to a macro-community.

A third lesson is that these processes of transmission have to be negotiated and enhanced by the creation of educational opportunities and tools, relying upon social and political decisions. Each macro-community is composed by different subcommunities. The possibility of members of subcommunities to access the macro-community is dependent upon the set of opportunities offered to them to engage with mathematical knowledge, linking context of origin and context of use.

We did not talk a lot about institutions, as we focussed on the knowledge communities and their environing epistemic, ecological and social-cultural—and political—parameters, which are the dynamic agents behind institutions. Engaging into a process of negotiating mathematical literacy as a human right is a dynamic way of questioning the role and function of existing institutions, as well as those institutions with a capital 'I' as those with a small 'i'. Institutions are but the products of human endeavour and commitment.

References

Ascher, M. (1998). *Ethnomathematics. A multicultural view of mathematical ideas*. New York: Chapman & Hall/CRC.

Ascher, M. (2002). *Mathematics elsewhere. An exploration of ideas across cultures*. Princeton, NJ: Princeton University Press.

Ascher, M., & Ascher, R. (1997). Ethnomathematics. In A. B. Powell & M. Frankenstein (Eds.), *Ethnomathematics, challenging Eurocentrism in mathematics education* (pp. 25–50). Albany, NY: State University of New York Press.

Baird, D. (2003). Thing knowledge. In H. Radder (Ed.), *The philosophy of scientific experimentation* (pp. 39–67). Pittsburgh, PA: University of Pittsburgh Press.

Bishop, A. J. (1988). The interactions of mathematics education with culture. *Cultural Dynamics, An International Journal for the Study of Processes and Temporality of Culture., 1*(2), 145–157.

Bishop, A. J. (1997). *Mathematical enculturation, a cultural perspective on mathematics education* (Mathematics education library, Vol. 6). Dordrecht, the Netherlands: Kluwer Academic.

Borba, M. C. (1997). Ethnomathematics and education. In A. B. Powell & M. Frankenstein (Eds.), *Ethnomathematics, challenging Eurocentrism in mathematics education* (pp. 261–272). Albany, NY: State University of New York Press.

Clancey, W. C. (1997). *Situated cognition: On human knowledge and computer representations*. Cambridge, UK: Cambridge University Press.

Coessens, K., & Van Bendegem, J. P. (2006). Expectations of what scientific research could (not) do: problems of translation, tool, lag of time and context. In P. Smeyers & M. Depaepe (Eds.), *Educational research: Why 'what works' doesn't work* (pp. 109–126). New York: Springer.

D'Ambrosio, U. (1997). Ethnomathematics and its place in the history and pedagogy of mathematics. In A. B. Powell & M. Frankenstein (Eds.), *Ethnomathematics, challenging Eurocentrism in mathematics education* (pp. 13–24). Albany, NY: State University of New York Press.

D'Ambrosio, U. (2001). *Ethnomathematics. Link between traditions and modernity*. Rotterdam, the Netherlands: Sense.

Dyer, M. J. (2010). Elementary roots and admissible subsets of Coxeter groups. *Journal of Group Theory, 13*(1), 95–107.

Francois, K. (2011a). On the notion of a phenomenological constitution of objectivity. In A.-T. Tymieniecka (Ed.), *Analecta Husserliana, transcendentalism overturned* (pp. 121–137). Dordrecht, the Netherlands: Springer.

Francois, K. (2011b). In-between science and politics. *Foundations of Science, 16*(2–3), 161–171.

Francois, K., & Pinxten, R. (2011). Etnowiskunde: ontstaan en betekenisverschuiving van een concept [Ethnomathematics: Development of a concept and its shifted meaning]. *Volkskunde, 112*(1), 33–54.

François, K., & Van Bendegem, J. P. (Eds.). (2007). *Philosophical dimensions in mathematics education*. New York: Springer.

François, K., & Van Kerkhove, B. (2010). Ethnomathematics and the philosophy of mathematics (education). In B. Löwe & T. Müller (Eds.), *Philosophy of mathematics: Sociological aspects and mathematical practice* (Texts in philosophy, pp. 121–154). London: College.

Freudenthal, H. (1960). *Lincos. Design of a language for cosmic intercourse. Part I*. Amsterdam: North-Holland.

Friedman, M. (2000). *The parting of the ways: Carnap, Cassirer, and Heidegger*. London: Open Court.

Haraway, D. J. (1991). Situated knowledges: The science question in feminism and the privilege of partial perspective. In D. J. Haraway (Ed.), *Simians, cyborgs, and women: The reinvention of nature* (pp. 183–201). London: Free Association Books.

Husserl, E. (1970a). *The crisis of European sciences and transcendental phenomenology* (D. Carr, Trans.). Evanston, IL: Northwestern University Press. (Original work published 1962)

Husserl, E. (1970b). Appendix VI: The origin of geometry. In *The crisis of European sciences and transcendental phenomenology. An introduction to phenomenological philosophy* (D. Carr, Trans., pp. 353–378). Evanston, IL: Northwestern University Press. (Original work published 1962)

Knuuttila, T., & Honkela, T. (2005). Questioning external and internal representation: The case of scientific models. In L. Magnani & R. Dossena (Eds.), *Computing, philosophy and cognition* (pp. 209–226). London: College.

Lang, J. C. (2011). Epistemologies of situated knowledges: "Troubling" knowledge in philosophy of education. *Educational Theory, 61*(1), 75–96.

Latour, B. (2008). The Netz-works of Greek deductions—A review of Reviel Netz's The shaping of deductions in Greek mathematics. *Social Studies of Science, 38*(3), 441–459.

Lave, J., & Wenger, E. (1991). *Situated learning: Legitimate peripheral participation*. Cambridge, UK: Cambridge University Press.

Menninger, K. (1969). *Number words and number symbols: A cultural history of numbers*. Cambridge, MA: MIT Press.

Netz, R. (2003). *The shaping of deduction in Greek mathematics. A study in cognitive history*. Cambridge, UK: Cambridge University Press.

Nussbaum, M. (2011). *Creating capabilities. The human development approach*. Cambridge, MA: The Belknap Press of Harvard University Press.

Pinxten, R., & François, K. (2011). Politics in an Indian canyon? Some thoughts on the implications of ethnomathematics. *Educational Studies in Mathematics, 78*(2), 261–273.

Powell, A. B., & Frankenstein, M. (Eds.). (1997). *Ethnomathematics, challenging Eurocentrism in mathematics education*. Albany, NY: State University of New York Press.

Rescher, N. (1999). *The limits of science*. Pittsburgh, PA: University of Pittsburgh Press.

Skovsmose, O. (2005). *Travelling through education: Uncertainty, mathematics, responsibility.* Rotterdam, the Netherlands: Sense.

Vithal, R., & Skovsmose, O. (1997). The end of innocence: A critique of ethnomathematics. *Educational Studies in Mathematics., 34*(2), 131–157.

Wilson, B. G., & Myers, K. M. (2000). Situated cognition in theoretical and practical context. In D. Jonassen & S. Land (Eds.), *Theoretical foundations of learning environments* (pp. 57–88). Mahwah, NJ: Erlbaum.

Wittgenstein L. (1956). *Remarks on the foundations of mathematics* (G. H. von Wright, R. Rhees, & G. E. M. Anscombe; G. M. Anscombe, Trans.). Oxford, UK: Basil Blackwell.

Chapter 11
The Classroom Space: A Problem or a Mystery?

Ian Munday

In the run up to the last UK general election, Michael Gove, the Secretary of State for Education in waiting, quoted Oakeshott and conjured up visions of a rich liberal education. Once in power and faced with spending cuts, Gove maintained that trainee teachers should be thought of as apprentices learning the tricks of the trade whilst on the job. Both these visions have quite different implications for how the classroom space is conceived, namely, a forum and a workshop, respectively. Research on classroom practice and indeed on education more generally throws up other configurations of the classroom. For critical educators it will be a potential space for emancipation. For those lucky enough to procure funding, it will most likely be treated as a space where 'effective learning' does (or does not) take place. On the other hand, those researchers who like to make analogies between schools and hospitals (see Darling-Hammond & Bransford, 2005) may see the classroom as a 'ward'—disappointingly, they never refer to wards. Perhaps the image is too depressing.

Though researchers from different backgrounds may perceive the classroom space in different ways, they often share one thing in common, namely, that they see it as a site for solving problems—teachers and children will be emancipated, students will become more effective learners and patients will be 'cured'. This chapter is concerned with what the classroom has become for both teachers and a particular species of research, namely, the kind in which teachers research their own practice. This form of research often goes by the name of 'teacher research', though it is sometimes described as 'action research' or 'practitioner enquiry'. Historically speaking, teacher research is deeply bound up with problem-solving approaches to educational matters.

As Biesta notes: "The nature of human problem solving has been studied for well over a century" (Biesta, 2009, p. 1). It has been conducted "both by psychologists interested in the principles and processes of problem solving and by educationalists

I. Munday (✉)
School of Education, University of Stirling, Stirling, UK
e-mail: ian.munday@stir.ac.uk

P. Smeyers et al. (eds.), *Educational Research: The Importance and Effects of Institutional Spaces*, Educational Research 7, DOI 10.1007/978-94-007-6247-3_11,
© Springer Science+Business Media Dordrecht 2013

interested in how problem solving can be learned" (ibid.). Influential figures in its emergence as a field of study include psychologists such as Karl Duncker (1935, 1945) and the pragmatist philosopher John Dewey (1909/1978). In the last five decades, approaches to problem solving have shifted from a focus on information processing to a concern with "more complex, semantically rich problems and on problems occurring in 'real life' contexts" (Biesta, 2009, p. 2). The emergence of teacher research (and its problem-solving approaches) largely coincides with this shift in emphasis. Teacher research arguably emerges from the action research of the 1950s and 1960s. However, it only started to become established as a movement following the work of Lawrence Stenhouse, who helped to establish the Centre for Applied Research at The University of East Anglia in 1970 and Patricia Carini at the Prospect Center and School in Bennington Vermont. Writing in 1993, Cochran-Smith and Lytle note that: "For almost two decades, the Prospect group has worked to develop a number of processes for documenting children's learning in school contexts, for helping teachers to uncover and clarify their implicit assumptions about teaching, learning and schooling, and for solving a variety of school-based educational problems". For Cochran-Smith and Lytle, teacher research draws on the role of the teacher that is heavily influenced by Dewey's educational writings. They note that Dewey was concerned that teachers had become fixated with "jumping from one technique to another" and felt that they had to be "adequately moved by their own ideas and intelligence" (ibid., p. 9) when reflecting on their practice. Taking his cue from Dewey, the notion of reflective practice was developed by Schön (1983, 1987) who maintained that professional practice should be "an intellectual process of posing and exploring problems identified by teachers themselves".

As is hopefully clear by now, 'problem solving' is at the heart of teacher research. In recent years, qualifications (usually Master's degrees) in teacher research have become a significant feature of professional development in the UK. Whether or not current approaches to teacher research capture the ambitions of the founders of the movement is another matter. The following quotation is taken from the first paragraph of *Practitioner Research and Professional Development in Education*:

> Let us assume that you have identified some aspect of your professional practice in your classroom that is puzzling you. You may have noticed that one particular technique you use to encourage effective learning does not appear to be working as well as it used to, or that another is working very effectively. You may have seen something in the news or read something in the educational press that reminded you of your classroom or at least caused you to wonder how it might apply to your own professional situation. At this point you have taken the first step as a researcher in that you have identified an educational issue that might need resolving. We could generalise by saying that much educational research focuses on interesting puzzles that have been identified by practitioners. (Campbell, McNamara, & Gilroy, 2004, p. 1)

Though there is no explicit mention of problem solving here, a problem-solving approach is surely being recommended. As a teacher you will be puzzled by whether or not the techniques you employ are working. You are confronted by an issue/problem that needs resolving/solving. Once this has been identified, the teacher/researcher can then play 'what's my epistemology' (am I a positivist or post-positivist?) and go on from there (this is certainly the route that Campbell et al. mark out for the budding teacher/researcher).

One way to critique the approach adopted by Campbell et al. is to draw on richer, less technicist accounts of what problem solving in the classroom can amount to. However, there might be another approach that is not concerned with problem solving at all. A note of caution here: Problem solving itself can take many different forms. Nevertheless, Biesta's definition of a problem would seem fairly uncontentious: "A problem occurs when we do not know how to proceed from a given state to a desired goal state. Problem solving then is the process through which we find a way to achieve the desired goal state" (Biesta, 2009, p. 1). To this, we might add that solving a problem must invariably involve overcoming some sort of obstacle.

11.1 Having Problems?

Drawing on the work of existentialist philosopher Gabriel Marcel, I want to consider what it might mean to think of the classroom as a space of 'mystery' rather than a site for problem solving. To get a better understanding of what is at stake in the distinction between problems and mysteries, it will be helpful to give an indication of how they figure in Marcel's wider project that features in *Être et Avoir* (in English, *Being and Having*). For Marcel mystery equates with being, problem solving with having. Let us begin with the phenomenology of having (Marcel, 1949, p. 169). Marcel notes that though there are different senses in which we can speak about 'having', he is not that interested in what he sees as peripheral or perhaps exceptional cases (such as having a cold) and moves on to consider more usual cases of having as possession such as having a bicycle or an idea.

In all unexceptional cases of 'having as possession', there seems to be a certain quid relating to a certain qui whereby the latter is treated as "a centre of inherence or apprehension" (p. 173). Why does Marcel speak of 'quis' and 'quids' here when a distinction between subject and object would seem to do just as well? It is perhaps because that very distinction and weight of intellectual history that accompanies it is something that he wants to eventually bypass. Moreover, the use of unusual terms brings strangeness to a distinction that would otherwise seem like a familiar and obvious way of dividing up the world. We will return to this shortly.

Anyway, when we think about 'having' something, the qui must therefore be, in some way, transcendent to the quid (ibid.). For Marcel, I can only "have, in the strict sense of the word, something whose existence is independent of me" and therefore what I have is "added to me" (p. 169). By the same token, "having" is "apt to reduce itself to the fact of containing" (pp. 173–174). By definition, to contain something is to enclose it and to oppose the tendency towards spreading or escaping. It is worth thinking here about how people tend to relate to their possessions. There is a precarious sense in which my possessions tend to simultaneously be both part of me and not part of me. This is not something we tend to think about until something unusual happens. Think, for example, of those occasions on which Pete Townshend from The Who would smash his guitar up. What is perhaps most powerful about this is that it looks and feels like an act of self-harm. It is, I think, more than just the destruction of an expensive instrument that can excite revulsion here. Similarly, people who are burgled or whose property is vandalised tend to be affected in ways which cannot be accounted for simply in terms of financial loss.

What does this reveal about 'having'? A dynamic is built into having that is coterminous with suppression. Our understanding of what it is to have a "secret" (p. 175) illustrates this. A secret is only a secret because I could reveal it. Here, one might think about the way in which we can covet secrets—to tell a secret is to give something of myself away, yet what I lose was never 'exactly' mine. Moreover, a secret ceases to be a secret as soon as I reveal it. This is what Marcel means when he argues that all assertions regarding having are "built on a prototypical statement where the qui is no other than myself" (ibid.)—the 'you have' depends on a kind of transference where something is always lost in the process. Let us pause for a moment. Earlier, I mentioned that the qui somehow stood in for 'the subject' but was not equivalent to it. In the 'phenomenology of having', 'the qui' is the subject but one troubled by her possessions, by what both is and is not external to her. It is worth thinking here of situations such as relationship break-ups and the madness and jealousy that so often accompany them. What do these feelings expose if not that our relationships are perhaps, simultaneously, not relationships—people can be part of us but also things that we 'have' and that we add and subtract from ourselves.

For Marcel, 'having' is damaging because of the dynamic of suppression and loss. It generates an economy in which the 'other' (particularly those closest to us to whom we are 'attached') is always posed as threatening. Her existence means that what is 'mine' can always be lost or destroyed. Indeed, through its negation, 'having' is coterminous with desire, covetousness and "a whirlpool of anxieties" (p. 78). Having indicates a will towards permanency. I struggle to make myself one with that which can always be taken away: "I hug myself to this thing which may be torn from me, and I desperately try to incorporate it in myself, to form myself and it into a single dissoluble complex" (ibid.). Through this process, I ironically become enslaved to the things 'I have'. The internal/external dialectic means that the relation to my things becomes technical. Though I believe that I have control over my instruments, in fact they blot me out (p. 179). The treatment of this idea is common in literature and popular culture—think of what happens to those who possess the ring in *Lord of the Rings* or the way in which Doctor Octopus from *Spiderman* becomes overwhelmed and dictated to by his new cyborg body parts.

11.2 *Endgame*

Earlier I mentioned that the phenomenology of having is inextricably linked to seeing things in terms of problems to be solved. Why should this be so? This is what Marcel has to say about problems: "A problem is something met with which bars my passage. It is therefore before me in its entirety". From this we can see the divide pertinent to having, for here I set an object (in this case a problem) against 'myself'. To 'overcome' it implies a will towards permanency. Of course, the permanency in question is 'empty'. Just as a secret disappears in the telling, a problem disappears in the solving. It has been eradicated. I anticipate an objection here—telling secrets is a rather detestable sort of behaviour, whereas solving problems looks like something we might pride ourselves on. We will return to this shortly. To get a flavour of what is wrong with the phenomenology of having and problem solving, let us turn to the theatre and Samuel Beckett's play *Endgame* which arguably takes issues of being and having as one of its principle themes.

The play focuses on Hamm, a blind man who is unable to stand up, and his servant Clov. They exist in a location that had once been by the sea though we come to understand that there is nothing left outside—no sea and no sun. The two characters have been arguing for years and continue to do so as the play progresses. Clov regularly threatens to leave but never seems to manage it. Also present are Hamm's parents Nagg and Nell, who live in rubbish bins and tend to either argue or request food. In this fragment, the characters turn to prayer:

Nagg: Me sugar-plum!
Clov: There's a rat in the kitchen!
Hamm: A rat! Are there still rats?
Clov: In the kitchen there's one.
Hamm: And you haven't exterminated him?
Clov: Half. You disturbed us.
Hamm: He can't get away?
Clov: No.
Hamm: You'll finish him later. Let us pray to God.
Clov: Again!
Nagg: Me sugar-plum!
Hamm: God first! (*Pause.*) Are you right?
Clov: (*resigned*). Off we go p.38
         Hamm (*to Nagg*) And you?
Nagg: (*clasping his hands, closing his eyes in a gabble*). Our Father which art –
Hamm: Silence! In silence! Where are your manners? (*Pause*) Off we go. (*Attitudes of prayer. Silence. Abandoning his attitude, discouraged.*) Well?
Clov: (*abandoning his attitude*) What a hope! And you?
         Hamm (Sweet damn all! (to Nagg.) And you?
Nagg: Wait! (*Pause. Abandoning his attitude.*) Nothing doing!
Hamm: The bastard! He doesn't exist!
Clov: Not yet.
Nagg: Me sugar-plum!
Hamm: There are no more sugar plums. (Beckett, 1958, p. 38)

There are, I think, obvious similarities between what Beckett is trying to show and Marcel's account of having/problems. If you like, *Endgame* would seem to be an extremely dark allegory of a world in which the effects of a phenomenology of having are presented in their most vulgar and stripped down form. The characters are filled with covetous desire for things that there are no more of. The things in question—sugar plums, God and famously in other sections 'biscuits'—do not figure in any sort of hierarchy; they just appear as a list of wants. Praying itself simply becomes a question of technique and etiquette, a means of solving a problem, though quite what the nature of that problem 'is' is unclear. Why do the characters pray? So that God brings them sugar plums? Out of force of habit or boredom? The point would seem to be that they don't really know. The characters are radically disconnected in space—only one of them can move. Such disconnection is symbolic of a general breakdown of communication. Nagg and Nell will fondly remember the same day, yet they talk about completely different events and seem oblivious to each others' recollections.

Beckett provides a dark allegory, but what an extreme set of circumstances he puts before the audience. Surely there are all sorts of situations in which problem solving is a pretty innocent business. Where is the harm in solving crosswords for example? There is no harm in it. The problem, as Beckett shows us, comes when a problem-solving approach is applied to the deepest and most significant aspects of our lives. Then again, if one is tired, or not in the best mood, crosswords can be pretty evil things. In other circumstances, solving them leads to mild anticlimax. On that note, but back to more 'serious' things, think of the end of *The Graduate*. The Dustin Hoffman character has overcome all sorts of obstacles to drag his ex-girlfriend away from the clutches of her rich husband-to-be. In the final scene, they sit at the back of a bus with no idea what to do next.

11.3   Being Mysterious

How might we escape the perdition that accompanies the phenomenology of having and its techniques? Marcel thinks there is a way, and it has everything to do with attunement towards being and mystery. At one point in *Being and Having*, he responds to a perceived objection to a claim discussed earlier in this chapter, namely, that our instruments/possessions eat us up. Could it not be said, 'In so far as you treat the instrument as pure instrument, it has no power over you. You control it yourself and it does not react on you'. Marcel says that this is perfectly true, however, when he says that when our possessions eat us up, this is:

> …truer of us, strangely enough, when we are in a state of inertia in face of objects which are themselves inert, but falser when we are more vitally and actively bound up with something serving as the immediate subject-matter of a personal creative act, a subject matter perpetually renewed. (It may be the garden of a keen gardener, the farm of a farmer, the violin of a musician, or the laboratory of a scientist.) In all these cases, we may say, having tends not to be destroyed, but to be sublimated and changed into being. (Marcel, 1949, p. 180)

If 'having' is to be sublimated into 'being', then this requires a suturing of the wound between me and the world. This is the essence of mystery: "A mystery… is something in which I find myself caught up, and whose essence is therefore not before me in its entirety. It is as though in this province the distinction between *in me* and *before me* loses its meaning" (p. 109). It is necessary to exercise caution here. This is quite a complicated idea and requires a degree of hesitancy on the part of the reader. It would seem that having and being are not two clearly delimited terms in a straightforward binary distinction. In the process of sublimation, 'having' (and therefore problem solving) is not eradicated exactly—some aspect of it persists. What might this mean? Heidegger (whose philosophy surely influences Marcel's) may help us here.

This distinction between a mystery/being and having/problem solving is very reminiscent of, though not identical to, Heidegger's distinction between things being 'ready-to-hand' and 'present-to-hand'. Ready-to-handness describes our normal everyday coping with the world in which we are not consciously directed towards the things that we're doing but are rather immersed in the activities we are involved in. This does not imply that we are acting as though under hypnosis and that there is no conscious dimension whatsoever to our activities. Rather, it denotes a situation in which the distinction between me and what I am engaged in doing becomes blurred. Things become present-to-hand when there is a problem and 'something bars my passage'. If things break or they malfunction, then they need to be fixed. This disrupts the ordinary flow of existence. So, when Marcel concedes that it is possible that one might control one's instruments, this may relate to those provisional cases in which problem solving is appropriate.

Though I think Heidegger's distinction is helpful here, as noted above, it is not identical to Marcel's. Though the former's work has a moral dimension, the distinction primarily deals with ontological concerns. Marcel blurs the divide between moral and ontological claims to reveal a paradox that Heidegger draws attention to more explicitly in his later writings.[1] The paradox can be stated in this way—a problem-solving approach to the world has ironically become ready-to-hand. We are immersed in a world view that is fundamentally bad for us. To see how Marcel demonstrates what is at stake here, let us start with his critique of Cartesianism.

To see things in problem-solving terms (or as present-to-hand) implies a kind of Cartesianism. For Marcel, to approach the world in terms of being and mystery requires a departure from Cartesianism and idealism more generally. He argues that Descartes' cogito assumes that whatever is thinking must be a coherent immaterial self, but if he was true to the spirit of his scepticism, he should also doubt the nature of the thing that was thinking, the thing that 'contained' the thought. It is not that Marcel wants to wallow in a more extreme form of scepticism but wants to show how such scepticism can create space for a more vital and immersive understanding of existence. Such an understanding throws a different light on how we think of the body (a theme that regularly recurs throughout *Being and Having*). I tend to think of myself as 'having' a body as though it were somehow external to 'me', as something 'I have'. For Marcel, the point is not that my body is 'me' but rather that the boundaries of the self when understood creatively are infinitely stretchable. This has clear implications for how we think about space, as people and objects can no longer be clearly distinguished as discrete-bounded entities. To think in terms of mystery sublimes the boundaries of a vulgar materialist approach to objects in space.

As mentioned above Marcel's ontological claims have a moral (and indeed spiritual) charge. For Marcel there is always a danger that we will pervert mysteries by turning them into problems. At various points in *Being and Having*, he argues that the mystery of evil is often turned into a problem whereby philosophers try "to make out its causes, the reason for its existence, and even its hidden ends". For Marcel, we can only grasp evil as evil when it touches us, when we do not try and externalise and emancipate ourselves from it. Treating it as a problem makes it into a kind of game or "intellectual sleight of hand" (p. 187). The same applies to philosophical discussion of the Divine attributes, diminishing, through dividing into pieces the immersive/transcendent experience of worship. Through their coldness, philosophers can get things just as wrong as the characters in *Endgame*.

At this point, it might be worth introducing a note of caution. It is easy to get carried away with the idea of 'mystery'—it may seem to imply a kind of perfectionism or vagueness that could be embraced by the happiness gurus or 'mystics' in general. Though Marcel's use of the word 'transcendence' may give the impression that he is some sort of mystic, I do not think that this is quite right. For Marcel mystery "lies at the heart of the every day" (p. 179). Moreover:

> We must carefully avoid all confusion between the mysterious and the unknowable. The unknowable is in fact only the limiting case of the problematic, which cannot be actualised without contradiction. The recognition of mystery, on the contrary, is an essentially positive act of the mind, the supremely positive act in virtue of which all positivity may perhaps be strictly defined. In this sphere everything seems to go on as if I found myself acting on an intuition which I possess without immediately knowing myself to possess it – an intuition which cannot be, strictly speaking, self-conscious and which can grasp itself only through the modes of experience in which its image is reflected, and which it lights up by being thus reflected in them. (p. 128)

Here, Marcel seems to be describing the ordinary flow of experience where things are already meaningful and rich (as opposed to 'unknowable'). Though the recognition of mystery is presented as 'an essentially positive act of the mind', this need not imply some state of permanent joy—our ordinary irritability with one another surely has its place here too. Fights also feature in the flow of ordinary experience. Also, due to the sheer cultural force of 'having', mystery is (as Marcel recognises in his discussion of evil) a necessarily fragile beast. Therefore, perhaps the experience of mystery is closer to McDowell's partial re-enchantment of the world than a more sugary form of perfectibility.

11.4 Some Ordinary Examples

Before saying what I think mystery might mean for teaching and the classroom space, I want to consider other contexts that might illuminate the distinction between treating things in terms of problems and mysteries. To provide an 'ordinary' example of this, I think of two old school friends of mine, Michael and Stuart, both guitarists. They were technically strong players, but Michael, who practised much harder, was capable of impressive shows of speed and agility. However, what he played did not sound like music. It was as though the instrument presented an obstacle that he had to overcome. In contrast when Stuart played, the guitar seemed, somehow, to be part of him (a cliché people often use when describing performances of revered musicians). More than this, those listening were drawn into an experience in a way that did not happen when Michael played (people felt he was simply showing off). Though we might say that Stuart 'had' a talent, this does not really capture how the distinctions between Stuart (mind/body?), the guitar and the audience were transcended.

To give another example, at some point in my early twenties, I worked in an Italian restaurant as a dishwasher. Three of us worked in the kitchen, the head chef and restaurant owner, his assistant and me. Both of my co-workers were extremely small, a little over 5 ft tall, nearly a foot shorter than me (the pertinence of this will become apparent in a moment). The chef/owner worked at the far end of the kitchen, and I washed dishes on the side wall with my back to him. Despite facing away from the chef, I had a blurred view of what he was doing in the reflective surface in front of me. He did a lot of cooking with wine—which meant a lot of flames. I often felt that I was about to be attacked by these flames as they appeared to almost spring from the reflective surface. When he had finished with one of the boiling hot pans, he would hurl it about 5 yards on to the surface to my left. I never got used to this and jumped every time. This annoyed the chef, as did my slowness in getting through the washing up. I was going as fast as I could but somehow or other.... After about 3 weeks, I was sacked. The chef was clearly quite upset and embarrassed about sacking me and struggled to explain why he'd chosen to do so. He began by saying that I didn't have the right 'you know what' and made a fluid gesture with his hands. I think he felt that this somehow wasn't clear enough and rather sheepishly told me that I had to go because I was too big—this was a small kitchen, he was small and everything was low down. How could I be expected to be fast or fluent enough? I received my wages and a couple of free beers and was then asked to leave.

What does this story say about problems and mysteries? Let us begin with the former. It would seem that a number of obstacles barred my path that, in several cases, might have been overcome. The reflective surface might have been taped over so that I couldn't see flames or pans flying in my direction. I could have practised dishwashing at home so as to speed up. Obviously, I couldn't shrink, though it is interesting that the chef presented my size as an insurmountable 'problem'. Though some of these 'solutions' may appear more sensible than others, I wonder whether this whole way of looking at my situation simply gets it wrong: "It is a proper characteristic of problems...to be reduced to detail. Mystery, on the other hand, is something which cannot be reduced to detail" (p. 109). I think that the chef came closest to putting his finger on the 'problem' with the (mysterious?) gesture. The kitchen could be thought of as a kind of living breathing organism in which, when things are going well, people and objects are bound together through fluid movement. I had given that organism asthma. That is not to say that, following my departure, an ordinary irritability did not make itself felt in that kitchen

It is important to stress that, in keeping with what has been said about mystery, there are moral as well as ontological concerns that emerge from the descriptions of these situations. It is not simply the case that my account of the guitarists raises questions about what music making 'is' (for it is questionable whether Michael is involved in music making). What I have tried to capture is the way in which the subliming of barriers between Stuart, the guitar and the audience enriches people's lives. In the case of dishwashing, a different orientation to working in the kitchen might have made my involvement a more meaningful and pleasurable experience for all those involved.

11.5   The Mysteries of the Classroom

To what extent if any can the above account have anything to say to a discussion of the classroom as opposed to, say, the kitchen. Let us consider the ways in which the classroom is often presented to 'trainee' teachers as a problem to be solved. Here are some of the things I was advised to do during my year of teacher education. I should (1) plan everything to the finest detail—some of us were given a book that outlined the 50 essential components of lesson planning—(2) create seating plans for students, (3) present clear learning objectives and outcomes, (4) differentiate materials to accommodate particular needs, (5) give the students rewards (if there were any) for good work/behaviour and (6) produce classroom contracts that students could sign in the first lesson.

This list of techniques seems to me to resonate strongly with Marcel's account of the phenomenology of having. It is as though the classroom presents itself as something that I must struggle to contain. What I 'have' can always be taken away, my control being the most obvious case in point. Things are always in danger of spilling over, and therefore, I must make every effort to try and instil a permanency in regard to order. Why not stick the unruly students in dustbins? This would probably be a popular move with David Cameron particularly if they have been engaged in any rioting. The students, indeed, the whole situation, the 'classroom' if you like, presents itself as a problem to be solved whereby each separate element could be suitably contained.

Perhaps this is an overly cynical portrayal of contemporary English approaches to teacher education. Maybe the various techniques presented above, once mastered and internalised, cease to be things I possess and become part of my extended self, therefore entering into the realm of mystery. Indeed, it could be argued that they help to instil the kind of confidence that allows for this. In response, might we not say that such confidence is necessarily fragile and simply represents an attempt to hug that which may be torn away thus forming a 'single dissoluble complex'? Indeed, we might ask what engenders the lack of confidence that teachers experience. It is perhaps nothing but the persecution felt by a culture (school and otherwise) caught in the grip of the phenomenology of having.

When I reflect on my own 'development' as a teacher, I believe that the technical elements listed above presented obstacles that, for a while, made life miserable. I found 'classroom management' difficult for quite a long time and tried out the various techniques. However, I think I only began to enjoy teaching when I stopped approaching what I was doing in terms of classroom management and began to relax. I stopped treating students (including those diagnosed as problem students) as obstacles to be overcome. Consequently, the classroom itself could become a living breathing organism. This would involve the kind of 'spillage' that could be affirmed. I am not suggesting here that this involve some sort of uniform coming together of hitherto disparate elements; each organism would be radically different and things would not always be smooth. That said, if children enter the classroom having spent all day being treated as 'problems', it is not surprising if situations become difficult.

Are there other objections to claims that teaching is caught up in the phenomenology of having? Constructivist approaches to teaching mean that it is no longer thought of in terms of a transmission of knowledge from teacher to student who comes to 'have' or 'not have' knowledge that the teacher already 'possessed'. However, this vision simply takes the emphasis on the bounded 'I' away from the teacher (who becomes a facilitator) and places it on the student (who supposedly 'creates' her own knowledge). It is up to the teacher to manufacture the conditions under which this can happen, to set the stage if you like. Bruner's 'scaffolding' metaphor is perhaps interesting here—scaffolding supports a building, the outlines of which have been determined in advance. It is worth considering that more old-fashioned approaches to teaching were not always about 'transmission' at all. In my 'best' memories of school, knowledge was creatively transformed within the 'vital' experience of teaching and learning whereby the notion of 'possession' somehow became redundant.

11.6 Classroom Research

As mentioned at the beginning of this chapter, classroom research is often thought of in terms of problem solving and the knowledge this produces. Many of the debates surrounding this kind of research focus on the validity, generalisability, etc., of such knowledge (see Bassey, 1999 and Fenstermacher, 1994). This approach to knowledge tends to include some sort of recognition of the problems with treating classroom research as though it were the same kind of objectifying practice as natural science. Often, researchers (who tend to characterise themselves as 'post-positivists') attend to these 'problems' by providing some glib autobiographical 'framing' of their lives and experiences. Given our discussion of being and having, problems and mysteries, I wonder if this particular focus on knowledge gets things wrong as it necessarily concentrates on what the teacher/researcher 'has or doesn't have' and therefore externalises knowledge itself. It takes it to a clean space away from the fray—as mentioned above, a certain emptiness accompanies the solutions to problems. The classroom becomes a 'clean space'.

The externalising practices described above are, it would seem, central to the way in which classroom research is so often conducted—create massive literature reviews in which there is no time or space to immerse yourself in anything, pick your epistemology as though you were grabbing sweets off a shelf, code your data and eliminate spillage, dissect what you have and conclude. So much of what goes on emphasises disconnection on numerous levels and distorts the mysterious aspects of teaching. Is it perhaps the case that contemporary approaches to teaching aim to eradicate 'mystery' in both Marcel's sense and indeed the more familiar sense of the term?

The clean lines of disconnection are perhaps the order of the day for the postmodern classroom in terms of both teaching and research. Let me 'reflect' on an instance of my own practice. In my last job, I taught on a course in which teachers researched theirs. Prior to the start of the course, students had to identify an aspect of their teaching that they were puzzled about (some of them found this extremely difficult) which they could 'tackle' in their dissertations. The course was run in accordance with a model of 'blended learning'. Most of the sessions were taught online. During the week before the seminar, students had to read online lecture materials and respond to questions contained in those materials in online forums. Every Thursday, my colleagues and I would sit in a computer suite (call centre?) and pose questions for discussion which we would then facilitate.

I have strong and rather unpleasant memories of the first session. To begin with, I posted a question that I had prepared in advance and waited. The first quite lengthy response was, as far as I could see, incoherent. Whilst I was trying to get the student to rephrase it, a stream of confused postings followed which read something like 'I thought I'd understood the question until I read Susan's reply and now I don't'. Consequently, much of the session seemed to involve everybody trying to clarify what they'd meant in response to utterances that may have been responses to one or numerous other postings. Following the session, I looked over the material. It read like a rather boring Beckett play (as mentioned earlier Beckett was of course most famous for writing dialogue illustrating a fundamental breakdown in communication). In later sessions, the only way I could think of to respond to this was to ask very simple/clear questions that were likely to elicit simple/clear answers. The business of posting became a much clearer/cleaner process.

In many respects, the virtual classroom chimed with the kind of research the students were undertaking. It provided a blueprint for the 'idealised' setting that they would never actually encounter. Of course, one might say that the very purpose of their research was to convert a living organism into the kind of bland rigid space that they encountered every Thursday night.

11.7 Conclusion

It is perhaps the moment to be more explicit about how what has been presented above is a meditation on educational space. On some level, getting too explicit about this issue jars with the general tone of the discussion. Nevertheless, it is perhaps worth emphasising that the spatial metaphor of 'having', whether this applies to objects or techniques, invariably feeds in to how one conceives of and treats spaces such as the classroom. The dislocation that accompanies 'having' is coterminous with the gap that now divides professional experience from other aspects of our lives. This manifests itself in a clear distinction between ways of being that are deemed appropriate in professional and private spaces. We do not, on the whole, order and contain our living rooms. Why does it seem so 'natural' to do this with the classroom? Might the infinitely extendable notion of the self offered by Marcel make a voyage across this divide? In so doing, it would of course be changed in the process. I am not suggesting that it is possible or desirable to map our interactions with our friends and family on to what happens with our students. However, need there be a clear division of personal and professional interactions and environments?

What has so far been discussed has implications for teaching, teacher education and classroom research. Making a case for mystery involves reimagining and hoping for the reanimation of all three. There may be good reason for abandoning classroom research altogether. If so, what, if anything should replace it? If teachers are to attend postgraduate programmes, they might be better served by courses in either their subjects or educational studies. Most teachers are given very little time or opportunity to engage with a deeper understanding of educational issues. Either option (or a combination of both) might aid them in becoming one with flows of knowledge that could stream through their classrooms. Of course, it is possible that a richer form of problem-solving approach to teacher research might follow on from this. In an anecdote about working on a teacher research course in Scotland, Biesta notes:

> One of the things that the teachers studying on this programme need to be able to do is show that through the conduct of small scale inquiry projects they can *improve* their practice. I have supervised a number of these projects, and what I found interesting and remarkable is that while most of the teachers were able to provide evidence about the fact that they had been able to *change* their practice, they found it quite difficult to articulate why such changes would count as an *improvement* of their practice. There is only one way in which we can answer this question, and that is through engagement with the question what education is *for*, that is, the question about the purpose of education. It is, after all, only if we are able to articulate what it is we want to achieve, that we can judge whether a change in practice gets us closer to this or further away from it. (Biesta, 2012, p. 11)

As mentioned earlier, thinking about what education is for was one of the ambitions of the influential figures at the beginnings of the teacher research movement. The problems solved would be genuinely educational ones. Moreover, there are much richer approaches to problem solving, advanced by the likes of Dewey that do not favour hard lines of disconnection: "Dewey not only rejected the dualism between cognition and action, but also the dualism between the mental and the material world. He took his point of departure in the ever-changing *transactions* of living organisms and their environments. Knowing is not outside of these processes but is part and parcel of it" (Biesta, 2009, p. 8). Though Dewey's problem solving makes a move towards subliming boundaries, he still thinks in terms 'transactions'. One is still left to 'reflect'. Marcel's account offers something more radical, immersive and vital.

In this chapter I have tried to show wariness in regard to the sentimentalism that may accompany a discussion of mystery. To acknowledge mystery is not to embrace naïf optimism where everything must be uplifting. That said if classrooms are allowed to be spaces of mystery, then a vitalism that has been exorcised from the profession may make a return. I wonder if such vitalism hovers over teaching as it seems to for Beckett's characters—when they pray, they are at least responding to one another in a communal though ill-defined goal. Students and teachers may appreciate something heartier than the pedagogical equivalent of sugar plums and biscuits.

Note

1. In *Being and Time*, Heidegger's moral concerns are mainly with freedom and authenticity in the face of Das Mann or 'The They' (Heidegger, 1962). The details of what 'The They' constitutes are not explicitly handled. The concern is more to do with the fact that if our fundamental condition is one of thrownness, how is it that we can achieve any freedom or authenticity given that we are not able to take an 'external' standpoint on things. In his essay *The Question Concerning Technology*, Heidegger shows that what we are thrown into is a condition in which things have become externalised and instrumentalised. Here

is Heidegger: In order that we may even remotely consider the monstrousness that reigns here, let us ponder for a moment the contrast that speaks out of the two titles, "The Rhine" as dammed up into the *power* works and "The Rhine" as uttered out of the *art* work, in Hölderin's hymn by that name. But, it will be replied, the Rhine is still a river in the landscape, is it not? Perhaps. But how? In no other way than as an object on call for inspection by a tour group ordered there by the vacation industry (Heidegger, 1977, p. 16). Here Heidegger introduces moral 'content' that is not a feature of *Being and Time*.

References

Bassey, M. (1999). *Case study research in educational settings*. Buckingham, UK: Open University Press.

Beckett, S. (1958). *Endgame*. London: Faber & Faber.

Biesta, G. J. (2009). Problemlösen. In S. Andresen, R. Casale, T. Gabriel, R. Horlacher, S. Larcher Klee, & J. Oelkers (Eds.), *Handwörterbuch Erziehungswissenschaft*. Weinheim, Germany: Beltz.

Biesta, G. J. J. (2012). The future of teacher education: Evidence, competence or wisdom? *Research on Steiner Education, 3*(1), 8–21.

Campbell, A., McNamara, O., & Gilroy, P. (2004). *Practitioner research and professional development in education*. New Delhi, India: Paul Chapman.

Cochran-Smith, M., & Lytle, S. L. (1993). *Inside/outside: Teacher research and knowledge*. New York: Teacher's College Press.

Darling-Hammond, L., & Bransford, J. (2005). *Preparing teachers for a changing world*. San Francisco: Jossey-Bass.

Dewey, J. (1978). How we think. In J. A. Boydston (Ed.), *The middle works (1899–1924)* (Vol. 6). Carbondale, IL/Edwardsville, IL: Southern Illinois University Press.

Duncker, K. (1935). *Zur Psychologie des produktiven Denkens*. Berlin: Springer.

Duncker, K. (1945). On problem solving. *Psychological Monographs, 58*(5).

Fenstermacher, G. (1994). The knower and the known: The nature of knowledge in research on teaching. *Review of Research in Education, 20*, 3–56.

Heidegger, M. (1962). *Being and time*. Oxford, UK: Blackwell.

Heidegger, M. (1977). *The question concerning technology and other essays*. New York: Harper and Row.

Marcel, G. (1949). *Being and having*. London/Glasgow, UK: A & C Black.

Schön, D. (1983). *The reflective practitioner*. New York: Basic Books.

Schön, D. (1987). *Educating the reflective practitioner*. San Francisco: Jossey-Bass.

Chapter 12
Spaces and Places in the Virtual University

Nicholas C. Burbules

12.1   I

The university with which we are familiar comprises spaces that define and are defined by the teaching and learning activities going on within them. In the seminar room, the lecture hall, the office, the library, and the laboratory, people come together and act out their different roles in relation to higher education. But today, universities comprise a range of technologically *virtual* spaces as well; this essay explores how they also are shaping and being shaped by new teaching and learning practices.

Elsewhere I have reviewed the distinction between *space* and *place* (Burbules, 2005). Spaces are relatively objective, defined by the contours of natural or architectural structures and locations. When I say 'relatively', I do not deny that spaces might already contain cultural markers and meanings. But *places* are spaces that have become personally or socially significant because of their history, uses, and cultural significance. A street corner is just a location on a map, but it becomes a *place* when it is where you proposed to your wife. A living room may be designed to be a gathering social space, but in many families, it is the kitchen that becomes the memorable *place* of familial gathering and bonding. Spaces are sometimes designed with the intention of making them places (a public square or a tourist attraction in a natural park), and sometimes they become so. But it is often the case that serendipitous events and circumstances make a space into a place that no one intended; other times, an existing place evolves over time to take on certain architectural or locational (spatial) features because it is where people actually gather and do things of cultural significance—here the place defines and reshapes the space. The notion of 'place', therefore, raises questions about the relation between natural or human structures and dynamic processes of historical, cultural, and social

N.C. Burbules (✉)
Department of Educational Policy, Organization and Leadership,
University of Illinois, Urbana-Champaign, IL, USA
e-mail: burbules@uiuc.edu

P. Smeyers et al. (eds.), *Educational Research: The Importance and Effects of Institutional Spaces*, Educational Research 7, DOI 10.1007/978-94-007-6247-3_12,
© Springer Science+Business Media Dordrecht 2013

change. Something can be a place and then lose that quality over time as people forget or as practices change; a space may acquire some new significance or meaning; or we might see 'place conflicts' when a particular space has different meaning and value as a place for different groups.

The university features a variety of places, significant because of what happens within them. Viewed as a whole, a university campus is itself a place, usually set apart from its environment, a place imagining itself as a site of contemplation and study. At other times, a university campus might be a site of protest, or of commerce, or of celebration. Because a campus brings together a large number of relatively young people to learn from and with their elders and each other, it has a certain atmosphere that can range from all-night study sessions to drunken festivals to candlelight vigils to graduation ceremonies. Here too, the importance of certain practices and rituals underscores the specialness of certain places in a university, just as those places in turn shape and provide continuity to the rituals that take place (and have taken place many times before) within particular spaces.

As in the work of Emile Durkheim, some of these places take on the character of the sacred—not only formally religious sites—though many universities have their origins in religious establishment and have the physical character of a seminary or monastic retreat. The sacred character of university places also derives from customs and ceremonies that are quasi-religious in character: the enforced silence of the library; the classroom that often looks like a place of worship, with the professor in an elevated or separate space that underscores his or her authority; the formal gowns and recessionals that mark the significance of graduation and other special events. This sacred character is further underscored by acts of privilege: who can stand during a class session, who can speak without permission, who can approach or touch the blackboard, the stage, the teacher's desk (or today, who can project images and information onto the screen in front of the room).

These markers, these privileges, and these formal places express and reinforce the values of a university around *knowledge, authority,* and *community.* They are inherently hierarchical, although increasingly faculty and students seek ways to contest or problematize them. These markers of place invest the values of knowledge, authority, and community with the aura of sacredness and tradition. Because they have the weight of history behind them, however, they affect faculty and students even in ways of which they might not be aware, and they continue to have force even in the face of contestation. Ironically, perhaps, for an institution founded on the principles of reason, these foundations of knowledge, authority, and community rest in part on institutional elements and the function of spaces and places that affect and motivate participants subrationally, through unconscious influences as much as through rational choice. What garners and sustains respect within the institution; what legitimates knowledge claims and assertions of authority; the dynamics of evaluation and who gets to issue such judgments, over whom, and how; the processes of approval and disapproval that motivate participants and establish a hierarchy of professional advancement; and so on, all have formal, explicit, and reasoned justifications—but all also rest upon the auras deriving from ceremony and tradition that abide in the distinctive spaces and places of the university.

The spaces and places of the university are also governed by norms about publicity and privacy. Universities comprise both open and closed spaces, giving them markedly different characters as *places*. It would be a remarkable event in a classroom for a stranger to walk in and start talking; faculty make choices about when to leave their office doors open or not, and these choices signify; some spaces are subject to degrees of surveillance and others less so. All of these characteristics give shape and meaning to the quality of teaching and learning interactions that take place within a university. In a broader sense, access to the university itself, through application, selection, and cost, creates a kind of enforced boundary marker; there is a reason we call it 'admission'.

Finally, these spaces and places also have certain material and even commercial significance. University buildings need to be heated, lit, and repaired. Their design entails efficiencies and inefficiencies that drive cost considerations (there are many reasons for the large tiered lecture hall, not all of them ritualistic). You now hear administrators talk about the price per seat in a classroom the way airlines talk about the price per seat on a plane. Large open campuses, depending on the region, require lawn care, leaf collection, and shoveling snow. Urban campuses increasingly require security barriers, lighting, and police. Many universities are feeling the costs of physical maintenance as a growing constraint on their budgets. And so it is not a great surprise that many institutions are intrigued by the idea of *virtual campuses* that extend the reach and influence of the institution without having to increase its physical size or facilities.

12.2   II

This essay examines the dynamics of space and place in the context of the 'virtual university'. If the foundations of knowledge, authority, and community within the university depend in part on the dynamics of space, place, and the traditions and rituals that accompany them, what happens when the physical character of those spaces and places is transformed into online contexts? Do those traditions and rituals, and the auras of significance and meaning they provide, disappear—or do other kinds of places, other kinds of traditions and rituals, come to take their place?

First, these changes involve new teaching and learning practices, as more and more universities are offering online courses and even complete online certificate and degree programs. Meanwhile, even on-campus students want access to these courses as part of their program of study because of their convenience (and sometimes, lower costs)—and so the on-campus experience itself becomes more 'blended' between different kinds of courses. And, of course, even traditional teaching on campus is relying more and more on uses of technology as a tool or complement, if not entirely as a platform for experimentation and transformation.

Online courses can be self-paced, they can be taken at flexible times, and some promise a more independent and individualized learning experience—and all of these can be attractive elements to students of all sorts. We are becoming increasingly aware, I think, that the virtues of the face-to-face, on-campus course or seminar are not experienced as beneficial by all kinds of learners. A certain romance or nostalgia for a kind of intensive, personal faculty/student bond needs to be balanced with a recognition of the difficulty (and cost) or trying to provide that sort of bond for every student. And in fact universities do not provide that sort of bond for every student. And not every student desires that sort of bond or can afford it. Student learning styles, interests, and motivations are eclectic, while the nature of the university has been to accustom them to a broadly similar set of educational options. Online courses and degrees can diversify those options, and students are showing through their choices that they want options.

While many online classes start out as regular classes 'delivered' through a different medium (still relying on video lectures, Powerpoint outlines and slides, quizzes and exams), over time many faculty see new technologies as a way of changing their instruction, moving courses more in the direction of inquiry, discovery learning, and collaboration that decenters the role of the teacher and enacts the potential for constructivist pedagogy and self-directed learning that many subscribe to at the level of principle but which can be difficult to create in traditional classrooms, especially given large numbers of students. Here is one prime way in which the physical spaces and ritualized places of the university, emerging out of a particular model of teaching and learning, over time become a constraint that limits imagination and innovation in teaching and learning in new ways. New technologies become an affordance that enables (though they do not guarantee) the possibility of rethinking these familiar teaching practices.

The term 'affordance' is useful here because it does not reinforce the notion that the transformation of teaching and learning is automatic. New technologies have capabilities just as adaptable to standardization as to diversification, to perpetuating traditional instructional practices as to overturning them, and to narrowing student choices as to opening them up. The crucial factor is not the new technology but the opportunity a new technology provides for reexamining and rethinking our assumptions and typical practices; in other words, the limiting factor is in ourselves, our imaginations, and our willingness as teachers to give up things that may be familiar and comfortable in order to embark on something uncertain, creative, and risky.

A related set of changes is happening on the side of learning. Portable devices and pervasive wireless connectivity mean that people can now carry the Internet in their pockets; this means more or less continual, 'anywhere, anytime' access to information and social connectivity with peers and with experts who possess knowledge one may not have. Access to information is not itself learning, of course. But it can facilitate learning that is situated in contexts where information can be used and applied, it can facilitate learning that is socially mediated and shared, and it can facilitate forms of lifelong learning and problem-solving that are continuous with the flow of life's activities in the workplace, in the home, and in public social spaces. I along with others call this 'ubiquitous learning' (Burbules, 2009). Some forms of ubiquitous learning involve access to online courses or other formal learning opportunities, others have much more the character of guided self-study through learning materials that can be accessed through the Internet, and some others involve collaborative learning through distributed networks of learners with similar interests in a subject—learning with and through each other without distinct teacher/student roles. Ubiquitous learning provides a way of rethinking the traditional idea of lifelong learning and making it more manifest; learning becomes a pervasive, continuous potential, seamlessly integrated into the flow of daily life and activity. The ubiquitous learning place is not freed from spatial location; rather, it participates in a variety of particular spatial locations—the workplace, the home, and the coffee house—and takes on different characters depending in part on the kinds of motivating questions and problems arising in those different locations.

These spaces are becoming significant educational *places,* places of meaning and purpose that inspire and motivate learning, within 'the virtual'. Often their capacity for meaning, purpose, and motivation derives from the extent to which they become *socially shared* educational places. It is not new that learning takes place in the workplace, the home, or the coffee house; what is new is the connection between these 'informal' sites of learning and the structured learning that takes place within formal, institutional settings and the ways in which these become places where socially networked and collaborative learning can take place.

Second, I have described some of the ways in which university spaces and places relate to traditions and rituals that enforce ways of thinking about knowledge, authority, and community within the institution. What happens in virtual learning places that may not support the same kinds of traditions and rituals?

Understandings and expectations about knowledge in the university are influenced by the places and practices through which knowledge claims are shared and validated. The lecture hall promotes a certain understanding of knowledge, who has it, and how it is communicated and learned. The laboratory promotes another, the library or the seminar room, still others. Knowledge in the virtual university has, I believe, much more the character of the Internet itself: the validating authority of any single knowledge source is more attenuated; there are multiple and openly conflicting knowledge claims to deal with; knowledge is often much more socially distributed in its validation and status. We see a shift from a search for the indubitable Cartesian claim of what 'I know' to the more distributed and negotiated claims of what 'We know'.

The very profligacy of information, of points of view, of dispersed and sometimes nonoverlapping communities of discourse on the Internet threatens a greater degree of epistemic relativism. The online learner is not a part of a captive audience quite as much as in a classroom, where the instructor has more latitude in shaping and controlling the information available to students (and this is one reason why some instructors feel very threatened when students bring their computers to class). This shift, in turn, means that learners may come to identify themselves with learning communities that are not bounded or defined institutionally in the same way that a university population is. The walls of the classroom and campus buildings are leaking in both directions, and for fully virtual students, there aren't any 'walls' in that sense at all.

What this means is that the instructor in a virtual learning place needs to intentionally promote new practices and new traditions and rituals to inspire and motivate student attitudes toward knowledge, authority, and community that will be productive toward learning. In part, certain traditions and rituals still persist from the traditional university (so far at least): there is still an aura and status to the teacher's authority and reputation; there are still markers in the provision of an online course syllabus or lecture that echo the traditional sources of meaning and significance that have inspired and motivated learners; and of course where students are 'blended', they are still members of the university environment, traditions, and customs even when they are taking some courses online.

Nevertheless, we are seeing a shift. Precisely because online courses and programs are designed to reach 'nontraditional' learners, to expand access to higher education, and to exploit the potential of a global marketplace for learning, the online course instructor is confronted with a much more eclectic population of learners, many of whom have not been socialized into the expectations about knowledge, authority, and community that the traditional university takes for granted and who are not particularly impressed with or motivated by the subtle auras of status and value that university places and university norms and rituals tend to promote. The very *feel* of tradition, of institutional authority, of exclusivity, which are the products of university buildings, impressive architecture, cloistered campuses, decorative privileged landscaping, and so on, is merely echoed in virtual places. In large part, this feeling—though it is not my main topic here—happens through the interaction of our embodied selves with the physical environments of the desk, the classroom, the building architecture, and the campus. And although we are still embodied even when we are online, the interactions between body, space, and sociality that give *virtual* contexts their verisimilitude and sense of place are different.

As a result, online instructors and designers need to consciously build in practices, structures, social processes, and rituals that have the capacity to motivate, inspire, and guide learning—which manifest valuations of knowledge, authority, and community that are appropriate to this new teaching and learning environment. Following are some of my own experiences and thoughts on this question, based on 15 years of online teaching.

12.3   III

The first way to adapt our ways of thinking of traditional university spaces and places is to think about the online class as a *learning space*. On the one hand, this means putting learning at the forefront of the course's purpose and direction. Online students approach classes much more with the question of what they will gain from it, and this means that their expectations are directed more toward specifiable learning outcomes. Where they are mature professionals, their very purpose in taking the course may be tied to professional development or advancement, which depends on demonstrable knowledge and skills they will have gained. Explicitness about the aims and purposes of the course also can provide a greater degree of transparency about the teacher's intentions and can establish a set of more explicit criteria by which teachers can be evaluated.

On the other hand, I find it is also fruitful to think of the course as a space: a space in which movement and exploration are possible and in which there can be surprises and serendipity—but most of all, a space in which student choices are possible that allow movement through the space in unique and personally differentiated ways. These choices, choices about importance and interest and choices about social connections and community building, are key to the processes by which this designed learning space can become a meaningful and valued *place* (or a set of places) for the students.

One way to think about this difference is in relation to two related Greek terms, *odos* and *poros* (Kofman, 1988). An *odos* is a path tracing a familiar route, where the direction and objective are known. A *poros* is a path of exploration, where the direction and outcome are more uncertain, a trailblazing path, oriented toward discovery. An *odos* can be provided by a map or a GPS device; a *poros* is more the way you learn your way around a new city. As Ludwig Wittgenstein (1958) says:

> Our language can be seen as an ancient city: a maze of little streets and squares, of old and new houses, and of houses with additions from various periods; and this surrounded by a multitude of new boroughs with straight regular streets and uniform houses. (see Wittgenstein, 1958, p. 18)

Language is a labyrinth of paths. You approach from *one* side and know your way about; you approach the same place from another side and no longer know your way about (see *ibid.*, p. 203).

In teaching you philosophy, I'm like a guide showing you how to find your way round London. I have to take you through the city from north to south, from east to west, from Euston to the embankment, and from Piccadilly to the Marble Arch. After I have taken you many journeys through the city, in all sorts of directions, we shall have passed through any given street a number of times—each time traversing the street as part of a different journey. At the end of this, you will know London; you will be able to find your way about like a Londoner (Wittgenstein, quoted in Gasking & Jackson, 1967, p. 51).

Putting this within a broader educational frame, we can ask: which are the kinds of learning goals that can be made explicit, and which are the kind that can only be gained in this more meandering, discovery-oriented manner? (Burbules, 2000) New technologies can facilitate both kinds of pedagogy: the directive *odos* of programmed instruction and the exploratory *poros* of an open learning system. And both, I hope it is clear, are ways of thinking about the design of learning spaces, with the potential to become activated and experienced by learners as kinds of learning *places*.

It is important, further, to see that the two sides of this discussion, the focus on learning and the focus on teaching as a process of designing kinds of spaces, are dependent on each other. The focus on learning means thinking about student questions, student needs, student learning styles, and student goals. The focus on the design of learning spaces means thinking about where learning needs to be (and can be) directed and where it requires a degree of choice and self-direction, and it means recognizing that different learners will go through the same material in different ways, at different paces, and for different purposes.

It is striking, when one examines the dominant *course management systems* (sometimes called *learning management systems*) provided for use in online teaching, how different the assumptions are, built into these applications, about the degree of directedness versus the degree of openness they tolerate. To the extent that teachers follow the implicit design assumptions that are built into them, as a path of least resistance (or because they simply take these implicit design elements as natural or inevitable), they not only cede important judgments they need to be making as teachers to the designers of the application; they also squander an opportunity to use the online environment to diversify the kinds of learning spaces available to students rather than standardizing them.

As I have stressed, the ways in which the instructor sets these design priorities (or allows them to be set for him or her) reflect implicit judgments about knowledge, authority, and community in the class. It reflects judgments about how far to emphasize (and encourage) student responsibility for the choices made possible in the learning space. It reflects judgments about decentering a more hierarchical view of knowledge without, I would say, falling into the opposite problem of relativism. It reflects, perhaps most of all, a willingness to give up a certain desire for control and determination as the teacher without giving up a broader responsibility to create and lead the class toward productive learning outcomes that, while not entirely determinable, still reflect one's own expertise and values in a distinctive way (otherwise, why teach the course at all?).

Second, spaces normally become places through a process of becoming *shared* spaces. While a space can acquire a particular meaning solely for a particular individual and so become a 'place' solely for him or her, that is not the usual pattern. For a learning space to become a *place* in any intentional, formal educational process, others must be involved. And so the teacher can find a valuable resource in emphasizing the social and *collaborative* nature of learning and find ways to promote this in the practices, discourses, and value systems of the classroom.

A social, collaborative environment is a more motivating environment for many students. Peer approval matters. A work project can be more satisfying and enjoyable when it becomes the focus for conversation and collective problem-solving. Pleasurable social relations often grow out of project-related interactions; people discover common interests, develop friendships, and so on. If one feels a commitment to the group and the group's success, this becomes an additional motivation beyond simple self-interest. Peer to peer teaching happens within these collaborations (Burbules, 2004).

Moreover, learning to collaborate is a crucial skill in more and more professional contexts; effective collaboration is itself a valuable learning outcome. This does not mean that collaboration is without difficulties and conflicts of its own, and it does not mean that for some learners a more social learning model may not be their preferred choice. No class has to be all one thing, but if learning to collaborate is a valued goal, then learning to adjust to collaborative environments, and contribute to them productively, is worth working at.

Third, if one takes the idea of ubiquity seriously, this also affects the way one thinks about teaching and learning in online environments. Some of these are extremely concrete: realizing that for some students the class is taking place late in the evening, after a long day at work, and for others, it is the first thing they are doing in the morning. Some may be interacting with the class while in the workplace; others may be at home breastfeeding their child. Whether the course is synchronous or asynchronous, time differences and people's schedules mean that their temporal environments may be widely disparate; they may all be 'in the class at the same time', *but it is not the same time for them*. Spatial arrangements may be similarly diverse—and as the above examples indicate, these temporal and spatial diversities are associated with each other.

These different locations also relate to different motivations and reactions to learning opportunities. Students may be distracted or 'multitasking' (or perhaps multitasking *means* distracted!). Some may be actively thinking about the class topic in relation to a more or less proximate need or problem; for others, the learning is more abstract and prospective. Some may be accessing the course together, as a group, others as individuals, and perhaps very solitary individuals.

A traditional classroom imposes a certain kind of uniformity among students, despite their personal differences: they are all in the same general environment, at the same time, in similar seats, and often arranged in very familiar ways. They all see the same instructor, the same blackboard, have the same textbook in front of them, etc. (They are usually even dressed similarly in broad fashion.) The online class is quite another thing: even down to the level of the kind of computer they are using, they may actually be seeing and experiencing very different learning environments, and they are certainly experiencing them within quite diverse contexts.

These three elements, the design of learning spaces (and the different things that can mean), the social nature of these spaces, and the spatial and temporal challenges presented by ubiquity, set up a set of similarities and contrasts with the familiar spaces and places of the university. They each provide challenges to rethink our practices of teaching and learning, while also providing affordances for doing teaching and learning in productive new ways. In this essay, I have discussed how these three elements shape the kind of spaces and places that characterize the *virtual university*; in some cases, there are analogies to the familiar, while in other cases, such analogies are constraining or misleading. Finally, they each refer back to changed understandings and values about knowledge, authority, and community, understandings and values that underlie and justify our approaches to thinking and learning. Unless we are willing to reexamine these, and rethink our ways of justifying them, I believe, we will fail to connect with a generation of learners who view them in quite different ways than we do.

References

Burbules, N. C. (2000). Aporias, webs, and passages: Doubt as an opportunity to learn. *Curriculum Inquiry, 30*, 171–187.
Burbules, N. C. (2004). Navigating the advantages and disadvantages of online pedagogy. In C. Haythornthwaite & M. M. Kazmer (Eds.), *Learning, culture, and community in online education: Research and practice* (pp. 3–17). New York: Peter Lang.

Burbules, N. C. (2005). Rethinking the virtual. In J. Weiss, J. Nolan, & P. Trifonas (Eds.), *The international handbook of virtual learning environments* (pp. 3–24). Dordrecht, the Netherlands: Kluwer.

Burbules, N. C. (2009). Meanings of ubiquitous learning. In B. Cope & M. Kalantzis (Eds.), *Ubiquitous learning* (pp. 15–20). Urbana, IL: University of Illinois Press.

Gasking, D. A. T., & Jackson, A. C. (1967). Wittgenstein as a teacher. In K. T. Fann (Ed.), *Ludwig Wittgenstein: The man and his philosophy* (pp. 49–55). Atlantic Highlands, NJ: Humanities Press.

Kofman, S. (1988). Beyond aporia? In A. Benjamin (Ed.), *Post-structuralist classics* (pp. 7–44). New York: Routledge.

Wittgenstein, L. (1958). *Philosophical investigations* (3rd ed., G. E. M. Anscombe, Trans.). New York: Macmillan.

Chapter 13
Material Contexts and Creation of Meaning in Virtual Places: Web 2.0 as a Space of Educational Research

Lynn Fendler and Karin Priem

In this chapter, we focus on the salient features of Web 2.0 as a space of research. By Web 2.0, we mean an interactive online environment in which readers are also writers. Reading and writing are also historical events: situated in time and space, requiring a medium of interaction, and based on historically specific tools and techniques. As such, the techniques and subjects of reading and writing are influenced by social and cultural contexts and highly dependent on the physical and intellectual capacities of a disciplined human body. Web 2.0 is a relatively new reading/writing platform that cannot be fully understood without examining the history of reading and writing. Therefore, our approach is very much influenced by material history (Latour & Woolgar, 1979) and the history of books (Burke, 1997; Chartier/Cavallo, 1995/1999; Genette, 1987/2001; Platteaux, 2002). We are especially interested in the historical shifts in reading and writing that are implicated in Web 2.0 research spaces. Within this focus, we highlight authorship and gatekeeping as salient cultural practices.

According to our historical and epistemological approach, our chapter has two main parts before the conclusion: (1) A Short History from Scroll to Screen: Materialities of Reading and Writing and (2) From Redaction to Compositionism: Epistemological Shifts in Web 2.0 Spaces.

L. Fendler (✉)
College of Education, Department of Teacher Education,
Michigan State University, East Lansing, MI, USA
e-mail: fendler@msu.edu

K. Priem
Faculté des Lettres, des Sciences Humaines, des Arts et des Sciences de l'Education,
Luxembourg University, Walferdange, Luxembourg

P. Smeyers et al. (eds.), *Educational Research: The Importance and Effects of Institutional Spaces*, Educational Research 7, DOI 10.1007/978-94-007-6247-3_13, © Springer Science+Business Media Dordrecht 2013

13.1   A Short History from Scroll to Screen: Materialities of Reading and Writing

The history of books and cultural practices has recently been analyzed as an important part of material culture and its strong influence on processes of knowledge and meaning production (see, e.g., Chartier & Cavallo, 1995/1999; Priem, 2012). Reading and writing first of all refer to physical objects that carry or contain text. Reading is seen as a practice of taking possession of a text and creating meaning. The formal structures and organization of texts influence the reading process and the understanding process. Identical texts are read, used, and understood in different ways under different historical circumstances. The meaning of a text therefore depends on the materiality of the text, the quality of the medium, the approach to reading, and the reader's spatial, social, and cultural circumstances. Writing as a cultural practice has very much in common with reading processes: writing is also situated in physical circumstances like the human body. Tools of writing and media carry the text while being produced. Writing and reading after all are cultural practices that create meaning, reflect relationships, and interpret reality.

The materiality of reading and writing becomes obvious if we look at some aspects of the history of books and reading, especially as this history has been put forward by Chartier and Cavallo (1995/1999). They note that in Hellenistic times, the practice of collecting books in libraries and categorizing them according to authors and contents was already well established. Texts were structured into volumina, or scrolls, which were defined by particular specifications of height and length. These first Hellenistic libraries were used only by a small group of scholars. Libraries were not established primarily for reading but to show political and ideological power.

According to Chartier and Cavallo, during the first and second centuries B.C., Greek books were brought to the Roman Empire, where they were collected in private libraries—still exclusive places, but by then part of everyday life. Thus, the Greco-Roman age marked an important turning point in the process of alphabetization. An increasing number of different sorts of texts and new practices of reading had become symbols of a cultivated way of life and sociability. The rise of reading corresponded to the rise of the codex, a type of book that consisted of and was divided into pages that were easier to handle than scrolls. The materiality of the text—from scroll to codex—had an impact on reading practices. Then in early medieval times, the modes of reading changed again. Medieval reading was practiced in rather closed spaces like churches and the covered walks and cells of monasteries. At this time, reading had come to mean religious edification and concentration. This shift also marked a change from reading aloud to reading silently.

From the late eleventh until the fourteenth centuries, another important turn was identified. The rise of cities and schools was accompanied by a huge increase in all sorts of texts and consequently also an increase in reading and writing skills. Reading came to be regarded not only as a way of picking up a text but also as a process of understanding its meaning. Reading at this time implied reflecting on texts.

As a result of this change, books became intellectual objects, not just political and ideological symbols. Efforts were made to provide the reader with new tools of reading, such as indices, tables of content, summaries, chapters, paragraphs, different and smaller formats, and so on. In their material form, texts became organized, structured, divided, and subdivided. The reading associated with these texts shifted gradually to mean selective reading. Increasingly, libraries became a place of silent reading and silent study.

In the middle of the fifteenth century, Gutenberg's invention of the printing press allowed not only a major reduction in the costs associated with the production of books but also a simple way of scaling up the production of books, which in turn led to changes in the distribution of books. These fundamental and quantitative changes then led to qualitative changes: that is, more popular journalistic and fictional genres became available, alongside more traditional scientific and religious texts.

As for reading, however, this proliferation of texts was not as important as is generally assumed by historians, since the organization and structures of texts were still the same as before the printing press. So from this perspective, it could be argued that Gutenberg's printing press did not constitute as dramatic a change as the earlier shift from scroll to codex. What is more meaningful for the history of reading at this time is the fact that silent reading became a more common practice (Chartier & Cavallo, 1995/1999). Reading became faster and more selective. Silent reading left the readers to their own thoughts, their individual use of books, and private understandings. In these circumstances, reading also became threatening. When reading became individual and private, it could no longer be monitored as public reading had been earlier. Private, silent reading then became an issue of governance and control, and women especially were accused of a kind of reading mania.

The most recent revolution in reading and writing occurred only recently, brought about by electronic media and the electronic transmission of texts on screens. Similar to the ancient scrolls, texts again are taking on a vertical appearance, while they are still fabricated and provided with the structuring means of pagination that came with the codex during the first and second century B.C. (Chartier & Cavallo, 1995/1999; Grossman, 2011). The traditional book is still one of the formats in which electronic reading and writing processes are performed, for example, Kindle editions of texts. Some electronic texts appear in scroll form, and other electronic texts appear in codex form. In addition, new forms of electronic communication and literacy are now being developed in response to market demands. All these new forms mark a change concerning aesthetic principles and material conditions such as the concept of authorship, the completeness of a text, its originality, and modes of protection from interference and from being copied into other texts.

The history of reading and writing refers not only to material shapes of text and modes of reading but also to historical changes in the concept of authorship and intellectual property. Gérard Genette (1987/2001) reminds us of the fact that the attribution of authorship, whether authentic or fictional, is a rather new necessity. To support his argument, Genette recalls the large number of anonymous texts, especially medieval manuscripts that often circulated without ever carrying titles or specifications about who wrote the text. According to Foucault, however, this was not the case in medieval science, since here the name of the author was a sign of reliability (Foucault, 1969/2003, p. 246). In medieval times, authorship had significance for scientific texts, but not for other genres of writing, a situation that has become almost completely reversed in modern times. In many cases, authors' names were added to texts only much later according to oral traditions or results of subsequent research. This attribution of authorship is especially true for Ancient Greek times but also occurred in other historical epochs.

Additionally, the invention of pseudonyms and the practice of ghost writing are still accepted practices, and they function as common means to mask or fabricate authorship. The recent understanding of authorship is, according to Genette, diffuse and clear-cut at the same time. On the one hand, the name of an author can be used in different ways to advertise a book or text; on the other hand, the author's name, when printed on front page and cover, is an official guarantee of the completeness and the canonized version of a text. The author's name therefore is often a gesture of powerful reputation within an established hierarchy of status and cultural tradition. An author's name can never be seen as neutral, and this is especially true with respect to gender (Hahn, 1991). Legally sanctioned authorship was established at the end of the eighteenth and the beginning of the nineteenth centuries, and this marks the fabrication of intellectual property as well as new possibilities for violation and plagiarism.

Following from these historical changes in conceptualizations of authorship, Roland Barthes (1968/2006) refers to authorship as an invention of modernity, a result of capitalism and the rise of individuality and individual prestige. Authorship was at one time powerful as well as dangerous, since, according to Barthes, even the critics followed the rule that only the author as its creator could authenticate and reveal the meaning of a text. Even though authorship is still a very powerful concept, Barthes dismisses the idea of it in most recent history and states that the author is disappearing even while he/she writes. Writing, in Barthes' opinion, always refers to what has been already written. Modern writing opens up a space of multidimensional meaning in which meaning no longer resides in the author's intentions; rather, it is fully up to the individual reader to produce a coherent meaning.

Another important contribution to the recent history of authorship was made by Michel Foucault (1969/2003). In his lecture, 'What is an Author?' at the Collège de France, Foucault argued that in present times, the transcendent qualities of authorship have not disappeared but have been shifted to the level of texts. In his view, a critical perspective on the location of 'authorship' can be found in discursive practices. Foucault argues that some authors are able to invent discourses and that those discourses themselves can take on the function and position of authorship in the sense that they structure and discipline further texts. One of Foucault's examples is Sigmund Freud and psychoanalysis, in which the discourse of psychoanalysis, rather than the person of Sigmund Freud, can be understood as the author of a text. The text is produced according to the rules of a particular discourse. It is the circulation of knowledge and power in discourse that creates the text and circumscribes possible meanings for a text.

In summary, this section has shown that reading has become important in new and different ways. Silent reading stressed the creation of meaning by the individual reader and, in the long run, even served to weaken the importance of authorship. The rise of text production and book markets culminated at the end of the eighteenth century.

Modern reading and writing are characterized by the strong position of individual authorship, which turned out to be another important aspect to the constitution of meaning in texts. This last approach to meaning production is being questioned currently by new modes of digital writing practices. We think that the establishment of discourse-oriented authorship by Foucault helps us to identify new networks of authorship and knowledge production, which might be a reaction to changes that are occurring now.

Electronic books, for example, can be read vertically and/or horizontally by adding several layers of information (like archival and visual material) to the author's original text. In Robert Darnton's (2004) view, the traditional hierarchy of writing and reading processes has been changed to a large degree as a function of textual architecture. As for writing history, he points out in an interview:

> This kind of book will create a new revolution between reader and author, a new kind of reading, one that empowers the reader, making him or her a collaborator and a critic of the author and opening up endless possibilities for enlarging our understanding of the past. (Darnton & Tamm, 2004, online version)

Historical shifts in reading practices have been accompanied by historical shifts in writing practices, as well. A first step of academic writing was made in the scriptoria of monasteries. Later writing became a cultural practice of knowledge production in secular spaces like universities and academies whose results were collected in libraries, which became spaces of reading and academic exchange. The medieval practice of copying of texts has regained some importance in present days, since Kenneth Goldsmith (2011) has recently argued that copying texts is an approach to teaching literacy. The materiality of writing has developed historically into various forms like handwriting, printing machines, typewriting, voice-to-text software, the use of keyboards, and touch screens. All stages of these forms (from handwriting to mechanization) coexist today as forms of interaction of body and mind. New writing practices have not tended to replace older ones sequentially; rather, new forms of reading and writing have accumulated so that now there is a whole array of reading/writing practices being used contemporaneously in the present day.

Authorship has not always belonged to the central aspects of a text, and the canonizing effects of authorship on the creation of meaning are historically inconsistent. One could thus venture a guess that another shift in authorship is happening now, and there are indications that the distinction between reading and writing is becoming increasingly blurred in the context of Web 2.0 text modalities.

13.2 From Redaction to Compositionism: Epistemological Shifts in Web 2.0 Spaces

Digital spaces of research exist now in several different modalities. Web 2.0 is distinguished from Web 1.0 and Web 3.0 modalities by the following characteristics:

- Interactive and dynamic reading/writing spaces
- Sites of polyvocality and complex practices of coauthorship
- Blurring of the distinction between 'reader' and 'writer'

Web 2.0 spaces include blogs, wikis, RSS feeds, mashups, open documents, and social media sites. Examples of Web 2.0 sites are Wikipedia, Weebly, Facebook, Blogster, YouTube, and GoogleDocs. One crucial feature is that Web 2.0 supports collective authorship, recently known as 'social scholarship', which we connect to Latour's (2010) term 'compositionism'. In this section, we describe how Web 2.0 research spaces are more interactive and different in quality from traditional read-only (or 1.0) spaces of research.[1]

We can characterize conventional reading/writing spaces as being shaped by processes of redaction. These editing practices—*redaktionelle Betreuung*—include deciding which topics should be discussed, controlling style, selecting content, and compiling or grouping texts. Redaction is the salient feature of research knowledge production in conventional research texts and in Web 1.0 spaces.

Research in Web 2.0 spaces is not subject to the same redaction processes; it is something different. To explicate the unique characteristics of reading and writing in Web 2.0 spaces, we employ Latour's (2010) term 'compositionism' to convey differences in reading/writing practices: "'composition' … underlines that things have to be put together (Latin *componere*) while retaining their heterogeneity" (Latour, 2010, pp. 473–474).

Web 2.0 research spaces exemplify Latour's idea of compositionism because in many blogs, social media, and wiki spaces, knowledge is assembled—composed—in a space without centralized or institutionally authorized redaction that aims to weave coherence or to reconcile oppositional viewpoints in a text. Depending on how public or private, open or closed, the Web 2.0 space is, the range of perspectives on an issue can be more or less diverse. At one extreme end, open public blogs become multiauthored, multi-perspective global texts that serve both as objects of study for research projects and as compositionist sites of research and publication. At another extreme end, a blog or wiki can be made available to only one or two authors, and not to the general public. In this latter case, one could argue that the space is similar to conventional coauthorship except for the simultaneity and accelerated rhythm of exchange between authors.

As a research space, Web 2.0 has the compositionist capacity to create and support collective authorship using mechanisms that have not been available in other research spaces. Production of knowledge in Web 2.0 spaces is not governed by the same regulatory mechanisms as previous modes of knowledge production,[2] and the distinction between readers/audience and writers/authors does not seem to fit so well any longer.

In North America, the term 'social scholarship' is used to capture the key feature of knowledge production in Web 2.0 spaces. Greenhow, Robelia, and Hughes (2009) define social scholarship as a bridge between formal and informal knowledge production:

Social scholarship capitalizes on Web 2.0 affordances to evolve the ways in which scholarship is accomplished in academia. It connects traditional formal scholarship practices (such as creating a peer-reviewed, print-based journal article) with more informal, social Internet-based practices (such as hosting an online video or audio conference discussion about a journal article). (Greenhow et al., 2009, p. 253)

Surprisingly, however, the field of education has very little grasp on the epistemological norms of compositionism because very little educational research has been conducted on Web 2.0 spaces. Compositionism, as a characteristic of Web 2.0 spaces, constitutes new forms and venues for production and dissemination of educational research, and there is vast potential, and possibly an urgent need, for future projects in educational research to focus more critically on the effects and affordances of compositionism in Web 2.0 environments. In this section, we begin to map some of the shifts in epistemology and politics that are implicated in Web 2.0 spaces of research.

13.2.1 Epistemology of Compositionism in Web 2.0 Research Spaces

Latour has suggested that compositionism may be replacing critique as a format for intellectual exchange in some research spaces: "In a first meaning, compositionism could stand as an alternative to *critique* …It is no more possible to compose with the paraphernalia of critique than it is to cook with a seesaw" (Latour, 2010, p. 475). When we consider possible differences between critique and compositionism, then certain epistemological issues are raised for consideration in educational research.

In conventional research spaces, critique and redaction (in the form of editing and peer review) have formed the basis for shaping and validating what is regarded as acceptable research-based knowledge. In contrast, Web 2.0 spaces allow information to be posted by anybody, and there are few (or no) authoritative mechanisms for safeguarding the space from falsehoods and ideological pollution. The most usual objection to Web 2.0-generated knowledge is the absence of quality control. It is assumed that information that has not been redacted by qualified reviewers is unreliable. The question of reliability in Web 2.0 spaces raises interesting epistemological and political conundrums regarding the role of academic institutions as producers and gatekeepers for scientific knowledge.

In traditional institutionally mediated spaces (off-line and Web 1.0), knowledge production is validated through culturally sanctioned mechanisms of redaction (peer review and editorial gatekeeping). Such mechanisms are an example of one kind of democratic procedure that allegedly adjudicates knowledge on qualified judgments of merit. At the same time, as we all know, knowledge production as it is manifested in traditional redaction practices is not based solely on some disinterested criteria of intellectual meritocracy. Rather, research knowledge is shaped by many forces in addition to intellectual merit including cultural traditions, institutional hierarchies, ideologies, careerism, funding trends, faddism, cronyism, and happenstance. From this perspective, then, the reliability of research produced through conventional mechanisms might be seen as being vulnerable to charges that are quite similar to those leveled against knowledge produced in Web 2.0 spaces.

In conventional research spaces, knowledge production tends to be concentrated in certain spatial centers, and peripheral sites of knowledge production—like online publications—tend to be devalued by university researchers. In a context of academically mediated knowledge production, the definition of 'reliable' is determined according to culturally specific norms of a cultural minority and established publication bureaucracies. This centralized and concentrated space of research refers not only to education but also to methodological, cultural, financial, and political hierarchies in the arts and sciences.

With the introduction of Web 2.0 spaces, schools, universities, and other conventional authorities no longer have the same unchallenged monopoly over gatekeeping, research production, and access to knowledge as they once had. The institutional boundaries around research and knowledge production have been redrawn in the context of openly available and user-created content. Authors who publish in Web 2.0 spaces are not always legitimated though institutional affiliations, or the institutional affiliation of an author may be invisible in the Web 2.0 publication space. The most famous example of this trend is Wikipedia, but the blogosphere is enormous, and Web 2.0 spaces are quickly out-publishing conventional spaces of knowledge production.[3]

The features of compositionism imply shifts in mechanisms deployed for evaluation of research and knowledge. Rather than judging intellectual merit on the basis of three handpicked peer reviews mediated by an institutionally appointed editor, evaluation in Web 2.0 spaces reflects the judgment of a random number of relatively random readers. There is extensive peer review in Web 2.0 spaces, even though the criteria and processes of review are quite different from those in conventional spaces (see, e.g., Critical Commons). The language of review has shifted from 'accept' to 'like' or '+1', and review commentary may come from dozens of people from various intellectual persuasions in any part of the world. In addition, compositionist features of the space are likely to reflect a much wider range of perspectives and contributions from a broad array of intellectual fields—for better or worse. Validation of knowledge in Web 2.0 spaces is unlike validation in conventional publication spaces; however, the difference is not simply that one space is characterized by rigorous quality control while the other space is characterized by willy-nilly opinions.

One salient factor of Web 2.0 peer review is the visibility of reader/writer commentary. Web 2.0 compositionist spaces display streams of time-stamped comments (and sometimes also votes or comments on comments) by reader/authors. There is usually no attempt in Web 2.0 spaces to reconcile an array of oppositional viewpoints expressed in comment threads. Because there is a visible record of many diverse perspectives in the space, the judgment of quality is left more to the reader/writer who is *within* the research space, and not to an editor who is hierarchically removed from the reading/writing space. Evaluation mechanisms in Web 2.0 spaces, then, operate within parameters that are unlike evaluation mechanisms in conventional research spaces.

Web 2.0 modalities have epistemological effects because they engender forms of knowledge production that are not available in other modalities or spaces of information technology. As Greenhow et al. (2009) summarize:

> Validity of knowledge in Web 2.0 environments is established through peer review in an engaged community, and *expertise* entails understanding disputes and offering syntheses widely accepted by the community…. In other words, knowledge is decentralized, accessible, and co-constructed by and among a broad base of users. (Greenhow et al., p. 247)

Practices of social scholarship in Web 2.0 spaces also contribute to the development of theory. Leu et al. (2009) have argued that the Internet in educational settings should no longer be framed as an issue of technology, but rather, research should be framed as an issue of literacy called 'New Literacy Theories':

> Recognizing the Internet as a literacy issue has prompted individuals from many disciplines to begin a collaborative approach to theory building.... This approach is coming to be referred to as New Literacies theory... It takes an open-source approach to theory development, at the highest level, inviting everyone who studies the Internet's impact on our literacy lives to contribute to theory development and to benefit from others' contributions. (Leu et al., 2009, p. 265)

Because of institutional shifts around validations of knowledge and knowledge production in Web 2.0 spaces, educational pathways and modes of credentialing are also being affected. University policies regarding publication and copyright are already in profound transition as they struggle to keep up with new definitions of research, peer review, authorship, plagiarism, and impact factors for publications (for an alternative to copyright, see, e.g., Creative Commons).

Web 2.0 spaces have facilitated new data-generating techniques for educational research. Crowdsourcing (a term coined in 2006 and applied most frequently to business ventures), for example, is now employed for research not only in commercial industries but also in sciences. To use crowdsourcing as a data-generation method means to post a research question into social media sites and then sift and analyze responses for usable data (see, e.g., The National Academies, 2011). Crowdsourcing is a data-generating mechanism that contributes compositionist features to research spaces. One recent example of crowdsourcing data generation is a historical project that is mapping the geographic origins of African-heritage people in North America. Researchers post onto social media sites the names and whatever limited family information is available, and then they ask readers to circulate the questions and reply with any anecdotal information they may have regarding these names and origins. Through snowballing and viral-like circulation, further identifying information associated with the names is provided by random informants in various parts of the world, and a map of the geographic origins of families is gradually being constructed on the basis of these responses (Smith, 2011).

Crowdsourcing, as a research technique associated with Web 2.0 spaces, also contributes to epistemological shifts because sources of information may not have an institutional affiliation and information cannot be validated using institutionalized redaction rubrics (McFarland & Klopfer, 2010). The potential of crowdsourcing contributions to research is multifaceted. There is a possibility for casting a very wide net in the search for particular information; there is also a possibility of capturing otherwise invisible or marginalized perspectives on an issue; in addition, it is possible that data generated will include nonsense or even vicious misinformation.[4]

The epistemological implications of Web 2.0 compositionist spaces have only begun to be recognized, and most of the research on knowledge production and epistemological shifts has not yet been addressed systematically by educational researchers.

13.2.2   Communities of Readers/Writers in Web 2.0 Spaces

Greenhow et al. (2009) commented on the potential for Web 2.0 spaces as a venue
for community building that will eventually include more minority points of view in
research production:

> In social operating systems, the emphasis on data and information is equal to or replaced by
> an emphasis on creating, developing, and sustaining human relationships.... Technology
> executives predict this next wave of social networking, social operating systems, will move
> technology systems away from restricting users to walled-off membership in a few sites
> (e.g., Facebook) toward a more open and flexible sharing among numerous niche communi-
> ties. (Greenhow et al., p. 255)

For example, there is now a Web 2.0 dimension to Kindle[5] readers. With Kindle
machines, it is possible for readers to mark up the text with highlighting and margin
notes. Readers can elect to make their marks publicly visible. So when you read a
Kindle text, you can elect to view other people's margin notes and highlighting as
you read. This interactive Web 2.0 feature creates new possibilities for interactive
reading experiences. It has never before been possible to 'read over someone else's
shoulder' from a distance, anonymously, and without ever having met the person.
This is a new technology of reading. This 'community of readers' is shaped by only
one point of connection, namely, people who are reading the same book on a Kindle
platform who have elected to make their reading notes publicly available. There are
no other cultural, demographic, or ideological connectors constituting this 'community of readers'. In this way, Web 2.0 constitutes a communal reading space, the
likes of which we have never seen before, and we do not yet know what literacy
practices may emerge from such communal reading experiences.

Web 2.0 shifts in authorship create different kinds of communities by blurring the
lines between reading and writing in a way that is analogous to newer forms of art
exhibition in which viewers become components of the artwork. For example, art
installations are now labeled as 'interactive' when viewers' presences become manifest as some aspect of the artwork itself (see, e.g., WHITEvoid). The artistic display
may be programmed to change with the number of people in the room or in response
to particular sounds produced by viewers in the space. This example of interactive art
is another historical example of trends that blur the distinction between readers and
writers or artists and audience and contribute to compositionist spaces of creation.

13.2.3   Communities of Surveillance in Web 2.0 Spaces

Web 2.0 technologies, with open access to data, compositionist structures, and user-
generated content have tremendous potential as mechanisms of surveillance and
new technologies of governance. We can already see the effects of Web 3.0 technologies in which user-generated information is manipulated through computer

algorithms primarily for entrepreneurial purposes. Corporate entities have been using Web 2.0-generated data to formulate profiles for use in marketing and advertising campaigns. In the United States, the provisions of the Patriot Act have given government authorities unprecedented access to people's private and pseudo-public correspondence, including email and social media sites (such as Twitter and Facebook). As a general rule, this surveillance has been exploited for marketing and policing purposes, but it has rarely been critically analyzed from an educational-research point of view.

There are new directions for research focused on the recent negotiations between freedom of information and intellectual property as presented by Web 2.0 technologies. A famous example of this, of course, is WikiLeaks. In addition, linking and embedding practices have already affected the definitions of plagiarism and academic integrity, and definitions of authorship are undergoing further transformations in Web 2.0 spaces characterized by open-data accessibility. Issues of governance and privacy in Web 2.0 spaces are unprecedented. Sophisticated software applications (e.g., Connotate; Oracle) now facilitate computerized Web 2.0 data mining analysis (see, e.g., Russell, 2011). Most of the data mining on Web 2.0 sites is being conducted by corporations for commercial purposes and Web 3.0 advertising. But scientific researchers are also using sophisticated analysis software focused on Web 2.0 spaces as data for generating knowledge about the world. Computational linguists are using Web 2.0 data to analyze shifts in language use (Ganapathibhotla & Liu, 2008), and sociologists are tracking new patterns of relationships and affiliations (Howard, 2011; Parry, 2011).

Surveillance has been critically studied, but primarily by technology experts and not by educational researchers. For example, Morozov argues that the mechanisms of surveillance and possibilities for cooptation through Web 2.0 have the potential to be oppressive mechanisms:

> First of all, my hope... is that policymakers will recognize that the Internet is not only a tool of liberation, but that it's also a tool of oppression. In many contexts, it oppresses more than it liberates. (Morozov 2011)

International comparison studies of Web 2.0 research spaces have investigated the complex dynamics of knowledge production, surveillance, and access in a global context. Case examples such as China's recent negotiations with Google are relevant for educational researchers in order to analyze variations in meanings of democracy and education in the face of cultural, linguistic, political, and religious diversity among Internet users. The Association for Internet Researchers (AIR) has published an ethics guide in an effort to analyze what constitutes privacy and ethical behavior with respect to data that is 'already public' in Web 2.0 spaces (Ess & the AoIR Ethics Working Group, 2002). The AIR maintains a wiki as a forum for discussions about ethical conduct of research in Web 2.0 spaces. In a legendary 2006 example, Harvard sociologists downloaded 1,700 Facebook profiles in order to study "how race and cultural tastes affect relationships" (Parry, 2011, online). Since that time and in response to accusations of breaches of privacy, Facebook archives have been pulled off-line, and those data are no longer publicly available.

13.3   From Parchment to Pixels: Web Spaces and the New Materiality of Research

Peter Burke (1997) once made the remark that one medium always tends to rise in importance above another, but without replacing older modalities. With the rise of libraries and printed texts, oral communication did not stop but rather increased considerably. Libraries became places of silent reading and centers of oral exchange on the meaning of texts. Electronic media again are adding new dimensions to reading and writing processes without forcing books to disappear and without diminishing the practices of oral communications. In the historical section of our chapter, it became evident that the creation of meaning is multidimensional: research is a function of the materiality of the text, the social and spatial context of the reader, reading and writing techniques, and concepts of authorship.

It seems to us that in this process, the importance of individual authorship is not historically constant. The new media could add tremendous new aspects to conceptualizations of authorship. Some of the writing practices even remind us of the past, when authorship was not so much valued as a transcendental process to create meaning and to authorize reliable knowledge but rather more valued as a way to participate in open community discussions. In Web 2.0 spaces of research, Barthes' conceptualization of authorship is particularly relevant in the context of social scholarship and collaborative authorship.

As for the materiality of texts, the new media have not changed the structure of texts in space; we do not yet consume texts through microchips surgically implanted and connected to our nervous systems. Web 2.0 however could and already does sometimes undermine the Western tradition of textual structure. Similar to changes in authorship, we see in textual architecture a tendency to go back to earlier forms when Web 2.0 formats have a more additive, compositionist style. Web 2.0 texts are less structured by disciplined reading tools and strong concepts of authorship. Their compositionist form has effects on the creation of meaning and possibilities for reflecting on texts. As for the arts and sciences, we would like to argue that modern or conventional research spaces have valued universalism in a global sense; science, classical authors, or arts are said to be universal or in other words, 'objective'. In contrast, compositionism does not lead to universal answers but to variations on answers or positions. Research in compositionist spaces does not necessarily aspire to coherence or objectivity. Rather, research in compositionist spaces values breadth of input and iterative approaches to knowledge production.

As for the spaces and social contexts of reading and writing, Web-based texts are often called 'virtual' texts in 'virtual' spaces; however, the term 'virtual' can be somewhat misleading. If we think in terms of essentialist definitions, then our tendency is to understand 'virtual spaces' as if they were completely different from 'real spaces'. On the other hand, if we think historically, virtual spaces are now real spaces. Web-based communications, reading, and writing have taken the place of previous material conditions. We can think of Baudrillard's (2010) hyperreality, in which it is no longer possible to think of 'real' and 'virtual' in oppositional terms. We regard Web-based reading and writing as situated within specific historical, material, and social contexts. Reading and writing still is subject to exercises of power in defining what should be seen as 'real'. In Web 2.0, power is more distributed in space and not a matter of a central redaction; Web 2.0 spaces are also dynamic and iterative, not captured and frozen in time as conventional works usually are. The fact that readers react differently to texts is not a matter of failed canonizing and lack of prestige but an absolutely appropriate response to reading and writing by socially and culturally different readers.

To summarize, Web 2.0 spaces represent a historical shift in reading and writing practices for educational research, a recent shift that follows a long historical trajectory of previous shifts in the materialities of reading and writing. The architecture of the texts tends to be vertical (scroll-like) and multidimensional (hyperlinked). Authorship in Web 2.0 spaces tends to be dispersed, iterative, and social rather than individual, institutionally validated, and static. The distinction between readers and writers has become blurred. The dynamic heterogeneity of compositionism is replacing hierarchical forms of redaction critique and authoritative reviewing mechanisms. Finally, Web 2.0 spaces have facilitated new research practices of data generation, community involvement, governance, and surveillance.

It will be interesting to watch in the near future how Web 2.0 spaces evolve and how compositionist practices do and do not become incorporated into educational research. There is much we do not know: To what degree are Web 2.0 spaces competing with and/or complementing conventional research spaces? Does participation in Web 2.0 spaces indicate a political choice? Is participation a matter of convenience and efficiency? Is platform related to research topic? A preference related to demographic features? Do Web 2.0 spaces coexist with conventional spaces in a shared ethos of knowledge production, and/or will reading/writing practices in Web 2.0 generate a historical transformation closer to the magnitude of Gutenberg's press? How will globalization become manifested in Web 2.0 spaces, and what new governmental legislation will be promoted in efforts to regulate reading and writing practices including intellectual property? All of these questions will become increasingly pertinent for educational research across spaces and places.

Reflexive note. This chapter was written in a Web 2.0 space over a period of six months by two people living 6,580 km and six time zones away from one another. Sometimes coauthorship and discussions about ideas occurred in real time; at other times, the exchanges occurred serially. The structure of this text shares some features of compositionism in its collage of narrative styles. Coauthoring the same document in real time across distance is a research-writing practice that has no precedent outside Web 2.0 spaces.

Notes

1. Previous spaces of research (including Web 1.0 and off-line research spaces) typically entail some degree of interactivity. For example, coauthorship has always been a feature of educational research, formal and informal peer review

practices add some degree of interactivity between readers and writers in the production of research, and various referential and citation practices serve as bridges between texts. However, we suggest here that compositionism in Web 2.0 spaces represents a notable shift for research reading and writing.

2. Of course, the production of knowledge in Web 2.0 spaces is still governed by cultural, religious, historical, and technological regimes; we do not mean to imply that Web 2.0 is an ungoverned space. In fact, many of the cultural imbalances of conventional writing have carried over into Web 2.0 spaces: more than two-thirds of bloggers are men, and 70 % of blogging activity originates in North America (Technorati, 2010).

3. There is an interesting emergence of a new category of Web 2.0 knowledge producers: Mom Bloggers. See, for example, Morris (2011).

4. Admittedly, conventional redaction processes of peer review are not immune to the influx of nonsense or vicious misinformation, either.

5. Kindle is an Amazon brand of electronic reader.

References

Barthes, R. (1968/2006). Der Tod des Autors. In *Das Rauschen der Sprache* (pp. 57–63). Frankfurt am Main, Germany: Suhrkamp.

Baudrillard, J. (2010). *Simulacra and simulation*. Ann Arbor, MI: University of Michigan Press.

Burke, P. (1997). *A social history of knowledge*. Cambridge, UK: Polity Press/Blackwell.

Chartier, R., & Cavallo, G. (Eds.). (1999). *Die Welt des Lesens. Von der Schriftrolle zum Bildschirm.* Frankfurt am Main, Germany/Paris: Campus, Editions de la Maison de Sciences de l'Homme. (Italian version published 1995)

Creative Commons. Retrieved November 17, 2011, from http://creativecommons.org/

Critical Commons. Retrieved November 17, 2011, from http://criticalcommons.org/

Darnton, R., & Tamm, M. (2004). Interview with Robert Darnton. *Eurozine.* Retrieved November 17, 2011, from http://www.eurozine.com/articles/2004-06-21-darnton-en.html

Ess, C., & the AoIR Ethics Working Group. (2002). *Ethical decision-making and internet research: Recommendations from the AoIR ethics working committee.* Retrieved November 17, 2011, from www.aoir.org/reports/ethics.pdf

Foucault, M. (1969/2003). Was ist ein Autor? In *Schriften zur Literatur* (pp. 234–270). Frankfurt am Main, Germany: Suhrkamp.

Ganapathibhotla, M., & Liu, B. (2008). Mining opinions in comparative sentences. In *Proceedings of the 22nd International Conference on Computational Linguistics* (pp. 241–248), Manchester, UK: Association for Computational Linguistics.

Genette, G. (2001). *Paratexte*. Frankfurt am Main, Germany: Suhrkamp. (French version published 1987)

Goldsmith, K. (2011). *Uncreative writing: Managing knowledge in the digital age*. New York: Columbia University Press.

Greenhow, C., Robelia, B., & Hughes, J. E. (2009). Learning, teaching, and scholarship in a digital age: Web 2.0 and classroom research: What path should we take now? *Educational Researcher, 38*(4), 246–259.

Grossman, L. (2011, September 2). From scroll to screen. *New York Times Sunday Book Review.* Retrieved November 17, 2011, from http://www.nytimes.com/2011/09/04/books/review/the-mechanic-muse-from-scroll-to-screen.html

Hahn, B. (1991). *Unter falschem Namen. Von der schwierigen Autorschaft von Frauen.* Frankfurt am Main, Germany: Suhrkamp.

Howard, J. (2011, September 11). Citation by citation: New maps chart hot research and scholarship's hidden terrain. *The Chronicle of Higher Education.* Retrieved November 17, 2011, from http://chronicle.com/article/Maps-of-Citations-Uncover-New/128938/

Latour, B. (2010). An attempt at a 'Compositionist Manifesto'. *New Literary History, 41*(3), 471–490.

Latour, B., & Woolgar, S. (1979). *Laboratory life: The construction of scientific facts.* Princeton, NJ: Princeton University Press.

Leu, D. L., O'Byrne, W. I., Zawilinski, L., McVerry, J. G., & Everett-Cacopardo, H. (2009). Comments on Greenhow, Robelia, and Hughes: Expanding the new literacies conversation. *Educational Researcher, 38,* 264–269.

McFarland, D., & Klopfer, E. (2010). Network search: A new way of seeing the education knowledge domain. *Teachers College Record, 112*(2), 2664–2702.

Morozov, E. (2011). *Fellows Friday with Evgeny Morozov.* Retrieved November 17, 2011, from http://blog.ted.com/2011/01/28/fellows-friday-with-evgeny-morozov/

Morris, A. (2011). *Technorati predicts continued growth within the blogosphere for 2011.* Retrieved November 17, 2011, from http://www.webpronewsde.com/webpronewsde-125-20110105TechnoratiPredictsContinuedGrowthWithinTheBlogosphereFor2011.html

National Academies. (2011, 13 June). *Crowdsourcing: Improving the quality of scientific data through social networking.* A public symposium organized by the Board on Research Data and Information. National Research Council, Washington, DC. Retrieved November 17, 2011, from http://www.nationalacademies.org/brdi

Parry, M. (2011, July 10). Harvard researchers accused of breaching students' privacy: Social-network project shows promise and peril of doing social science online. *The Chronicle of Higher Education.* Retrieved November 17, 2011, from http://chronicle.com/article/Harvards-Privacy-Meltdown/128166/

Platteaux, H. (2002). What can we learn about hypermedia navigation from a book history study? *Information Search and Knowledge Acquisition in Electronic Environments.* Retrieved November 17, 2011, from http://nte.unifr.ch/IMG/pdf/earli_sig2_article_2002.pdf

Priem, K. (2012). Sehen, Lesen, Schreiben, Sprechen und die Dinge: Eine Didaktik der "Stunde Null". In K. Priem, G. M. König, & R. Casale (Eds.), *Die Materialität der Erziehung: Kulturelle und soziale Aspekte pädagogischer Objekte* [Materiality of education: Cultural and social aspects of education. *Beiheft, Zeitschrift für Pädaogigk, 58,* 7–13]. Weinheim, Germany: Beltz.

Russell, M. A. (2011). *Mining the social web: Analyzing data from Facebook, Twitter, LinkedIn, and other social media sites.* Sebastopol, CA: O'Reilly Media.

Smith, S. L. (2011). Emory University tracks slave origins via online database, crowdsourcing. *BlackWeb 2.0.* Retrieved November 17, 2011, from http://www.blackweb20.com/2011/04/27/emory-university-tracks-slave-origins-via-online-database-crowdsourcing/

Technorati. (2010). *State of the blogosphere.* Retrieved November 17, 2011, from http://social-easemarketing.com/2011/03/08/what-is-the-state-of-the-blogosphere/

WHITEvoid interactive art & design. Retrieved November 17, 2011, from http://www.whitevoid.com/

Chapter 14
From Entrepreneurialism to Innovation: Research, Critique, and the Innovation Union

Naomi Hodgson

> *Innovation: something newly introduced, such as a new method or device (thefreedictionary.com)*
>
> *We must rewrite the contract between the researcher and society, so that freedom of thought is balanced by responsibility for action. (European Research Area Board)*

14.1 Introduction

Over recent years, Europe has continually been renamed, for example, the change from European Community to European Union. In the process of integration, it has been reframed as a different space. In its constitution as a knowledge economy, further spaces have been created, for example, the European Research Area and the European Area of Higher Education. More recently, the European Union has recast itself as an Innovation Union. The Lisbon Strategy, which aimed to make the EU the most competitive and dynamic knowledge economy in the world, has been superseded by strategies for the creation of the Innovation Union.

While policies relating to this new space may be driven by the need for austerity, they can also be seen as commensurate with the existing governmental rationality that has emerged in recent decades, characterised by, for example, the introduction of market principles to public services and the demand for mobility, adaptability, and permanent (self-) improvement in the name of quality and excellence. The shifts in policy driven by the emphasis on innovation will not, then, be approached here in economic terms, for example, in terms of saving money, increasing GDP, or privatisation, but rather in terms of how they continue or adapt an existing mode of government.

N. Hodgson (✉)
Institute of Education, University of London, London, UK
e-mail: naomihodgson@hotmail.com

P. Smeyers et al. (eds.), *Educational Research: The Importance and Effects of Institutional Spaces*, Educational Research 7, DOI 10.1007/978-94-007-6247-3_14,
© Springer Science+Business Media Dordrecht 2013

The recasting of the European Union as an Innovation Union recasts the role of the university and of the researcher therein. But the shift not only affects institutions *usually* associated with knowledge production; innovation is now a priority across all policy areas and for all actors—governments, institutions, businesses, and individuals—in order to be able to adapt to and survive in current conditions.

Research from the perspective of governmentality has shown how, in the creation of the knowledge economy or learning society, learning becomes governmentalised (see, e.g. Delanty, 2003; Masschelein, Simons, Brockling, & Pongratz, 2007). It is suggested in this chapter that, in the shift of emphasis to innovation, research has displaced learning as the imperative according to which we are governed and called upon to understand ourselves. 'Research', in this sense, refers not only to the formal practices and institutions of scientific and academic inquiry but to an attitude of permanent self-improvement applicable to all aspects of our lives, driven by responsibilisation of the individual not only for their own achievement, as in the learning society, but also for the survival of society itself.

Governmentality studies have also shown how the current regimes of performance, requiring transparency, accountability, and permanent feedback, effect an immunisation and thus a stifling, or domestication, of critique (Heid, 2004; Masschelein & Simons, 2002). That is to say that critique, as feedback in a variety of forms and functions, becomes part of the operation of government and self-government today and thus only reinforces, rather than disrupts, its performativity (see Masschelein, 2004).

The purpose of this chapter, then, is twofold. One aim is to show how the creation of the European Union as an Innovation Union brings about shifts of emphasis from a general entrepreneurialism to a more focussed innovation and from learning to research. I will illustrate this with particular reference to the university. A second aim is to explore the possibility of critique in this context: as a researcher, how is it possible to be critical when (a) critique forms part of the functioning of government and (b) one's survival depends on meeting the (measurable) demands of the innovative university?

In this exploration, critique is understood in Foucauldian terms and thus emphasises the analysis of the functioning of power rather than the suggestion of alternative policy solutions. The early sections of the chapter discuss the subtle shift from entrepreneurialism to innovation and document how the Innovation Union becomes a reality through the discourses and practices it introduces; the later sections explore the possibility of resisting this. The possibility of resistance is illustrated with reference to the reconceptualisation of the space of the university offered by Jan Masschelein and Maarten Simons' proposal for a 'world university' (Masschelein & Simons, 2009). Their proposal is illustrative not only as a productive account of new possibilities for thinking about the public role of the university but also as an example of the particular form of critique—as an attitude—espoused in the work of Foucault and also of Bruno Latour. A critique of Masschelein and Simons' account (Allen, 2011) is discussed to indicate the ways in which what they say is uncomfortable (and necessarily so) due, it is argued, to a particular understanding of the role of the researcher and the university *vis-à-vis* society or the public. Masschelein and

Simons, following Latour, displace established notions of critique and of expertise. The chapter concludes by considering how to proceed in light of this.

14.2 The University in the Learning Society

The notion of the learning society is not new. The demands placed on the individual and the form of self-understanding it requires are well-documented, particularly from the perspective of governmentality. I will provide a brief summary here to lay the way for the discussion of innovation in the next section.

As part of the move to become 'the most competitive and dynamic knowledge-based economy in the world',[1] Europe has implemented structures and measures that enable governance in terms of lifelong learning. For example, the creation of the European Research Area, the European Area of Higher Education, lifelong learning policy, and the schemes that have facilitated these have been analysed in terms of the governmentalisation of learning (Delanty, 2003; Simons & Masschelein, 2008b, p. 192). These shifting configurations of space are marked by simultaneous shifts in the objects of government. For example, education is no longer confined to the fixed space of the institution; we now access learning environments (ibid.).

With the recasting of society as a learning society or knowledge economy, individuals have been addressed in terms of their responsibility for their own lifelong learning, which takes the form of a particular attitude towards work and education characterised by mobility, adaptability, and entrepreneurialism.

The policy objectives relating to the knowledge economy, formalised in the Lisbon Treaty in 2009 and according to which Europe has been governed, mean that the research function served by the university is now also carried out by various other institutions, and the university now exists within the triangle of education, research, and innovation.

Governance of education in terms of quality and excellence has contributed to a domestication of critique (Masschelein & Simons, 2009). That is, critique becomes a constitutive part of the permanent feedback mechanisms informing rankings of quality and excellence. We must all be critical, but in the name of the rationale of performativity or as Simons and Masschelein describe it: "the 'university of excellence'…is a habitat which demands an entrepreneurial ethos of *obedience* or *submission* to a permanent quality tribunal" (Masschelein & Simons, 2009, p. 239).

A European Council Communication on the modernisation agenda for universities in 2006 stated the need for universities to respond to the rapidly changing global context, which entails harnessing their particular societal role (Council of European the Communities [CEC], 2006).[2] Jan Masschelein and Maarten Simons point out that, despite reference to the 'modernisation' of universities in European policy and to the modern traditions of Humboldt and Newman, the ethos of the university has shifted:

> The modern university is an institution which committed itself to a transcendent idea of 'universal reason', 'humanity' or 'civil service'…Listening to the current European discourses on the university, the conception of the university that orients itself to a transcendent idea of humanity (including universal reason) or a particular vision of (civil) society through the integration of research, education, and public service is no longer embraced… the orientation is 'excellence'. (Masschelein & Simons, 2009, p. 238)

The university is now oriented not to progress and emancipation, as in the modern period, but to innovation and empowerment (ibid.).

The European Council modernisation agenda identifies universities and "their interlinked roles of education, research, and innovation" to be core conditions for the success of the Lisbon Strategy (CEC, 2006, p. 2). In order to achieve the creation of a "competitive, dynamic, knowledge-based economy" as set out by this strategy, the university is called upon to "create the necessary conditions… to improve their performance, to modernise themselves, and to become more competitive" (p. 4). This 'entrepreneurial' university is characterised by innovation, responsiveness, and flexibility, enabled by autonomy and accountability in the form of "new internal governance systems" (p. 5). It encourages mobility, interdisciplinarity, and transdisciplinarity and recognises the 'strategic importance' of partnership with business in the name of both the "pro-active diversification of…research funding portfolios" (p. 8) and the addition of "entrepreneurial skills to students' and researchers' scientific expertise" (p. 6). It must also recognise its role in making lifelong learning a reality in Europe and offer greater flexibility to accommodate those entering higher education at different stages of life and with differing learning needs. It is focussed on achieving and rewarding excellence and convincing the public, politicians, and business that it is worth investing in through effective stakeholder engagement.

Discussion of the university, the researcher, and the student in theses terms is now very familiar in Europe and elsewhere. Innovation has already been integral to the understanding of modernisation at work in recent years. The recasting of the European Union as an Innovation Union marks a shift of emphasis, however, and an intensification of these demands. In the documentation discussed below, innovation refers clearly to the demand to capitalise knowledge and to produce marketable research. This demand is not only made of all sectors but also requires a displacement of the understanding of the roles and functions of these sectors. The university, then, must also rethink its purpose and actions. The demand for innovation insists that this rethinking must be along the lines of strategies for the pursuit of excellence in the capitalisation of knowledge. The citation from the European Research Area Board makes clear that the researcher must also rethink her actions in these terms: "We must rewrite the contract between the researcher and society, so that freedom of thought is balanced by responsibility for action" (European Research Area Board). At every level, innovation is required; it is incumbent on every actor—governments, institutions, individuals—to adapt.

The understanding of time and space found in Foucault's analysis of territory and population as the objects of government of emergent nation-states cannot be applied today therefore (Simons & Masschelein, 2008a). The linear, evolutionary understanding of time and of education as progression through set stages operative in the modern period has been displaced by the individual learning trajectory of the mobile, adaptable, and entrepreneurial learner (Simons & Masschelein).

14.3 Making the Innovation Union a Reality

The recasting of Europe as an Innovation Union entails not only a focus on the businesses and institutions ordinarily concerned with education, research, and innovation. Europe seeks a distinctive approach to innovation, which entails:

> Involving all actors and all regions in the innovation cycle: not only major companies but also SMEs in all sectors, including the public sector, the social economy, and citizens themselves ('social innovation'); not only a few high-tech areas, but all regions in Europe and every Member State, each focussing on its own strengths ('smart specialisation') with Europe, Member States and regions acting in partnership. (European Commission [EC], 2010, p. 8)

In fact, it seems innovation, located within current structures and as articulated in the earlier modernisation agenda, is not enough. In the global competition for resources and power, Europe must find innovative ways to innovate. This entails an all-encompassing approach in which all aspects of economic and social life are subject to this demand.

While the central concern here is with how this shift changes the role of the university and the researcher, the focus is not only on how research is governed but also on how the governance of research forms part of how society is governed today. The discussion here focuses on the European Commission Communication on Innovation Union (EC, 2010). It is important to note that the policies under discussion here relate to the period to 2020. Making the Innovation Union a reality (EC, p. 5), then, represents not the final stage in the development of Europe or its ongoing project but the necessary response now. Europe must innovate in order to survive in today's global conditions.

The modernisation of higher education remains central to Europe's and to the institutions' own survival. This discussion will show, however, that what counts as modernisation has changed with the shift of emphasis from the entrepreneurial to the innovative university. European policy for the period to 2020 seeks not only to consolidate existing structures constitutive of Europe as a knowledge economy (e.g. the European Research Area) but to ensure their adaptation to current conditions. The further consolidation of the European Research Area, for which a deadline has been set, requires not only adaptability and the ease of mobility (of individuals/knowledge, i.e. assets) between member states as in the modernisation agenda but also the optimisation of the use of these assets:

> Researchers and innovators must be able to work and cooperate across the EU as easily as within national borders. The European Research Area must be completed within four years – putting in place the frameworks for a truly free movement of knowledge. (EC, 2010, p. 4)

We must, however, avoid 'fragmentation of effort', which amounts to the same or similar work being carried out by different actors within the Union: "national and regional research and innovation systems are still working along separate tracks with only a marginal European dimension" (p. 8). One aspect of the shift is evident here, that from competition to specialisation. Being an Innovation Union requires not simply national/regional/institutional/individual competition but being so attuned to the marketplace that if similar activity is being done elsewhere, the answer is either formally to collaborate (or merge) or to channel your resources into a different activity, that is, a more distinct and more productive niche: "By better pooling our efforts and focussing on excellence, and by creating a true European Research Area the EU can enhance the quality of research and Europe's potential for major breakthroughs and increase the effectiveness of the investments needed to get ideas to market" (p. 8). The duplication and overlap that arise from working separately are "unacceptable at a time of tight finances" (p. 8). China and South Korea are cited as examples of the competition, which are catching up fast and moving from being imitators to leaders in innovation (p. 8). Europe must become an "innovation-friendly environment", which requires it to become a coherent, efficient whole (p. 8). This requires instituting a new form of, what might be termed, inclusion (see Fejes, 2008) by ensuring that each region identifies its own distinctive means for innovation: "Europe must avoid an 'innovation divide' between the strongest innovating regions and others", and Structural Funds will be used "to support the development of 'smart specialisation' to avoid overlap" (EC, 2010, p. 22).

Ensuring sustainable development through specialisation is central to the reform of universities:

> Higher education reform is especially urgent. Most European universities do not attract enough top global talent, with relatively few in leading positions in existing international rankings. European universities should be freed from over-regulation and micro-management in return for full institutional accountability. Universities also need more diversity in their missions and outlook, with smarter specialisation across different fields. (p. 10)

Excellence under the auspices of innovation refers not only to higher ranking, higher research ratings, better retention, higher student satisfaction, etc. compared to other universities or nations but the wholesale review of a university's areas of expertise internally in comparison to other universities, other research institutes, and private companies. With the demand for specialisation, innovation intensifies the demand for excellence.

One way in which universities can adapt is to establish links with business. The Innovation Union actively encourages such collaboration, for example, in the proposal to form Knowledge Alliances, linkages "between education and business to develop new curricula addressing innovation skills gaps" (p. 10). These Knowledge Alliances will help universities to modernise towards interdisciplinarity, entrepreneurship, and stronger business partnerships (p. 10). In response to the demand for interdisciplinarity, precursors to such alliances are already visible in many universities and research organisations that have been restructured around what are often termed research-oriented 'clusters'. More publicly visible are the research centres or science parks funded through joint university/public/private partnership or by a consortium of universities. Where previously competition has been fiercely fought between universities, the competition for resources means that pooling strengths by interuniversity collaboration at an organisational/infrastructural level—to become specialist—is more likely to ensure survival.

References to research, innovation, and specialisation in the Innovation Union document are not only concerned with universities and other institutions concerned with knowledge production. Innovation is necessary for adaptation and survival for all actors. The Communication on Innovation Union (EC, 2010) states:

> Perhaps the biggest challenge for the EU and its Member States is to adopt a much more strategic approach to innovation. An approach whereby innovation is the overarching policy objective, where we take a medium-to-longer term perspective, where all policy instruments, measures and funding are designed to contribute to innovation, where EU and national/regional policies are closely aligned and mutually reinforcing, and last but not least, where the highest political level sets a strategic agenda, regularly monitors progress and tackles delays. (EC, 2010, p. 2)

The mobility required of this space is to be facilitated by the formalisation of a fifth freedom (in addition to the four existing freedoms of movement of goods, capital, services, and persons): the free circulation of knowledge. There are to be no barriers to the movement of innovative goods, people, and services. This mobility appears not as an option but as necessary for survival. This refers not only to geographical barriers but also to institutional or infrastructural barriers. The distinction between institutions and the assumption of an institution such as the university as a discrete, bounded entity is broken down. What counts is the ability of skilled, adaptable actors to respond to the identified challenges.

The production of knowledge is being reorganised around a flexible, 'challenge-driven' structure (p. 24). The definition of societal challenges (e.g. climate change, a growing elderly population ('healthy ageing')) determines the validity—the innovation potential—of research as these are the areas in which the market seeks to invest. To facilitate innovative collaboration research organisations and businesses can form Innovation Partnerships, which must meet the following criteria:

- Focus on a specific societal challenge that is shared across the EU, with clear, ambitious, and measurable goals which will bring important benefits for citizens and the society as a whole before 2020, and where there is a large new market potential for EU businesses [such challenges are identified—and have targets set—by the Europe 2020 strategy[3]].
- Have strong political and stakeholder commitment.
- Have clear EU-added value, bringing efficiency gains and large-scale impact through critical mass.
- Have a strong focus on results, outcomes, and impacts: "partnerships must be result-oriented and should therefore not be all-encompassing in scope. Societal challenges should be broken down into smaller 'work packages'…Clear targets, milestones, and deliverables should be defined in advance".
- There must be adequate financial support.

Although, these conditions refer to a specific form of collaboration, Innovation Partnerships, it is possible to say that these conditions provide a benchmark for research excellence for all actors in the Innovation Union.

The success of the Innovation Union will be proved or not by the devices implemented to measure it. As with the measures of comparability that already exist within Europe and globally, innovation requires the introduction of new measures of impact, benefit, added value, etc. The success of the Innovation Union will be subject to various measures: each sector will have innovation benchmarks; research should be challenge-led, that is, responsive to identified social problems; these priority areas will be the focus of Innovation Partnerships; the funding of such collaborative relationships will be conditional on identifying outcomes and impacts in advance.

The Communication provides examples of a number of such devices, such as the European Design Leadership Board, measuring excellence in the field of design, and the European Public Sector Innovation Scoreboard. The demand for innovation in the public sector, and on the part of organisations and individuals not usually associated with knowledge production, is now integrated into the demand for the continual recalibration of work in response to rapidly changing global socioeconomic pressures.[4]

The Communication on Innovation Union recasts research as an essential aspect of the labour market in general, and in this respect, education—assisted by collaboration with business—must provide everyone with research and innovation skills:

> The shift to an innovative economy has major implications for the world of work. Employers need workers who actively and constantly seek out new and better ways of doing things. This requires not only higher skills levels, but a new, trust-based relationship between employer and employee. This kind of approach is needed at all occupational levels, and must extend to sectors not usually thought of as 'knowledge sectors' [e.g. the caring sector]. (p. 22)

Policies relating to the Innovation Union concern not only the productivity of universities, other higher education and research institutions, and businesses, then, but also the public sector and civil society ('social innovation'): "Against a backdrop of fiscal austerity, the public sector needs to innovate more than ever" (p. 22). This demand to innovate entails becoming more efficient, more productive, and even profitable. As the Communication notes, "more and more governments are embracing more citizen-centred approaches to service delivery"[5] (p. 22). What is (traditionally) public is now understood in terms of its accountability to the entrepreneurial citizen and is thus governed in terms of the rationality of the market and the efficiencies this brings. The logic of performativity is such that criticism forms part of its functioning, the constant feedback mechanisms that drive its performance.

Innovation appears, then, not only as vital to the survival of the university and research organisations but also to all actors in Europe today. Research becomes the means by which to permanently improve, to find new, more efficient and productive ways of working. Success or failure is measured by sector-specific innovation scoreboards, winning or losing jobs or funds, and ultimately survival ('sustainability'). Permanent critique—feedback, comparison, and appraisal—is essential to this. In this context, then, how are we to understand critique as an academic practice? What is distinctive about what could happen in the university and what the academic researcher could do, when every actor must concern themselves with this. The following section takes up these questions.

14.4 Composing a 'World University'

The innovative researcher, then, is a mobile, adaptable individual seeking permanently to rethink how she does what she does in the name of efficiency, sustainability, and responsibility, for which she requires permanent feedback. So what can it mean to provide critique when it is constitutive of the system in question? For Bruno Latour, it requires a reorienting of our attitude to the present by focussing not on matters of fact but on matters of concern, that is, thinking not in the name of 'quality', 'excellence', and 'innovation' but in the name of our seeking a common world and thus in response to the conditions in which we find ourselves. Maarten Simons, Olssen, and Peters, (2009) explain Latour's distinction as follows:

> Whereas matters of fact and problems are always already being taken care of – by the available expertise and agencies in society – matters of concern, because no-one can claim them, can become everyone's concern, and therefore a public concern. (Simons et al., 2009, p. x)

This takes seriously the demand to rethink the question of 'how we are going to live together' (ibid.). Latour's distinction is motivated in part by his identification of critique as having 'run out of steam' (Latour, 2010, p. 474). He refers to critique as having done 'a wonderful job of debunking prejudices, enlightening nations, and prodding minds' (ibid.) in the modern period but suggests that it gained its force from the difference between appearance and reality:

> With critique, you may debunk, reveal, unveil, but only as long as you establish, through this process of creative destruction, a privileged access to the world of reality behind the veils of appearances. Critique, in other words, has all the limits of utopia: it relies on the certainty of the world *beyond* this world. (p. 475)

The Utopianism providing the difference of potential belongs to the time of time, the time of an orientation of unilinear movement away from savagery and barbarism towards Progress and Enlightenment. In contrast to critique, Latour offers the notion of composition: "for compositionism, there is no world of beyond. It is all about *immanence*" (ibid.). Composition is concerned not with debunking and revealing a reality behind a veil of appearances but with repairing, taking care, assembling, reassembling, and stitching together: "it is achieved only by the slow process of composition and compromise, not by the revelation of the world of beyond" (p. 478). From this perspective, the assumption of the expertise of the academic is also displaced.

The practice of composition and the rethinking of the role of the academic in relation to knowledge are present in Masschelein and Simons' (2009) proposal for a world university. Their proposal illustrates the necessity of moving beyond 'critique' and to attempt composition as a way of responding to our current conditions. This entails an attitude of resistance not as opposition but as 'ex-position', putting oneself at risk in the composition of—simultaneously—our academic work and our common world. The questioning of the assumed authority of the academic entails seeing the academic first and foremost as a member of the public.

The attitude of exposition this entails derives from Foucault's thought. Masschelein and Simons' account is perhaps unusual in that it does offer an alternative. This alternative, however, is not simply a comfortable shift from one mode of understanding the university to another. Nor is it a grand Utopian conception of what the university should be. For this reason, the proposal for a world university has been subject to critique (in the modern sense, we might say) for failure to gain critical distance and to deal with real-world problems. I will explore the criticism levelled by Ansgar Allen (2011) here to illustrate further how 'proposing' and 'composing' differ from critique.

14.4.1   The Idea of the World University

The world university is presented as an alternative to the entrepreneurial university and thus is concerned with how "universities, due to the specific scope of their teaching and research, can constitute a public of *world citizens* around specific *concerns* as opposed to *possible active* citizens with particular *competencies*" (Masschelein & Simons, 2009, p. 236). Academics in the world university are understood as "[l]earned individuals acting as world citizens" (ibid.): "He/she is a world citizen because and as far as he/she conceives of him-/herself as a member of the world, which he/she calls into being through and *in the use* of his/her own reasoning, through and in the way he/she speaks" (p. 238). The notion of membership of the world called in to being through one's reasoning derives from Kant's distinction between public and private reason.

In his essay 'What is Enlightenment?' (1977), Kant distinguishes between the public use of one's reason and its private use—"by the public use of one's reason he means the 'use which anyone may make of it as a *man of learning* [*Gelehrte*] addressing the entire reading public' (p. 55, original emphasis)" (Kant cited in Masschelein & Simons, 2009, p. 237):

> Hence, as a man of learning one is a world citizen who…is not instructing pupils but 'publicly voices his thoughts', 'imparts them to the public' (p. 56). A man of learning (a 'scholar', in the English translation of his text) is 'addressing the real public' (i.e. the world at large, *die Welt*) and speaks 'in his own person' (p. 57). Indeed, learned individuals are putting before the public their thoughts', with 'no fear of phantoms' (p. 59). (ibid., p. 237)

For Kant, enlightenment is related to the freedom "to make public use of one's reason in all matters" (Kant, 1977, p. 55). Private use of one's reason, by contrast, refers to:

> the use one makes of it when one acts in 'a particular civil post or office' (Kant, 1977, p. 55) that is 'employed by the government for public ends' (p. 56). In that case, one acts as part of the machine' (p. 56). And as part of a public institution (a machine with public ends), one speaks 'in someone's else's name' (p. 56) and speaking becomes some kind of teaching or instruction. According to Kant, the use one makes of one's reason as part of a social machine or institution (and the main example he gives besides the army and the state is that of the Church) is purely private, since these, however, large they may be, are 'never more than a domestic gathering [*häusliche Versammlung*]' (p. 57). (ibid., p. 237)

The domestic gathering refers then to 'a particular domain or sphere with clear limits and laws of operation' and hence is conceived of as a machine. This may refer not only to the state but also, Masschelein and Simons suggest, "a scientific discipline or cultural community" (p. 238). Reason used in this way, then, is referred to as the private use of reason as it is limited by the domestic operation of that machine and its audience. The public as constituted by the state can be seen to be governed by the private use of reason, as public in this sense refers to members of a particular territory.

The private use of reason, or domesticated thought, relates to what Latour terms 'matters of fact', understandings that are no longer questions or are questioned and taken care of according to existing expertise. Matters of concern, by contrast, appear or are made visible by one's public use of reason in which one is answerable not to a policy, an academic field, or an existing strategy but to the world.

In the world university, the work of the academic is not oriented to gaining mastery of that world and recommending what to do in light of the evidence but to acknowledging the power of things in the world to shape that world. It entails an experimental attitude that is open to the uncertainty of the world. Masschelein and Simons write: "inventing a world university means to invent measures, strategies, practices and exercises that give power to things (to matters) which oblige us to think (and to think about what to do in the face of an idiotic question)" (Masschelein & Simons, 2009, p. 241). Such invention can 'constrain the protective manoeuvres of immunisation' (ibid.).

Invention arises not or not only in the use of experimental methods (which might act to immunise). On this understanding:

> The text or reality is not just a playground for one's thoughts and actions, but becomes something to which people are exposed and in the presence of which they have to think. This kind of exposition through research or study is uncomfortable, not just because there are no criteria or there is no tribunal to judge the things one is confronted with (one is outside 'the machine', to use Kant's terminology), but also because one's own position is always at stake.

The academic and the university then are not understood strictly as professional roles or institutions and as discrete, bounded, authoritative entities. They are answerable to the world and constitutive of it and thus, in order to compose it collectively, must be exposed to it: not immunised against it by existing practices, criteria, or 'matters of fact'.

The conception of the world university entails the assumption of equality between all members of the public as citizens of the world (see Rancière, 1991). The academic understood as a learned individual acting as a world citizen does not mean merely that she must devise a new experimental methodology that will include the public in its deliberations and in the dissemination of its authoritative conclusion. On this view:

> The inhabitants (academics/professors) are not representatives in this sense; they are not speaking 'in the name of', and thus cannot say 'and so…'. They are not addressing students or the public as those who are in need of guidance or orientation (for example, in need of the light of [universal] reason). They are not experts saying, 'these are the facts, this is the

case (and cause), and so…'. At the world university this 'and so…' is precisely *suspended*. (Masschelein & Simons, 2009, p. 241)

It is at this point that the act of disruption, of ex-position, appears more radical. This suspension is the basis for Allen's (2011) critique of Masschelein and Simons' account, to which I now turn.

14.4.2 Critique, Proposal, and Composition

The root of the problem, Allen argues, is the Foucauldian framework on which the conception of the world university is based. Its refusal to make recommendations leaves it politically inert. Allen writes of Foucault that:

> [H]is approach is limited by the fact that it has nothing to recommend. It deliberately avoids prescriptive thought and alternative visions that might indicate how education, which is our concern, should be reformed. The world university proposed by Simons and Masschelein is a little eccentric in this respect offering an alternative blueprint of sorts, yet it fails to escape the limitations of Foucauldian thought. (Allen, 2011, p. 378)

In view of seeking future political possibilities and solutions to inequality, Allen argues:

> It may, on the contrary, be time to occupy a position and speak in the name of a political dream. It might be worth adopting a mode of scholarship that is committed rather than abstracted, or when scholarship is abstracted, ensuring such abstraction has a specific commitment in mind. (Allen, 2011)

Allen suggests that being confined to the limits of Foucault's thought itself imposes an immunisation, one that is reflected in the abstraction and privilege of the position of the learned individual in the world university. Education in Allen's critique refers to its institutional form, while reform, in keeping with his position, seems to refer to improvement and outcomes sought in the name of an ideal. In Masschelein and Simons' account, education is not dealt with only in the formal sense. They are discussing the university and illustrate their proposal with the example of the lecture, but education refers also to our common experience, as inherent in our being human and thus as not necessarily governed in the name of something other.

Part of Allen's criticism is that such work is abstracted and privileged. This does not recognise the assumption of equality in the proposal. The position of the academic in the world university is uncomfortable precisely because it acknowledges the activities of their academic life as activities constitutive of their citizenship and thus carries the ethical and political implications of this.

Both Masschelein and Simons' paper and the notion of the academic in the world university therein illustrate Foucault's conception of his works as experience books. He draws a distinction between these and what he terms 'truth' or 'demonstration books', which aim to inform, to put forward a truth, and thereby to justify it. This implies what Foucault terms a 'pastoral attitude': the writer assumes the role of the knowing teacher and addresses the reader as one who takes the position of the learner. An inequality is thereby installed, which gains its legitimacy from a particular regime of truth organised according to such binary distinctions (Masschelein, 2007, p. 152). Neither reader nor writer is, in the process, put at stake.

The writing of an experience book was for Foucault a philosophical exercise, one of *askesis*, in which he did not take the stance of the teacher but assumed an attitude of ex-position, suggesting the destabilising of one's subjectivity, testing its limits. Writing and reading the experience book are referred to rather as a 'limit experience', which entails an attitude that entails work that puts itself "to the test of… contemporary reality" (Foucault, 2000, p. 316). This attitude is not a "grand gesture of transgression or liberation, but a certain modest philosophical and pragmatic work on ourselves", a work that is "both banal and profound, which we carry out upon ourselves in the very real practices within which we are constituted as beings of a certain type, as beings simultaneously constrained and obligated to be free, in our own present" (Rabinow & Rose, 2003, p. 27).

The discomfort that Foucault's thought, and Masschelein and Simons proposal, brings about is due to a sense that withdrawal is a withdrawal from the public, from lived reality, and from active political commitment. Rather, what is at stake is something both as banal and profound as how to live (Rabinow & Rose, 2003, p. 27). As such, the approach requires a voice that does not speak in the name of a Utopian ideal and does not recognise an outside in which the 'researcher' can take refuge. As Allen argues, the Foucauldian approach does not recommend. Rather, it assumes potentiality and equality (Foucault, 2000, pp. 240–242). He "writes under the democratic *assumption* that power over others cannot be exercised in the name of expertise or any other qualifications—or, at least, that it should be possible to question how power is exercised" (Simons & Masschelein, 2010, p. 602).

This presents a challenge to refuse to assume the pastoral attitude of the expert. The provision of expertise in marketable, accessible form furthers a form of immunisation effected by the belief in the possibility that every aspect of ourselves can be made fully accountable:

> To criticize the present without anesthetizing those who must act within it, to make conventional actions problematic without portraying them as acts of bad faith or cowardice, to open a space for movement without slipping into a prophetic posture, to make it possible to act but making it more, not less difficult to 'know what to do' – this, it seems, is the ethic of discomfort that Foucault seeks to introduce into our relation to the present and to ourselves in the present. (p. 23)

The notion of making it more difficult to know what to do is at odds with a problem-solving orientation to research, in which the academic is responsible to its stakeholders to provide solutions, as expressed by the European Research Area Board. The notion of the world university returns the academic to the role of thinking but does not therein exclude others from this role. On the contrary, she makes things public as an invitation to think together. The possibility of thinking, while it may appear abstract, acknowledges what is—or could be—distinctive about what the university can offer with regard to citizenship. This refusal of the self-understanding of the innovative researcher is by no means a traditionalist critique that seeks to restore the university and the researcher to a golden age of freedom of thought and that engages in a lament for times past. Rather it takes seriously the need to ask again what it means to do research and puts our knowledge to the test of the reality we seek to understand.

14.5 Conclusion: Finding a Way to Proceed

This chapter has begun to explore what it means to be governed in terms of innovation. In particular, the focus here is on the way that the demand for innovation is reshaping the university and the researcher. Innovation in the policy documents discussed here refers to the capitalisation of knowledge, the marketability of research outputs. This understanding is located within a discourse of financial austerity, sustainability, and social responsibility. Policies relating to the knowledge economy, or learning society, have now been recast by the shift to a focus on innovation. The orientation of all actors according to the non-referential notions of quality and excellence has been upgraded; the strategies implemented by the most innovative actors must now be applied by and to us all. Public service or public responsibility now refers not to the universal provision of particular services by state-funded institutions but to the responsibility of each actor to contribute to economic growth and therefore to employment, productivity, adaptability, and well-being. Failure to achieve targets will result in the transfer of that responsibility to another actor.[6] New devices standardise measurement and comparison in terms of innovation. Devices such as sector-specific scoreboards and schemes to facilitate collaboration between sectors such as Innovation Partnerships are examples of the means for governing (through) innovation.

The recasting of Europe as an Innovation Union marks a shift from the entrepreneurial to the innovative university. It is apparent in the policy discussed here that the focus on learning has been rationalised as a focus on research: that is, not just responsibility to invest in one's own knowledge and skills but also responsibility for rethinking how we do what we do for maximum (economic and therefore social) benefit.

Making the Innovation Union a reality entails the introduction of new methods and devices for governing. The document indicates the ways in which the actors in the knowledge economy (institutions, businesses, governments, individuals) are reorganising and ways in which innovation will be encouraged, organised, and managed. In response to this, the shifts that are apparent in the reordering of space, or in the creation of new spaces, to facilitate innovation (and further facilitate the Europeanisation of Europe) illustrate the ways in which knowledge—through education, research, innovation, and its capture, storage, and sharing through digitisation—is now a primary object of government.

The policies for governing (through) innovation intensify the demand for excellence across all sectors and for all actors. The Innovation Union effects not only a shift in how research is governed but also makes research and innovation a means for the governance of society. It demands a particular self-understanding of the citizen not as simply as a learner but as a researcher, taking responsibility for how best to continually adapt her life to current conditions and seeking strategies to maximally capitalise it.

In the context of the permanent demand for feedback and the immediate ability to comment, petition, and share information, critique becomes ubiquitous. To speak out is to have a voice and thus to evidence a particular form of participatory democracy. To speak out of turn is to show oneself to be a potential risk to oneself or society and in need of reform.

The free movement of knowledge is, of course, not the same as the free movement of thought. To seek this is not to seek thought that is unrestrained or unfocused. A certain mode of (self) discipline is required. This is freedom of thought that refers to the freedom to look, to identify the object of that focus, and how it will be brought into view. To seek to refuse the self-understanding of the innovative researcher is not a refusal to innovate but rather a refusal to do so solely in the name of innovation as a marker of the equally non-referential notions of quality and excellence. If critique is ubiquitous, how then are we to speak differently? Innovation conceived not as the capitalisation of knowledge but as new thought requires not accepting predefined social problems and thus the register in which those problems can be discussed.

Masschelein and Simons provide a rethinking of the space of the university and its public. The proposal for a world university raises insistent questions for the new researcher whose success in her academic career will be determined in part on her ability to innovate. The quote from the European Area Research Board above suggests that in exchange for her freedom of thought, the researcher must produce something—but something whose value can be calculated according to the current order. To do otherwise is framed as existing in isolation, acting without consideration for her fellow citizens. Her actions then must be visible; they must produce tangible (measurable) benefit. This rewriting of the contract might serve as a challenge to consider her public role as a researcher and to take responsibility for her actions by rethinking them in terms of matters of concern. What does it mean to be a researcher today? What is the reality I am faced with? What questions does it raise? Freedom of thought and responsibility for action are not mutually exclusive. Rather, the challenge today is to restate the public role of the researcher, as constitutive of the university, and of the society to which she is responsible. This is to take seriously the statement of the European Area Research Board: claiming one's freedom of thought by taking responsibility for one's actions and acting in accordance with a different ethic of research.

Notes

1. http://www.europarl.europa.eu/summits/lis1_en.htm
2. http://eur-lex.europa.eu/LexUriServ/LexUriServ.do?uri=COM:2006:0208:
   FIN:EN:PDF
3. http://ec.europa.eu/europe2020/targets/eu-targets/index_en.htm
4. The Europe 2020 strategy defines the challenges to which innovation should be
   oriented until 2020, with targets set for employment, research and development/

innovation, climate change, education, and poverty/social exclusion (http://ec.
europa.eu/europe2020/targets/eu-targets/index_en.htm).
5. This can be seen in the move towards e-government and in the discourse of
   'choice'. One example of this is the raising of the cap on university tuition fees
   in the UK. Criticism of this move focuses on the exclusions it (re-)introduces.
   Students protested against this largely fuelled by the belief that many would not
   be able to afford to go to university as a result. The policy however does not
   require any up-front payment. Universities have largely been forced to raise fees
   to the £9,000 per year maximum due to the reduction of direct payments by government to universities for teaching. Rather than governments funding universities directly 'the money follows the student'—the universities that will receive
   the funding therefore are those that attract the students, placing even greater
   emphasis on international league table rankings, not only for research excellence, and academic success, or the employment records of graduates but also on
   the increasingly emphasised student satisfaction survey.
6. In the UK, for example, local authorities have targets for the speed at which
   children are allocated to adoptive families. If they do not achieve these targets,
   adoption services will be taken over by other better performing local authorities
   or by private organisations. In universities, failure to achieve a particular standard of international research excellence according to the Research Assessment
   Exercise has resulted in the wholesale closure of academic departments.

References

Allen, A. (2011). The idea of a world university: Can Foucauldian research offer a vision of edu-
    cational futures. *Pedagogy, Culture and Society, 19*(3), 367–383.
Council of European the Communities. (2006). *Delivering on the modernisation agenda for uni-
    versities: Education, research, and innovation.* Brussels, Belgium: Council of European the
    Communities. http://eur-lex.europa.eu/LexUriServ/LexUriServ.do?uri=COM:2006:0208:FIN:
    EN:PDF. Last accessed 17 May 2012.
Delanty, G. (2003). Citizenship as a learning process: Disciplinary citizenship versus cultural
    citizenship. *International Journal of Lifelong Education, 22*(6), 597–605.
European Commission. (2010). *Europe 2020 flagship initiative: Innovation Union.* Brussels,
    Belgium: European Commission. http://ec.europa.eu/research/innovation-union/pdf/innovation-
    union-communication_en.pdf#view=fit&pagemode=none. Last accessed 17 May 2012.
Fejes, A. (2008). European citizens under construction: The Bologna process analysed from a
    governmentality perspective. *Educational Philosophy and Theory, 40*(4), 515–530.
Foucault, M. (2000). What is enlightenment? In P. Rabinow (Ed.), *Essential works of Foucault
    1954–1984 Vol. 1: Ethics.* London: Penguin.
Heid, H. (2004). The domestication of critique: Problems of justifying the critical in the context
    of educationally relevant thought and action. *Journal of Philosophy of Education, 38*(3),
    323–340.
Kant, I. (1977). An answer to the question: "What is Enlightenment?". In H. Reiss (Ed.), *Kant's
    political writings* (H. B. Nisbet, Trans.). Cambridge, UK: Cambridge University Press.
    (Original work published 1784).

Latour, B. (2010). An attempt at a "compositionist manifesto". *New Literary History, 41,* 471–490.

Masschelein, J. (2004). How to conceive of critical educational theory today? *Journal of Philosophy of Education, 38*(3), 351–367.

Masschelein, J. (2007). Experience and the limits of governmentality. In J. Masschelein, M. Simons, U. Brockling, & L. Pongratz (Eds.), *The learning society from the perspective of governmentality* (pp. 147–161). Oxford, UK: Blackwell.

Masschelein, J., & Simons, M. (2002). An adequate education in a globalised world? A note on immunisation against being-together. *Journal of Philosophy of Education, 36*(4), 589–608.

Masschelein, J., & Simons, M. (2009). From active citizenship to world citizenship: A proposal for a world university. *European Educational Research Journal, 8*(2), 236–248.

Masschelein, M., Simons, M., Brockling, U., & Pongratz, L. (Eds.). (2007). *The learning society from the perspective of governmentality.* Oxford, UK: Blackwell.

Rabinow, P., & Rose, N. (2003). Foucault today. In P. Rabinow & N. Rose (Eds.), *The essential Foucault: Selections from the essential works of Foucault* (pp. 1954–1984). New York: New Press.

Rancière, J. (1991). *The ignorant schoolmaster* (K. Ross, Trans.). Stanford, CA: Stanford University Press.

Simons, M., & Masschelein, J. (2008a). From schools to learning environments: The dark side of being exceptional. *Journal of Philosophy of Education, 42*(3–4), 687–704.

Simons, M., & Masschelein, J. (2008b). "It makes us believe it is about our freedom": Notes on the irony of the learning apparatus. In P. Smeyers & M. Depaepe (Eds.), *Educational research: The educationalisation of social problems.* Dordrecht, the Netherlands: Springer.

Simons, M., & Masschelein, J. (2010). Governmental, political, and pedagogic subjectivation: Foucault with Rancière. *Educational Philosophy and Theory, 42*(5–6), 588–605.

Simons, M., Olssen, M., & Peters, M. (2009). *Re-reading education policies.* Rotterdam, the Netherlands: Sense.

About the Authors

Nicholas C. Burbules is the Gutgsell professor in the Department of Educational Policy, Organization and Leadership at the University of Illinois, Urbana-Champaign. His primary research focuses on philosophy of education, teaching though dialogue and technology and education. He is the Director of the Ubiquitous Learning Institute, dedicated to the study of new models of 'anywhere, anytime' teaching and learning, given the proliferation of mobile technologies and pervasive wireless connectivity. He has published several papers and given numerous talks on 'ubiquitous learning'. He is currently the Education Director for the National Center on Professional and Research Ethics, located at Illinois. His most recent books are *Showing and Doing: Wittgenstein as a Pedagogical Philosopher*, coauthored with Michael Peters and Paul Smeyers (2010, Paradigm Press) and *Feminisms and Educational Research*, coauthored with Wendy Kohli (2012, Rowman and Littlefield). He is also editor of the journal, *Educational Theory*.

Kathleen Coessens' research is situated at the crossings of science and art, human creativity and cultural representations, embodiment and epistemology. She graduated in piano and chamber music at the Ecole Cortot in Paris and the Conservatory in Brussels and in philosophy, sociology and psychology at the Vrije Universiteit Brussel (VUB). She was awarded her doctorate in 2003 'The human being as a cartographer'. With a background in both art and human sciences, she works now as a professor and researcher at the Vrije Universiteit Brussel (VUB) in the Centre for Logic and Philosophy of Science (CLWF), at the Orpheus Research Centre in Music (ORCIM), Ghent, and at the Conservatory, Antwerp. She teaches semiotics, sociology of artistic practice and arts and performance culture. She publishes artistic research work and collaborates in artistic projects (with Champ d'Action, Antwerp; Grays School of art, Aberdeen; ORCIM, Gent) merging visual and performance arts. Recent publications are *The Artistic Turn: A Manifesto* with Darla Crispin and Anne Douglas (2009) and *On Calendar Variations* (2011) with Anne Douglas.

Lieven D'hulst is a professor of French and Francophone literature and of translation studies at the KU Leuven. His actual research topics include the discursive construction of Flemish migrant identities in Northern France (1850–1900), literary

P. Smeyers et al. (eds.), *Educational Research: The Importance and Effects of Institutional Spaces*, Educational Research 7, DOI 10.1007/978-94-007-6247-3,
© Springer Science+Business Media Dordrecht 2013

relations in Belgium (nineteenth century), transfer techniques (including translation), and the history and historiography of translation and of translation studies. He is a member of the editorial board of *Target: International Journal of Translation Studies* and the codirector of a series 'Traductologie' at 'Artois Presses Université' (France). He is also a member of the Research Council of KU Leuven.

Jeroen J.H. Dekker is full professor of History and Theory of Education at the University of Groningen. In 1998 and 2005, he was a visiting professor at the History and Civilisation Department of the European University Institute in Florence, and in 2010 at the European Institute of Columbia University in New York. A former President of the International Association for the History of Education (ISCHE), he is coeditor in chief of *Paedagogica Historica* and visiting member of the Editorial Board of *History of Education*. His publications deal with the social and cultural history of education, childhood and parenting. Among his publications are *Educational Ambitions in History: Childhood and Education in an Expanding Educational Space from the Seventeenth to the Twentieth Century* (2010), *Het verlangen naar opvoeden: Over de groei van de pedagogische ruimte in Nederland sinds de Gouden Eeuw tot omstreeks 1900* [From Educational Aspiration to Educational Supervision: Childhood and Education in the Netherlands from the Golden Age until 1900] (2006), *The Will to Change the Child. Re-education Homes for Children at Risk in Nineteenth Century Western Europe* (2001), and numerous articles.

Marc Depaepe (1953) is full professor at the *Katholieke Universiteit Leuven*, where he teaches courses in the history of education and in the history of behavioural sciences at the campuses Kortrijk and Leuven. He is a coeditor in chief of *Paedagogica Historica* since 2005 and member of the editorial board of *Bildungsgeschichte: International Journal of the Historiography of Education* (Germany); *Historia de la Educación: Revista Interuniversitaria* (Spain); *History of Education Review* (Australia); *Ricerche Pedagogiche* (Italy); and *Revista Historia Caribe* (Colombia). He is a former president of the *International Standing Conference for the History of Education* and former vice president of the *Internationale Gesellschaft für Historische und Systematische Schulbuchforschung* and a fellow and member of the Board of Directors of the *International Academy of Education*. His research interests are theory, methodology and historiography of education; history of the educational sciences; educational history in Belgium; colonial history of education; history of migration; and intercultural education. He has published a lot of books and articles on these topics in several languages.

Pieter Dhondt (1976) is university lecturer at the University of Eastern Finland. His current research focuses on the history of university celebrations and on medical history, including medical education at universities and colleges of higher education and the process of medicalisation in pre-school, primary education and secondary education. Among his recent publications are *Un double compromis. Enjeux et débats relatifs à l'enseignement universitaire en Belgique au XIXe siècle* (Gent: Academia Press 2011) and as editor National, Nordic or European? Nineteenth-Century University Jubilees and Nordic Cooperation (Leiden: Brill 2011).

Lynn Fendler is an associate professor in the Department of Teacher Education at Michigan State University, USA. In 2010–2011, she served as a visiting professor in Languages, Culture, Media, and Identities at the University of Luxembourg. Her research interests include curriculum theory, historiography, genealogy, and the philosophy of food. Her most recent book introduces the work of Michel Foucault to teachers; it was published in 2010 in the series Continuum Library of Educational Thought. Lynn is also interested in the political and epistemological implications of Web 2.0 technologies, and she maintains a wiki to serve as an open, public and interactive resource on educational theories for teachers and educational researchers. Her current research projects include studies of empiricism, methodologies for humanities-oriented research and the educational problems of aesthetic taste.

Karen François is part-time professor at the University Brussels (Vrije Universiteit Brussel –VUB). She is the director of the Doctoral School of the Human Sciences (http://www.vub.ac.be/phd/doctoralschools/dsh/index.html), and she is part-time postdoctoral researcher at the Centre for Logic and Philosophy of Science (www.vub.ac.be/CLWF/). Her doctoral research (2008) was on the politics of mathematics. She now focuses on statistical and mathematical literacy, ethnomathematics, the intersection of science and politics, social constructivism, and actor-network theory. She has published several papers, most recently: François, K., Coessens, K., & Van Bendegem, J. P. (2012, in press). The interplay of psychology and mathematics education: From the attraction of psychology to the discovery of the social. *Journal of Philosophy of Education, 46*(3); François, K. (2012, in press). Pro-latour. *Foundations of Science, 16*(3–4); Pinxten, R., & François, K. (2012). Etnowiskunde: een maatschappelijke en wetenschappelijke keuze (Ethnomathematics: A social and scientific issue). *Volkskunde, 114*(1), 74–93; François K. (2011). In-between science and politics. *Foundations of Science, 16*(2–3), 161–171; François, K. (2011). On the notion of a phenomenological constitution of objectivity. In A-T. Tymieniecka et al. (Eds.), *Analecta Husserliana* (Vol. CVIII), pp. 121–137; Goeminne, G., Francois, K. (2010). The thing called environment: What it is and how to be concerned with it. *Oxford Literary Review, 32*(1), 109–130.

Naomi Hodgson is a visiting research associate at the Centre for Philosophy, Institute of Education, University of London. Her current research focuses on European education policy and the shifting role of the university and the researcher, drawing on the work of Foucault, Latour, Emerson and Cavell. She has published a number of journal articles and contributed to a number of edited volumes. She is current reviews editor (UK) for the *Journal of Philosophy of Education*.

David F. Labaree is a professor in the Stanford University School of Education (USA). He was president of the US History of Education Society (2004–2005) and vice president for Division F (history of education) of the American Educational Research Association (2003–2006). His research focuses on the history of American education. His most recent book is *Someone Has to Fail: The Zero-Sum Game of Public Schooling* (Harvard University Press, 2010).

Ian Munday is lecturer in Education at the University of Stirling. He teaches on the Initial Teacher Education and Doctoral School programmes. Ian's research activities testify to an engagement with philosophical issues in education, particularly those concerning teaching and learning. His publications have tended to focus on various approaches to performatives and performativities and demonstrate the significance of these ideas for education. The themes explored in these terms include race, gender, the construction of authority, power relationships and the language of schooling. Here, philosophical ideas are treated in regard to their relevance to the details of educational practice. Ian's forthcoming research will focus on theorising 'creativity' in education.

Stijn Mus is a doctoral student at the Department of Foundations of Education at Ghent University, Belgium. His research centres around the question to what extent qualitative research in education could be challenged, informed and (re)vitalised by the literary arts.

Karin Priem is professor of education at Luxembourg University. Her current work focuses on Visual and Material History of Education, History of Cultural Practices, History of Industrialization and Education and Educational Theory. Karin Priem was president of the German History of Education Association (2007–2011), is member of the international advisory board of the 'Educational Review', and the 'Revue Suisse des sciences de l'éducation'. She is coeditor of the book series 'Beiträge zur Historischen Bildungsforschung' (Böhlau, Köln) and of the 'Jahrbuch für Historische Bildungsforschung' (Klinkhardt, Bad Heilbrunn). She initiated and collaborates in conferences and research projects, such as a project on the analysis of visual representations of the family in portraits and Genre Paintings from the sixteenth to the nineteenth centuries, the conferences 'Materiality of Education' (2009; recently published in *Zeitschrift für Pädagogik,* Beiheft 58, 2012) and 'Visual Politics, Material Culture, and Public Education' (2011).

Pauline R. Schreuder is assistant professor at the University of Groningen, where she teaches courses in philosophy of education and early childhood education, particularly in relation to gender and diversity. Her primary areas of research include professionalisation of early childhood education, (notions on) quality in day care and the pedagogical relationship between professional and (young) child.

Frank Simon has, since the beginning of the 1970s, been professor in history of education at Ghent University (retired in 2010). He is doing sociohistorical research on education, more specifically on pre-school and primary education. Most of his research is in collaboration with the research group on the history of education of the Katholieke Universiteit Leuven (M. Depaepe, A. Van Gorp) and deals with education policy, teacher unions, the teaching profession, and Progressive Education (Ovide Decroly). In the last decade, the research has focused on everyday educational practice, classroom history and curriculum history. Since August 2006, he has served as chairperson of the 'International Standing Conference for the History of Education' (ISCHE).